# HANDYMAN

For Maeve and Catha

First published 1981
Text and illustrations © 1981 by Patrick Keegan and Ian Layzell
Whittet Books Ltd, The Oil Mills, Weybridge, Surrey

Design by Alan Kitching
Illustrations by Ian Layzell

The information in this book is given in good faith and is correct at the time of going to press, as far as can be ascertained. The authors stress that extreme care must be taken when carrying out any of the work described in this book. It is necessary to observe the relevant regulations that apply and to take all reasonable steps to ensure your safety - especially when working with electricity and gas.

This edition published 1994 by Magna Books, Magna Road, Wigston, Leicester LE18 4ZH, produced by the Promotional Reprint Company Limited.

ISBN 1 85422 770 X

Acknowledgments
The author would like to thank Anne Archer and Penny Gardiner for their long hours at the typewriter. Patrick Keegan is indebted to Peter Mount and Richard Kaminski, who helped him rebuild his house, greatly expanding his knowledge of building. Special thanks are due to Annabel Whittet for help, forbearance and liquid refreshment.

Printed in Spain

# CONTENTS

# HELLO!

You know how demanding your home is — it seems constantly to
need repairs and maintenance, let alone improvements. All of which
are expensive, so you have to undertake them yourself. While some
people find this easy, others are reluctant handymen; if you are one,
this book is for you.

We set out to give you the basic skills and knowledge to make the
right decisions : when to use an expert, how to find him, when a job
is so easy that you can do it yourself, how to do so, and how to avoid
doing anything at all.

Patrick Keegan and Ian Layzell

# HOME
# SURVEYING

## 1

If you really are reluctant to do household repairs, it's obvious that you should buy a house that doesn't need them. The right house would be one that has recently been decorated to your taste, has all the built-in storage you require and all the plumbing, electrics and roofing in working order. This will then enable you to spend more time watching the video.

Ah! Easier said than done. It is difficult, as most house hunters will tell you, to find a house in good condition, in a suitable location, at the right price. Most people accept that certain repairs and modifications will be necessary.

However, this will probably be only the beginning. Too often as a result of being ill-informed, we do not appreciate the implications of such a decision. I was recently asked by a new householder to give an opinion on an architect's estimate for some small alterations to his house, namely a loft conversion and a conservatory. After some discussion, the architect's estimate of £30,000, plus fees at 15% seemed realistic to me. The householder was aghast, he had already stretched his resources to buy the house and had estimated that at the most his alterations would cost a quarter of the architect's estimate. Probably this householder will reluctantly attempt to do the alterations himself over the next few years.

So wise up, become your own 'home surveyor' and understand more fully what you're letting yourself in for. When viewing a bijou property, ask yourself questions like, 'Will the roof keep the rain out for the next thirty years?' or 'When will the outside of the house need redecorating?' If there is some small task you think you will be able to handle, quadruple the time and cost you estimate will be involved.

### Mm! Your dream come true?

Having located the house of your dreams, quickly apply the 'Top 20 Questions' listed in this chapter. Your survey will, we hope, show how well your potential dream home will stand up in terms of maintenance and running costs, or regretfully tell you that it should be knocked down.

The questions are far from comprehensive and should in no way be considered as a substitute for a surveyor's report; they can indicate when you should decide against a house and help you understand the construction of houses and some common problems. Having made up your mind about a particular house, you should approach a surveyor — but be sure, as you can probably only afford a surveyor once. The following list will also help you to understand the surveyor's report, which should be read on receipt avidly for a couple of days.

Before setting out on your survey safari, you will need to collect together a small survey kit and a basic knowledge of how houses are constructed.

### Surveyors

Most people confuse building society surveyors with building surveyors, assuming wrongly that if the building society agrees to a loan, the house has a moderately clean bill of health from their surveyor (whose report will not be divulged to you). However, the purpose of the building society sending its surveyor round — at your expense — is to discover if their loan will be secure should you default on the mortgage payments. Then in theory they would sell the house, take back the money they loaned you plus costs and pass on to you the change.
The only part of the building society's survey that may reach you is any repairs they consider essential to maintaining the value of the property, such as broken roof tiles that may let the rain in and cause dry rot.

You really need in addition a 'building surveyor' or chartered surveyor employed directly by you to prepare a comprehensive report, which should note any defects that you may have overlooked in your own '20 questions' survey. Suitable surveyors in the area where the property is can be found from the Information Dept. of the Royal Institute of Chartered Surveyors, 12 George Street, London SW1 (Tel. 01 222 7000). Ask for three names and ring each to find out how much they will charge (I'm afraid it's not cheap).

As well as finding any defects you may have missed and confirming those you found, a surveyor's report can be very useful; your solicitor can ask that the price of the house be reduced by the cost of essential repairs. You should have made your offer to the vendor 'subject to survey' for just this reason.

Your surveyor should be able to advise on local builders if you need them.

Finally, your surveyor's report acts as an insurance policy. If the surveyor has failed to inform you of defects in the house that he ought reasonably to have noted, you may be able to recover the costs of repairs through his insurance policy, if you're unable to get them on your insurance policy. As a result, surveyors' reports are pretty gloomy.

### Local Authority Planning Department

Before doing anything else, whizz down to the Town Hall to see if the chaps in the Planning Department have plans to drive an inter-galactic highway through your dream home. Whilst there, inspect the council's approved master plan for your neighbourhood, to see what they intend to build in the way of schools, shops and playing fields or other amenities.

### National House Building Council (NHBC)

Since 1964 the NHBC has run an insurance scheme, primarily for owners of new houses, to cover builders' mistakes (such as forgetting to put in the foundations). This insurance runs for a ten-year period after the NHBC surveyors, who will have inspected the house during construction, have issued their certificate. The scheme is now so extensive that virtually all houses built for sale are insured, and many building societies make it a condition for a mortgage.

If you are buying a 'second-hand' house built after 1964 you can find out from the NHBC (58 Portland Place, London W1N 4BU; tel. 01 637 1248) if the house was inspected and certified, and also, if you are interested, who the builder was.

The cost of the insurance scheme is borne by a lump sum paid by the builder before he starts work — you don't have to worry about premiums. Recently the NHBC have index-linked the insurance.

### Home owners

Why not apply the 20 questions to your house? You may conclude that you should move.

### The survey kit

Before setting out on your survey safari, you will need to collect a small survey kit and a basic knowledge of how houses are constructed. Top of the list for the kit is a good camera with flash for indoors and, if possible, a wide-angle lens. You can then study the house at your leisure from the photographs; and don't be mean, take the whole film. Next on the list is a damp meter which you will have to send for (see Where to Find It), and thirdly a powerful torch for looking in cellars and roof spaces. Other useful items are notebook for noting essential repair work, penknife for prodding render and timber window sills and tape measure to see if the four-poster will fit in, or if you can put another bedroom in the loft.

To carry out even a modest survey as outlined later on a semi-detached will take at least four hours, and that's without being interrupted by endless cups of tea with the vendors. So first ask the vendors if they mind you carrying out the survey and explain what you're going to do. Above all, stress that you intend to make an offer when you've done your survey. Of course with a vacant house there isn't a problem.

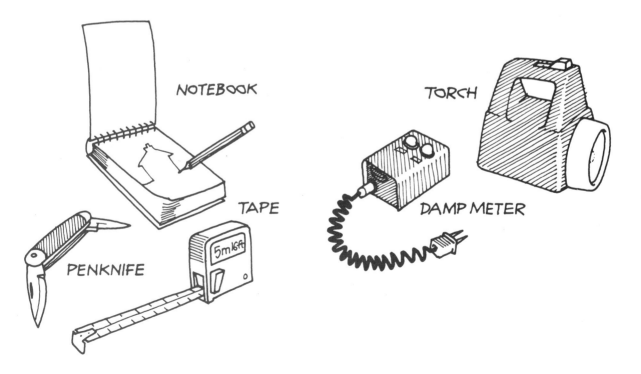

NOTEBOOK

TORCH

TAPE

DAMP METER

PENKNIFE

# Basic knowledge of typical Victorian house construction

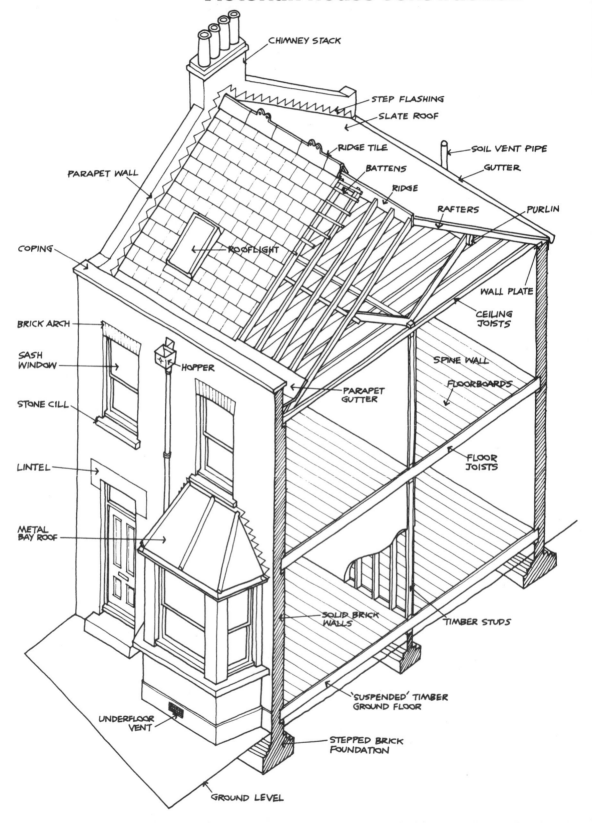

CHIMNEY STACK

STEP FLASHING

SLATE ROOF

RIDGE TILE

BATTENS

RIDGE

SOIL VENT PIPE

GUTTER

PARAPET WALL

RAFTERS

PURLIN

COPING

ROOFLIGHT

WALL PLATE

CEILING JOISTS

BRICK ARCH

SPINE WALL

SASH WINDOW

HOPPER

FLOORBOARDS

PARAPET GUTTER

STONE CILL

LINTEL

FLOOR JOISTS

METAL BAY ROOF

SOLID BRICK WALLS

TIMBER STUDS

UNDERFLOOR VENT

'SUSPENDED' TIMBER GROUND FLOOR

STEPPED BRICK FOUNDATION

GROUND LEVEL

**Roofs**: pitched roof structures are simply constructed with short wooden rafters 16"-20" apart, supported between a wooden ridge board and notched over wooden wall plates built into the external wall, and tied together at mid span with wooden purlins. Over the rafters wooden cross battens are nailed to receive the roof slates. Roof slates are nailed to the battens so that they overlap to avoid rainwater coming through the joints between the slates, clay tiles are either nailed or hooked over the battens. The junction of the slates to vertical brickwork parapets is protected with sheet lead flashings.

**External walls**: are constructed from solid brickwork increasing in thickness towards the ground. A typical house would have 9" solid brickwork on the upper floors (one brick length thick) increasing to 13½" thick on the lower floors (one and a half brick lengths' thick). The mortar used for laying is made from one part lime (which was used instead of cement) to three parts sand.

**External openings**: are formed by 4" wide timber lintels on the internal face with brick arches or stone lintels on the outside. Window sills are either made of stone or bricks plastered over with lime/sand mortar to look like stone.

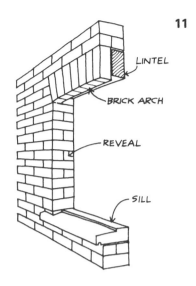

**Floors**: are constructed with 2" wide timber joists (the large bits of wood onto which floorboards are fixed) supported on wall plates built into the external brickwork and on the internal partitions. Floor joists generally span the shortest distance possible — usually from the front and back walls to the main partition or spine wall in the middle of the house. This wall will be built more solidly since it is load bearing. Joists are spaced approximately 16" apart and covered with 1" thick floor boards. At the mid-point of the floor, the joists are stiffened with 'herringbone' timber struts to prevent the joists from twisting. The ceilings are formed with thin strips of wood — laths about ¼" thick by 1" wide, nailed to the underside of the joists 1" apart. These laths are covered in a plaster consisting of lime, sand and goat's hair. This plaster is finished with a ¼" thick 'lime putty' which consists of pure lime. The ornate mouldings are made of cast plaster of Paris.

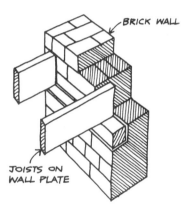

**Internal partitions**: are usually of timber-framed construction, with 2" x 4" upright timber studs, diagonal braces and timber plates spanning over floor joists. Both sides are finished with lath and plaster like the ceilings. On the lower floors the spaces between the upright studs are sometimes filled with bricks. Occasionally you might find partitions in basements are solid brickwork.

**Ground or basement floors**: similarly constructed to upper floors but with less deep joists. Spanning over small brick walls spaced at 4'0" centres built on the ground. Airvents are located in the external walls, providing through ventilation and preventing timber decay. Occasionally you may find solid floors formed with York stone slabs.

**Foundations**: of Georgian and Victorian buildings are rarely deeper than two feet below the lowest floor. However, it was considered good practice to remove the topsoil from the area of the building, which could mean the foundations would be anything between 2'0" and 6'0" below the original level of the ground. The foundations are formed by broadening the width of the brickwalls to spread the load.

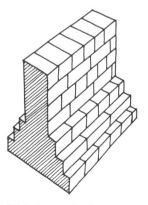

Brick stepped footing

# Basic knowledge of post-1930 house construction

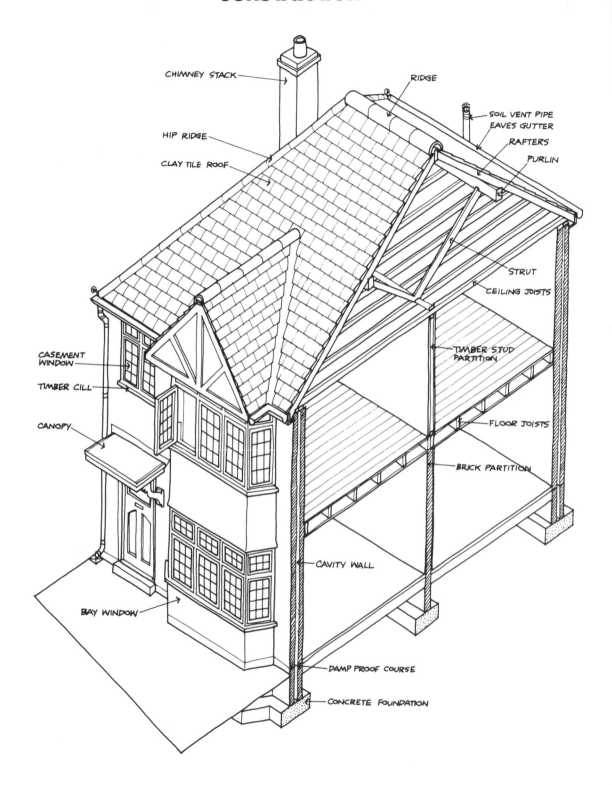

CHIMNEY STACK

RIDGE

SOIL VENT PIPE

EAVES GUTTER

HIP RIDGE

RAFTERS

CLAY TILE ROOF

PURLIN

STRUT

CEILING JOISTS

CASEMENT WINDOW

TIMBER STUD PARTITION

TIMBER CILL

FLOOR JOISTS

CANOPY

BRICK PARTITION

CAVITY WALL

BAY WINDOW

DAMP PROOF COURSE

CONCRETE FOUNDATION

**Roofs**: are constructed, generally, with wooden struts taking the weight onto the load-bearing spine wall to avoid outward thrusts on external walls. Rafters are of 2″ x 4″ timber, spaced at 16″ centres, and span over heavy timber purlins or collar supported by struts onto the spine wall of the house. Battens nailed to the rafters support clay tiles which are hooked over the batten with projecting nibs. The junctions of the tiles to the brickwork parapets are protected with either lead or zinc flashings.

**External walls**: there is no specific date when contractors switched from building solid external walls to cavity construction. However the majority after 1930 have cavity wall construction formed with two 4½″ brick walls (one brick width) with a 2″ gap between, making an overall width of 11″. The mortar used is sand and cement mix, with lime sometimes added. Because of the cement the wall is very rigid. The two walls are tied together with metal wall ties, which are built into the brickwork (3′ apart horizontally; 1′6″ vertically).

**External openings**: are formed with reinforced concrete lintels in the inner wall and concrete lintels or brick arches in the outer wall. As the windows are generally located on the face of the wall rather than being recessed as they were in previous eras, the timber window sill can deflect rainwater without the need of a masonry sill.

**Upper floors**: the floor joists are built into the inner brick wall of the cavity and generally span across the house over load-bearing internal partitions. Joists are spaced at 16″ centres, stiffened with herringbone timber struts at mid-point and covered with 1″ thick floorboards. The ceilings are usually of plasterboard coated with a ¼″ thick finishing plaster. Decorative mouldings are simply curved plasterboard sections nailed into position.

**Internal walls**: on the ground floor are generally 4½″ thick brickwork (one brick width thick) plastered on both sides with a sand, cement and lime mix, and then finishing plaster. In the last twenty years this has been replaced with lightweight plasters made from gypsum. On the first floor partitions are constructed with timber framework, using 2″ x 4″ timber studs at 16″ centres, faced both sides with plasterboards coated with a ¼″ thick finishing plaster.

**Ground floors**: are similarly constructed to upper floors but using 2″ x 4″ floor joists spanning over 4¼″ thick honeycombed brick walls built off 4″ thick concrete slabs, called 'oversite', laid over the ground; the void between the timber floors and the oversite is ventilated to avoid timber decay by means of airvents located in the external walls.

**Foundations**: are formed by digging 3′0″ deep trenches in the ground beneath both external and internal load-bearing partitions. The base of the trench is filled with 9″ of solid concrete from which the walls are built up using hard non-porous bricks until the wall is above the finished ground level.

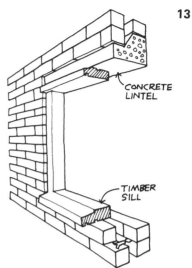

CONCRETE LINTEL

TIMBER SILL

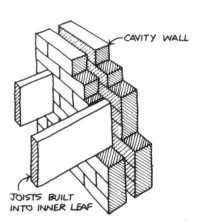

CAVITY WALL

JOISTS BUILT INTO INNER LEAF

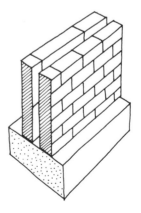

Concrete stripfooting

# Basic knowledge of
# timber-frame 'modern' house

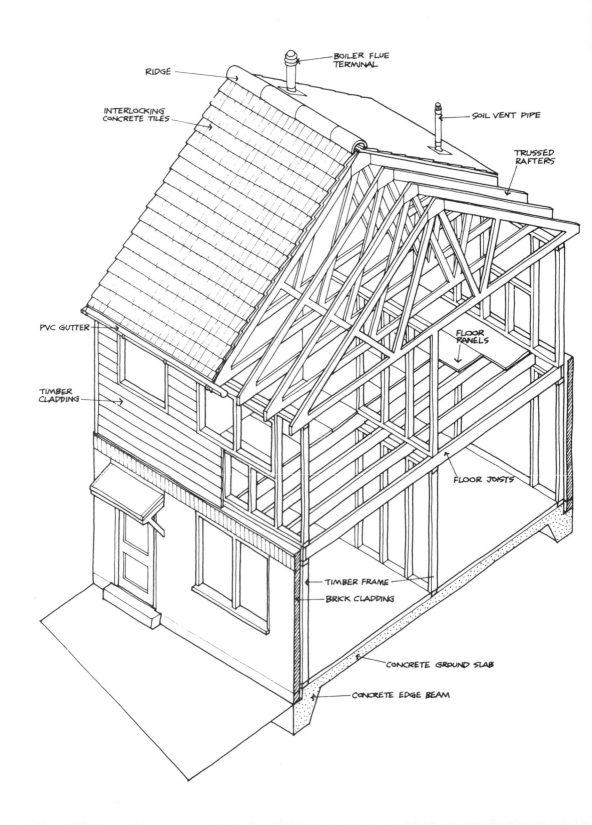

RIDGE

BOILER FLUE
TERMINAL

INTERLOCKING
CONCRETE TILES

SOIL VENT PIPE

TRUSSED
RAFTERS

PVC GUTTER

FLOOR
PANELS

TIMBER
CLADDING

FLOOR JOISTS

TIMBER FRAME

BRICK CLADDING

CONCRETE GROUND SLAB

CONCRETE EDGE BEAM

**Roofs**: are constructed from light-weight factory-made trusses held together with metal plates and spaced at 24" centres; battens are 1" x 2" nailed over roofing felt to trusses. Tiles made of concrete.

**External walls**: the basic structure is pre-fabricated of timber, with 2" x 4" studwork faced with ¾" ply panels which are simply nailed together on site. The framework is then clad with a variety of materials, such as 4½" brickwork on the lower floors or timber boarding on the first floors — neither of which are used for structural support. The cavity formed is filled with fibreglass insulation.

**External openings**: are simply formed in the timber structure by leaving openings where required in the panels. Openings in the external cladding, where brickwork is used, are formed with light-weight pressed metal lintels.

**Upper floors**: are either constructed with timber joists set out on site and covered with ¾" tongue-and-groove chipboard sheets or with panels constructed at the factory. Ceilings are lined with plasterboard, with the joints filled; no plastering at all is used.

**Internal walls**: are part of the structure and are formed in the same way as the external walls. Additional partitioning may be made by plasterboards.

**Ground floors**: constructed from 4" concrete slabs cast in situ.

**Foundations**: usually dug with a trench digger, which cuts a neat trench, which is filled with mass concrete composite with the ground floor concrete slab.

Movement fractures

Foundations

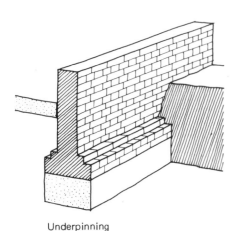

Underpinning

## 1 Is the house falling down?

If your dream house is falling down as a result of foundation failure, however much you may like it, please avoid it because it may well turn into a nightmare. The reasons for settlement may be difficult to ascertain but the following may help to establish if the house has suffered, or is suffering from subsidence.

In surveying for signs of movement, look at the external walls. In houses up to the 1930s where the brickwork was laid with soft sand/lime mortar, the structure can be considered to be 'flexible'. As a result the structure distorts before showing dramatic fracture lines with windows and door openings becoming out of square. Fractures develop later at the corners of the structural openings. With the introduction of cement in post-1930 construction, buildings have become substantially more 'rigid' and tend to show dramatic fracture lines through the brickwork.

The purpose of a foundation is simply to spread the load of the building over the ground so the load down is equal or less than the load bearing capacity of the ground. For instance a building sitting directly on rock needs little or no foundation whereas a building on sand needs to spread the load as much as possible or it will simply sink. The majority of buildings in Britain sit on clay.

There are four major causes for subsidence: design errors, a change in the bearing capacity of the ground, collapse of mining works, and land slippage.

The most obvious and much spoken about cause for subsidence recently was the drought of 1976, when a massive £80 million worth of claims were made to insurance companies for subsidence of houses on clay soils. The cause was that the clay shrank as a result of the drought, which was aggravated by trees and other plant life sucking up all the spare water.

Trees, however much we may like them, can seriously affect clay soils as they grow, even without a drought. The tiny fleshy roots which gather the ground water radiate from the tree at a distance equal to the height of the tree. Contrary to popular opinion there are no 'safe' trees. It is more a question of how fast and how tall a tree grows. Trees to be treated with respect are elms, willows and poplars, which reach mature heights of 27m, 24m and 30m respectively. The distance roots travel can be increased by hardstanding areas which prevent rainwater reaching the roots. Another reason for the clay shrinking may be the drying up of an underground stream covered over by building works. If you live in the London area, a useful book to establish if your house is built on top of an old river is *The Lost Rivers of London* by Nicholas Barton (Phoenix House and Leicester University Press, London).

In a number of cases settlement of the foundations happened many years ago, particularly with Victorian houses. This was caused by some walls being heavier than others, notably those with the chimneys. The heavier walls have compressed the ground more and have thereby sunk lower than the lighter surrounding walls. If the cracks have been made good and haven't opened up again the building is probably quite safe. With the modern desire for open living many houses are losing some of their internal load-bearing walls, which in turn is increasing the load on the remaining foundations. Check with the present owners if the District Surveyor or Building Inspector required the foundations to be strengthened as part of any modifications that have been done.

Houses built on hills occasionally slide down as a result of the foundations not being adequately built into the ground.

Depending on how far the settlement has gone, most foundation problems can be halted by underpinning. This is a process of digging, in sections of 3'0" at a time, under the existing foundation and putting another foundation in at a lower level. This is a costly and time-consuming business, making the majority of home owners quite insecure during the process. At current prices underpinning a semi-D could be several thousands of pounds. If the cause of the settlement has been a tree, the underpinning company could require that all trees around the building, within a distance equal to their fully grown height, be cut down.

If you are suffering settlement in your present place, most causes of subsidence are covered by house insurances and you should contact your insurance agent. Refer to Chapter 10.

### 2 Are the outside walls bulging or leaning or the chimney stacks leaning over?

These problems apply mainly to houses built before the 1930s and are a result of design errors of our forefathers and simply time, although we are suffering from similar problems on recently built high-rise buildings from poor workmanship.

In looking for bulges initially inspect the upper storeys. If you stand as close as possible to the outside of the house and look up, this may make the bulges more noticeable. If the house is at the end of a terrace, inspect carefully the end wall, 'flank wall' to surveyors, as you may be surprised to see it leaning out quite dramatically. Parapets and chimney stacks can, of course, be inspected through the binoculars in the survey kit. If you are really keen and you are not afraid to go on the roof, you could do a proper inspection by dropping a plumb line. If you fall off don't blame me.

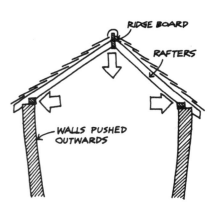

The major causes for failing brickwork are as follows:

A very common failing is the bulging out of the top-floor brickwork on the front elevation of terrace houses. Where the roofs are of the butterfly construction (see Valley gutters, p. 19), the brickwork is so slender that it is pushed out by the weight of the roof timbers. Such areas of brickwork are often rebuilt and you may notice the appearance of new brickwork in that dubious area on adjacent houses.

Another problem caused by roof structures is in connection with pitched roofs, where the same panel of brickwork is pushed out by the lateral thrust of the roof. Unlike modern timber truss roofs, Georgian and Victorian roofs don't have the benefit of the principles of triangulation, which prevent the outward thrust.

The most alarming design error of our forefathers was the lack of restraint they offered to the flank walls of their houses. We hope you are aware from the 'Basic knowledge of typical Victorian house construction' that the floor joists run back to front and are built into the back and front walls, thereby tying the brickwork into the body of the house. However, with the flank walls the brickwork rises from the ground to roof level without any such restraint. This is, in theory, similar to brickwork standing freely some 30-40 feet high without anything to prop it. Eventually flank walls either buckle or lean over under their own weight.

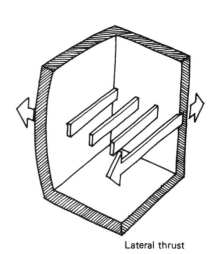

Lateral thrust

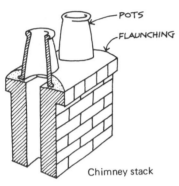

POTS

FLAUNCHING

Chimney stack

Decayed lintels

Dry rot

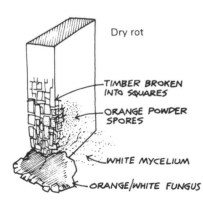

TIMBER BROKEN INTO SQUARES

ORANGE POWDER SPORES

WHITE MYCELIUM

ORANGE/WHITE FUNGUS

Parapets and chimney stacks start leaning over because of their severe exposure to weathering and because of the action of calcium sulphate from fires on mortar. Over the years the rain saturates the brickwork, the frost and the sun alternately expand and dry out the mortar. Chimney stacks, you may notice, tend to lean one way and this is a result of the prevailing winds.

Although I personally have not had any experience of the metal corrosion of wall ties used in cavity walls, there is a tendency by Building Inspectors and District Surveyors to require nowadays stainless steel to be used in external walls. Even assuming the worst — that the wall ties of the cavity walls have corroded into a pile of rust — I wouldn't suspect this would turn into a serious defect, as the majority of post-1930 houses are only two storeys high.

The first question asked by all home-owners with bulging brickwork is: when will the house fall down? The answer is generally couched in eloquent language but essentially means, I don't know. The real decision makers are the Building Inspectors and District Surveyors who have a legal obligation to place an order on the building owner when, in their opinion, the structure is dangerous. One of the rules they use is when the brickwork is more than 2" out of plumb.

As you have probably seen with the new spate of rehabilitation, bulging brickwork can be rebuilt in sections and panels as required. The only drawback is the cost: starting prices are in the range of £1,000 for a few square yards of rebuilding. If you have a leaning flank wall you may be able to strap it back with steel plates on the outside of walls tied to the inside of the house for a lot less.

### 3 Are the floors collapsing?

Timber that is attacked by dry rot becomes structurally unsound and eventually turns to dust. Moreover it spreads throughout a house alarmingly fast. A dry rot outbreak is something to worry about in any property, although more so in pre-1930 houses because of the extent of timber they have built into brickwork, which easily gets damp.

One sign of dry rot is a gap between the bottom of the skirting board and the floorboards. Tell-tale evidence of dry rot in wood is vertical cracks in the paintwork and a curving of the timber; if you can push your finger into the timber window sills it's a pretty good sign, or you may be fortunate enough to put your foot through the floor. In pre-1930 houses look for the slipping of brickwork over window and door openings where the timber lintels behind may have decayed. If you are brave, do the surveyor's trick of the 'Jump Test' on all floors. If the whole house rattles, there is a good chance that the joist ends built into the brickwork have decayed. If you suspect dry rot call in the timber treatment specialists who will provide a free estimate and survey.

Dry rot is simply fungus — mushrooms — growing in the dark humid areas of the house. Classic places in which dry rot is nurtured are in ground floors where the ventilation to the sub-floor has been blocked off. The mushrooms grow by eating the cellulose and drinking the water in the timber; when they've consumed all the food in one piece, they send their wispy white tendrils in search of more food and water. You may even see the actual mushrooms when surveying. They are orange, pancake-like objects.

The prime instigator of dry rot is dampness. If a house has not been properly maintained and gutters, downpipes, overflows or timber window sills have allowed water to keep brickwork and timber constantly damp, there is very high risk of an outbreak. The most essential action to prevent outbreaks is to ensure that all walls are free from dampness and that areas such as roofs and ground floors are well ventilated.

Depending upon the extent of an outbreak, a building can be treated to prevent further outbreaks. But serious treatment with a guarantee can only be effectively carried out by specialists, and it usually means tearing out the affected timbers and replacing with new — very messy and expensive!

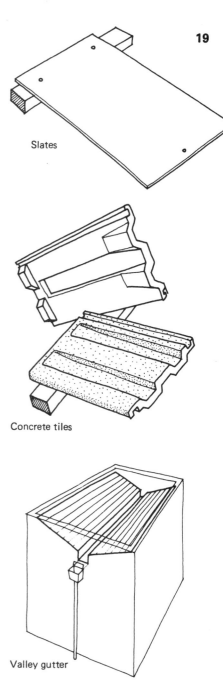

Slates

### 4  Is the roof collapsing?

The majority of roof coverings are designed on the principle of falls, so that the rain runs off them, be they severe pitches or gentle sloping flat roofs. If the roof structures start sagging the rainwater may not be shed as originally intended. To use that familiar builder's phrase, ensure that you go and have 'a look see' by getting onto the roof and looking inside, and then most of the problems discussed below will be obvious.

The major roof structure problems in my knowledge are as follows:

A common defect concerns re-tiling old slate roofs. With the increasing scarcity and price of slate, many roofs that were previously slated are being re-tiled with cheap, heavier concrete tiles. Unless either the existing roof structure is strengthened, by putting in struts, or was originally strong enough to take the load, then the roof structure will slowly settle, causing the roof covering to leak and pushing, as previously mentioned, brickwork in one or another direction. The District Surveyor or Building Inspector would require an inspection of the re-roofing work. But much of this work is carried out by 'cowboys' so he may never get involved, much to the disadvantage of property owners.

Concrete tiles

However popular Georgian architects may be today with those who readily reject modern architects' apparent stupidity in providing flat roofs in a wet country, the Georgians created similar problems with their desire to hide their pitched roofs behind parapets. In doing so they created valley gutter roofs, which, instead of simply shooting the rainwater off, collected it and carried it in a lead-lined channel across the house. The channel is formed with timber joists either side of a flat board. These joists have had a tendency to sag and, in doing so, have allowed the rainwater to pond, which in turn has rotted the timber. This sagging has been aggravated in some cases by settlement of the spine wall.

Valley gutter

It seems to me that the best roof constructions were built between the wars. The roof structures were soundly constructed and good timber was used. All of which might have led us to believe everything was going in the right direction, as far as roofs were concerned.

However, with more recent buildings the lightweight roof trusses, which you have probably noticed going around the country, stacked on articulated lorries, use the simplest joints and minimal timber sections. There have been problems with the metal plates which hold the timbers together, rusting or popping out, and of course once this has happened you should think about popping out yourself.

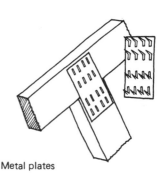

Metal plates

Roof structure problems can be cured, but obviously if a roof requires extensive work, it is unwise to be in occupation. If the roof is opened up for works, considerable damage can ensue in the house below, unless extensive precautions are taken. There can also be considerable damage to your pocket.

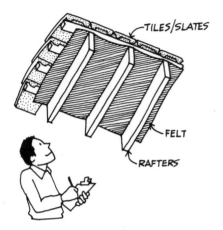

### 5 Is the roof leaking?

It may not come as a great surprise to you that the main objective of a house is to protect you from the inclement weather of this country. It will certainly drive you insane if, the moment you move, the roof starts leaking. A thorough inspection is required.

There are two main types of pitched roof covering, slates and clay tiles. Nowadays there are asbestos slates and concrete tiles, these having been introduced in the early 1950s.

Roof coverings of slates or tiles, except the variety with nibs that hook over the battens, become defective primarily as a result of the nails holding them to the roof battens rusting away and allowing them to slip. It can therefore be assumed that if a few tiles have slipped the remainder are on the way.

To establish if an old, pre-1950s, roof has been re-covered, go into the loft and look at the underside of the tiles. If you see a black felt covering below them, it's been re-roofed. The practice of putting felt below roof tiles started about thirty years ago and provides a second barrier to rainwater penetration. More recently, this felt is being combined with fibreglass insulation. In some cases roof structures are covered in timber boards with the slates fixed over — this may confuse you.

The problem of nails rusting away is recognized by the Building Inspectors who have, since 1960, required tiles to be fixed with non-ferrous nails, such as copper, stainless steel and aluminium alloy. If a roof has been re-covered, ask the owners when, who did it, and if there is any guarantee. It could come in handy.

Both tiles and slates can be re-used in roofing if they're in good condition. Replacing a slate roof with new slates costs a fortune. Just one new slate costs about £2 and this is why substitutes have been introduced. If the roof looks a little suspect contact a local roofing contractor and obtain a free quotation for a new roof covering.

There are three main categories of flat-roof covering: layers of felt stuck together with bitumen, termed 'built-up' roofing by surveyors, asphalt and sheet metal.

Felt roof

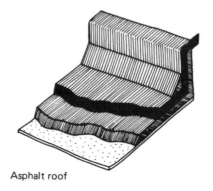

Asphalt roof

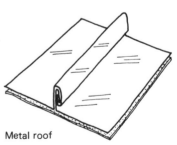

Metal roof

The least effective of these are the cheaper forms of 3-layer felt built-up roofing which, depending on how well laid they were in the first place, have a short life expectancy of between ten and fifteen years. The felts expand and contract daily and, over the years, tend to crack as they become more brittle. However in recent years manufacturers of built-up roofing have introduced plastic sheeting, which is more able to take the stresses of everyday life.

The second best is the asphalt roof, which is simply made from 1" thick asphalt laid on a felt over the timber roof boards and carried up at the edges to form upstands. Good asphalt roofs have white granite chippings to reflect the sun and prevent melting. Most people, I am sure, have noticed how easily asphalt softens on hot days and certainly asphalt roofs should not have objects lying about on them, as the asphalt will dent very easily and form a weak spot. Look over an asphalt roof for dents, blisters and cracking, especially at the edges. I like asphalt roofs because, depending how old they are, they can be quite simple to repair and maintain.

The Rolls Royce of flat-roof coverings is the metal roof. Metals used in order of cost are zinc and zinc substitutes, the cheapest, copper and lead, the most expensive. The main cause for concern is electrolytic action caused by the closeness of dissimilar metals that cause corrosion of the metal. With all flat roofs inspect both the covering and the ceiling below closely. If the ceiling has been recently patched and decorated be a bit suspicious.

The most common weak spot of both flat and pitched roofs is the junction between the wall and the roof. This is where we find the flashings and soakers which join the two together. The problems are corrosion of the metals used, loosening of the mortar that keeps the flashing tucked into the wall and movement of the roof structure timbers, away from the wall. The most common remedy for these problems is to fill in with cement fillets and in simple language 'they ain't no good', as the last thing cement fillets allow for is movement. Flat timber roofs should have 6" timber upstands around the edge to keep the roof covering away from the brickwork and a simple flashing covering the gap. It would probably cost about £20 a yard to replace flashings in zinc or lead.

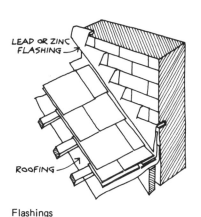

Flashings

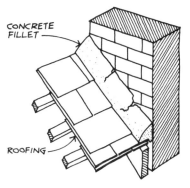

Cement fillets

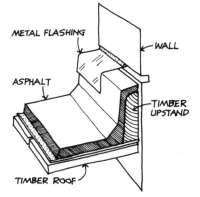

Timber upstand

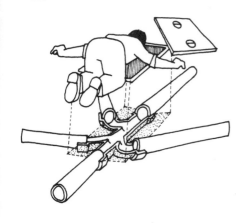

### 6 Are the drains broken?

Are the drains in working order or are they fractured, or do they get blocked up often? If, after you've bought the house, you find that the drains are getting blocked up, you'll want to commit *hara-kiri*.

Before purchasing, therefore, look for the manhole covers in the garden; it might be more easily said than done, for some misguided chaps go and concrete them over and just think of the headache that will cause when you have your first blockage. When found, have a look inside. If it's full there's something wrong, as your nose will tell you. If you have difficulties in locating manhole covers you could try going to the local council and having a look at the drainage plans kept by the Building Inspector.

It is imperative to have the drains tested by the surveyor. He may choose to test them in various ways, the simplest test being to fill the drain with water by putting a plug in and seeing how quickly the water seeps away; slowly — say a jam jar's worth over an hour — is OK. The cause of cracked drains is either settlement of the ground, the reasons for which are discussed in question one, or, as happened to the grandmother of an acquaintance of mine, a tree root growing inside the drain — the root eventually appeared in the loo!

If a drain fails a test you may be able to have it lined by a specialist firm which you will be able to locate through the yellow pages. Arrange for an inspection and ask for a quotation. Drains are lined by a process of dragging a canister full of cement through the drain and forcing the cement into the cracks. Costs would vary, but £25 a yard is a guideline, and that's much cheaper than laying new drains.

### 7 Gutter problems?

We have already mentioned the evils of allowing water to dribble all over the outside of the house. Here we assume that leaking gutters have not yet caused the serious side effects of dry rot. But for how long?

If the downpipes and gutters are plastic or aluminium look no further, but make sure the joints are tight and the fixings secure. However, if they are cast iron, give them a thorough check, even by getting a ladder to look in the gutters. Be careful not to lean the ladder against the gutter; as you can imagine, the cast iron could now be very thin from rusting.

The cost of replacing pipework with maintenance-free plastic depends on accessibility more than anything else. The easy bits you should be able to do yourself. It's more complicated, however, to replace cast-iron waste drainage, as you obviously have to get to the bath, WC and basin indoors.

You may find that the decay has not gone too far and can be saved by a nice bit of regular maintenance. See long-term drainage maintenance for gutter maintenance.

### 8 Is there dampness?

All dampness, although you may take a bit of convincing, has a cause. Establishing the fault that causes it is the most difficult bit. Most faults are simple to rectify.

For your survey take the damp meter from your kit and go round inside the house prodding in different places, not just the obvious places to find dampness, which are above and below windows, in chimney breasts and ground floor walls. Remember a wall can be

Damp meter

damp and still not be showing signs, such as peeling wallpaper — especially if it was only wallpapered last week in time for your visit. If dampness has been hanging about for a long time it may have caused considerable damage that cannot be seen.

We list below five common causes of dampness. Of course any patch of damp could be a result of more than one. For instance moderate condensation on the inside of a wall will be aggravated by dampness on the outside, as moisture in the brickwork lowers the thermal insulation of the wall.

Rising damp is certainly the most discussed and familiar of all damp problems leading to its very own TV programme. As most people know, the reason is the breakdown or lack of a damp-proof course. Damp-proof courses abound in houses and are located in places where water would, unless prevented by an impervious material, simply be sucked by capillary action up the brickwork into the house. Capillary action is the sucking effect of the porous bricks. The Victorians used slates as damp-proof courses (DPCs), laid within the brickwork courses at best, or just allowed the basement to get damp. However, the best is still leadcore, a combination of a thin sheet of lead sandwiched between layers of bitumen coatings.

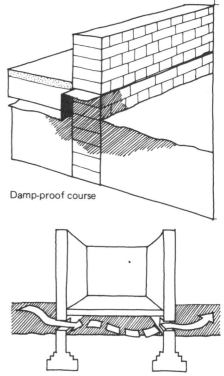
Damp-proof course

If you establish that the cause of dampness is failure or absence of a damp-proof course, you can now go to a whole industry set up for inserting or injecting damp-proof courses; for the price of £250, or thereabouts, a specialist firm will block up your capillaries with silicone and guarantee it for no less than 20 years. However, they also recommend — and probably will not guarantee their work unless you do — extensive re-plastering to stop the water already in the brickwork from damaging your wallpaper, and this will cost, at current rates, about £8.00 per square metre, of the equivalent of carpeting the walls. If you are inspecting a Victorian house and everything is dry, it could be for two reasons. Either that the present owners have inserted a chemical DPC, or the house is sitting on well drained land. Obviously location affects rising damp, and if you are sitting on a hill the ground water below is going to be substantially less than if you are in a valley.

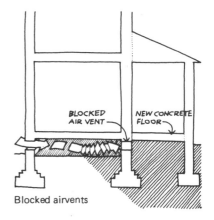
Sub-floor ventilation

Rising damp of course does not just come up walls, it can also percolate through floors. The way of solving this originally was to suspend the ground floor and ventilate the cavity by means of airbricks in the outside wall. Quickly walk around the house looking for them. Some people, however, don't understand the principle of sub-floor ventilation and merrily go and provide concrete floors in the back room, thereby blocking existing airvents, or add an extension at the back which prevents the flow of air.

Blocked airvents

In more recent years there has been a tendency to provide solid concrete ground floors and this brings us on to something called a damp-proof membrane, which uses materials like polythene or bituminous paint. Stick in the prongs of your damp meter to see if the water is coming through the floor. Even the slightest reading will play havoc with most carpets. Especially the foam-back kind. I also strongly advise home owners not to stick their carpets down. Dampness through a concrete floor can be cured at a cost by hacking up the screed, laying down a more expensive membrane and putting back a screed. However, this will effectively involve taking out all the skirtings, doors, kitchen and sanitary fittings, and joining the membrane to the damp-proof course in the solid walls. There is also a problem with the internal walls and staircases. I suppose the bill for doing it could be as much as £2,000-£3,000 for the whole of the ground floor of the average house and the result would be dependent on exemplary workmanship.

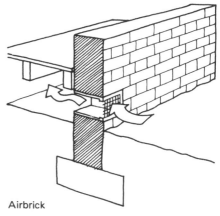
Airbrick

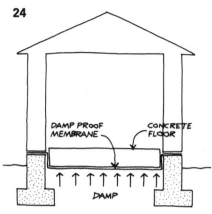

Falling damp is the failure of a damp-proof course in reverse and is most common in cavity brickwork above and below window openings. It means the builder forgot to put the damp proofing in. There is a lot of water floating about in cavities and as it falls it rests on window frames, unless it is directed away by a cavity DPC through weepholes in the brickwork. Below windows is another place to test; water on the external sill can soak through.

Next we have penetrating damp. Exposure is the greatest problem here because, as you may have gathered, brickwork is porous. Driving rain can penetrate cavity walls just as well as solid brickwork though it's difficult to believe. The condition of pointing and rendering is important. The pointing (the layer of mortar that sticks the bricks together) should not be cracking or flaking away. To test the rendering (the surface coating, if any, over the bricks), tap it; if it sounds hollow, it's deteriorating. Also watch out for earth banked up against a wall above the DPC, if there is no vertical protection or 'tanking' against damp.

Damp-proof membrane

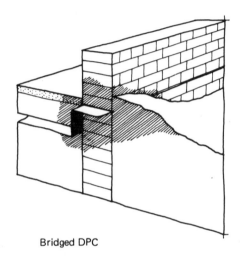

Bridged DPC

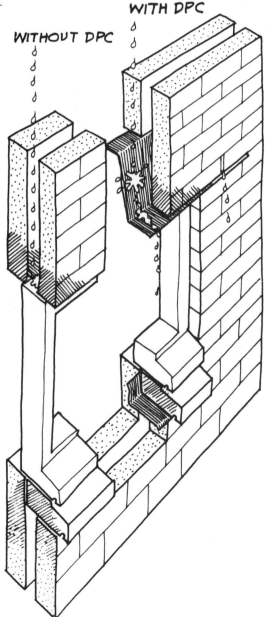

Falling damp

Thirdly, there is hygroscopic damp; this refers to a particular plaster used in houses nowadays called 'Carlite'. This plaster behaves like a sponge and will suck moisture from damp brickwork; you will see crystals on the inside of the wall. Used on a wall that cannot get damp, it's a perfectly suitable plaster, but on solid external walls it will simply suck the damp in and this is stated clearly in the manufacturer's instructions. It is used because it is cheaper than traditional methods as the plaster dries quickly, is light and therefore easy to put on. But it's expensive to replace. Alternatives to this plaster in damp situations are sand/cement/lime rendering. If the present owners have carried out re-plastering ask with what, by whom and why.

Hygroscopic damp

Air carries water as vapour which, as we all know, turns into rainclouds and, when either the pressure or the temperature changes, rapidly forms rain or condensation. With houses becoming warmer and more draught-proof, they are therefore less ventilated, and the air within a house accumulates more water vapour. When it meets the cold surface of a wall it condenses either on the surface or, more dangerously, within the fabric of the wall. We have three contributory elements — the amount of water we put into the air, the amount of air to carry the water and the temperature drop within the fabric of the house's external walls.

If you conclude that the dampness is a result of condensation you may also note that the present owners' use of the house is the main reason. For they may never open a window, wash the children's nappies in a bucket on the kitchen stove, like endless hot baths, heat the house with paraffin stoves or they may just be heavy breathers.

A classic place for condensation within the structure is where people have blocked up the fireplaces but not provided through ventilation. Cold, damp air comes down the chimney and condenses inside the flue.

Lastly the cause may be simply leaking plumbing, blocked downpipes or defective guttering, something never really noticed unless you like standing in the rain.

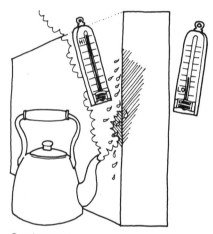

Condensation

Blocked gutter

Q: HOW MANY BRICKS PER SQ. YD?
A: TOO MANY....

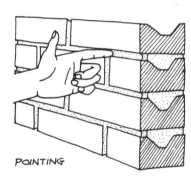

POINTING

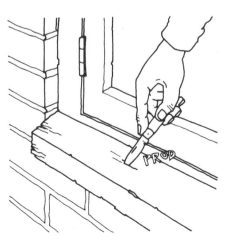

### 9 Will the outside of the house need constant maintenance?

Sure it looks pretty, but for how long and will it then mean you spending several weeks decorating it to return the house to the picture it was when you bought it. Really for us reluctant chaps a pretty house is one that has lovely plastic or aluminium windows, plastic rainwater goods and is built in brickwork, all requiring little or no maintenance.

A small caution. Not all bricks last for ever, there are some soft red bricks — the Victorians were keen on them — which flake after fifty or sixty years permitting dampness to come in. The proper solution to this problem is to cut out the brick and replace it with a new one, which, as you can appreciate, will cost anything from £2 a brick upwards. Oh, by the way, there are 48 bricks to every square yard.

Whilst looking at the brickwork, check the pointing. The house may need re-pointing, and if it does it'll cost yer at least £5 per square yard at current prices, plus the cost of scaffolding, and you will have to find somebody reliable (you certainly won't be doing it yourself, as you will go out of your mind within two hours). If the house has pebbledash all over the walls, it may be OK, but tap it with your penknife to see if it is sound. If the house has been rendered and it is obvious that it wasn't when it was originally built — something you can see by looking next door — find out why, because it might be covering something evil. Competent external rendering is rarely carried out nowadays; if it isn't competent it might be about to fall off.

Well that's put a little colour into those charming houses painted in nice pastel shades which get all those civic trust awards.

### 10 What is the condition of the windows and external doors?

Flash out your penknife from the old survey kit and start surreptitiously prodding away at door and window sills in search of rotten timber. Be sure to open all doors and windows.

Firstly let us deal with old sash windows. You may have found that the sashes wouldn't open because of the cords having broken. No big problem, it's quite easy to repair them, it will only take you a day for each. (For 'How to replace sash' see Techniques.) You may find that the sashes don't stay where you put them: this will probably be because some of the panes have been replaced with heavier glass, upsetting the balance. This too is no big problem. What is a big problem, or rather cost, is if you conclude that the window needs replacing, i.e. the sill has decayed. Replacement sash windows start at about £150 each and if all the windows need renewing there will be quite a bill. In the case of sash windows in bays it'll probably cost even more as they hold up the bay structure and it's very difficult to replace them without the whole

ONLY
£150!

thing coming down. Before considering cheaper alternatives to sash windows, be sure to check with the planners.

Then there is the casement or outward opening window; check for decaying sills, squareness of the casement and decay on the bottom rail. Rarely do decorators paint where it's really needed at the top and bottom of the casement and this leads to decay.

If you have metal windows, tap the metal vigorously and try to detect from the sound any rusting patches. Check the hinges aren't rusted solid or about to fall apart.

Roof lights and skylights are generally in poor condition as they are difficult to decorate from the outside and yet get the most severe exposure.

Especially check the lowest section of the ground-floor door frames to see if they are rotten. If the frames were inadequately primed before installation, the grain abutting the ground will be like a sponge.

If doors and windows fit poorly but are sound, you will nowadays be able to draught-proof them effectively and cheaply with one of the purpose-made draught excluders (see Chapter 9).

Casement window

### 11  Are the ceilings falling down?

This is simply to do with lath and plaster and lime plaster, which tends to have a varying lifespan of 60 to 200 years — fabulous stuff, as it's very good for sound insulation. If only I could think of some simple substitute I'd be a rich man. Around about the 1930s the evil plasterboard was introduced. As most people will agree, it is like building houses out of paper and it leads to articles in newspapers about hearing the neighbours four doors away going through their conjugal rites.

Firstly establish if the house has lath and plaster walls by tapping them; lath and plaster will sound dull, like a heavy blanket. You'll know if it's solid brick because you will hurt your hand, or if plasterboard because the whole house will rattle. If it's lath and plaster ask if the house has been re-plastered and if so what with. If it's 'Carlite' check with your surveyor. Look to see if the ceiling is covered in glorious polystyrene tiles which most likely means the ceiling has cracked. A close look at the ceilings should enable you to discover if there are cracks and crazing. You may be in the fortunate position of seeing some appear whilst you are visiting the house.

If ceiling or wall plaster is beginning to fall off, don't contemplate patch and repair as a simple course because it will lead you into a very frustrating period of your life. If it is coming down, well, it's going to come soon enough.

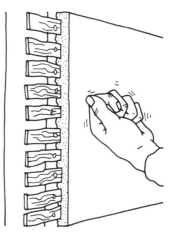

Lath and plaster

Re-plastering is expensive, partly because of the lack of skilled plasterers and partly because it is labour intensive. It will cost between £5 and £10 per square metre for re-plastering, producing a £3,000 bill for re-plastering a two-storeyed Victorian house with rear extension.

A tip, save money and don't take the laths off. Have the house re-plastered with Limelite on the existing laths with a spot of goat's hair mixed up in it. Remember, added to the bill will be the cost of removing and replacing skirtings and architraves (mouldings that go round doors and windows).

If the house is covered in plasterboard, there is not much to worry about. The only problem is if it ever gets damp, or you have a bath overflow. But plasterboard is very easy to patch and repair. The only other problem I know of with it is that skim coats of plaster blow off because the solid wall plaster gets damp. Here again not much harm is done.

....IMMERSION HEATER SEEMS FINE........

### 12 Is the plumbing inadequate?

There was a time not so long ago when it was considered good practice to have cold-water storage tanks in the roof to which a pipe from the water main in the street would rise, only stopping off to give drinking water at the kitchen sink. From the tank the house would be served. However all this is changing and to the best of my knowledge only one water authority still requires tanks, the Thames Water Authority. A plumbing system is therefore only inadequate if it doesn't supply the water where you want it, at the pressure you are looking for (particularly in the case of showers).

Start your survey by turning on all the taps and flushing the WC and cistern; gurgling noises are a bad sign. Then look for a cold-water storage tank, which will probably be in the roof. If you are in an area where the Water Board require storage you'll need a tank capable of holding 50 gallons of water, which a tank 2'0" high x 2'6" wide x 4'0" long will do. Have a look inside the tank, especially if it's galvanized, because it may be filthy, rusting and in need of replacement with a nice plastic tank. Whilst you're there look for an overflow pipe and see it is insulated.

If the house hasn't a central heating system find out how the water is heated; if it is an immersion heater inside a copper hot-water cylinder, run the bath to see if there is sufficient hot water and then run it again half an hour later, if you're still there and haven't already been thrown out.

If the house doesn't have a bathroom or a kitchen and you are intending to put them in, just remember that you are jumping in at the deep end. To install the cheapest bathroom, kitchen sink and some form of water heating is going to cost £1,000 and that's with white bath fittings and no allowance for drainage, which could cost anything depending on the existing drainage system.

### 13 Are the electrics out of date?

There we were only ten years ago sitting in the centre of white heat technology and being constantly bombarded by the idea of 'all electric' homes and still hundreds of homes throughout the country have barely more than one light in the centre of the room. I even know of homes in the centre of London with gas lighting.

The obvious first sign is the sockets. If they have round holes the system is out of date. However, there are chaps who go round removing the old sockets and putting new square three-point sockets, without replacing the wiring behind the sockets, which can be a bit misleading. So up to the loft where you should be able to see some cables going between the ceiling lights. If the house has been re-wired in recent times you should see white or grey flat PVC cables. There are two other types of cable: lead-covered cable and rubber insulated cloth-bound cable, both of which are way out of date and mean the system is certainly due for re-wiring.

If you are unsure of the electrics, call in the local Electricity Board, who will carry out a survey, and should give a simple answer of yes or no. If the answer is no, ask for a quotation for re-wiring. I should think for the average two-bedroomed house, it would be about £1,000.

Even if the electrics are satisfactory, they may not provide you with all the outlets you require. For instance if you are contemplating electric central heating you will need a new ring main. Or there may not be enough sockets in the kitchen for your culinary arts. You may find that it's simpler to have the whole house re-wired to meet your require-

ROUND PIN          SQUARE PIN

ments; adjustments to existing electrics are time-consuming as it is so difficult to know what cable is what when you lift a floorboard. For a better understanding of electrics, see Chapter 2, Turning On The Electrics.

### 14 Incompetent central heating system?

We have all heard stories of cowboy central-heating firms from Esther Rantzen and her gang and there is, of course, the growth of DIY heating engineers. So there is a pretty good chance you'll be getting one of these systems.

A tip from our publisher, don't buy a house without having the central-heating system run in your presence so that you can feel the hot radiators and hot water.

If it's a gas system you could contact the local Gas Board for a free survey.

Wet systems, that is, radiators filled with water, don't last for ever, especially pressed steel panel radiators and low water content boilers. Try and find out when the system was installed.

Pressed steel panel radiators can rust away in a very short time if air continually gets into the system. Look around to see if there are any rust marks around the radiators or the valves at either end. Radiators can be replaced quite easily, but do remember that the current price of a 4'0" x 2'0" double panel radiator is £55, and the average house needs at least seven radiators.

Low water content boilers, much heralded about ten to fifteen years ago as providing quick heat-up time and lower running costs, relied on a copper/aluminium heat exchanger, that is, the kettle the water is boiled up in. However, these lightweight exchangers suffer from the constant expansion and contraction and inevitably have short lives. More popular nowadays is the tested and tried faithful old cast-iron exchanger.

Try to establish who put the installation in, when and if it has been regularly maintained, that is once a year, under a service contract. Refer to turning on the central heating in Chapter 2.

It might also be helpful to ask to see old bills for gas or oil so that you know what the system will cost to run.

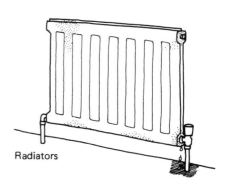

Radiators

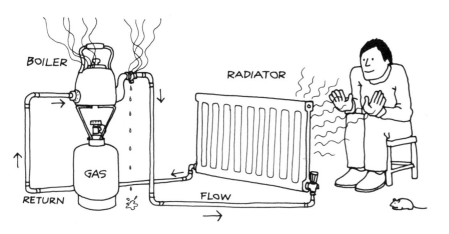

BOILER

RADIATOR

GAS

RETURN

FLOW

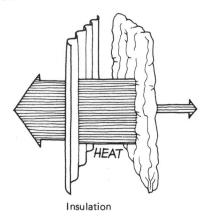

Insulation

## 15 Is it warm and cosy?

Everywhere you look nowadays there is someone telling you to wrap up and get insulated; turn on the TV and there it is again. It doesn't matter what sort of house you occupy, you will have been told to do it. So before you start buying a house on the basis that it's fully insulated because it has double glazing, here is a short explanation about how heat is lost from houses, which may help you to assess the level of insulation in the house you are inspecting.

Heat is obviously lost through the external walls, the roof and the ground by simple conduction. It is also wasted in the heating up of fresh air that is brought into the house to sustain life. If you lived in a completely air-sealed box you wouldn't last long. What allows heat to pass quickly or slowly through the outside envelope is the thermal resistance of the material it's made of. For instance metal lets heat through it very quickly but a nice fluffy duvet lets it through very slowly and therefore keeps your heat in.

So in theory it's better to build a house out of duvet covers than, say, corrugated metal sheeting. Nowadays we have a new measure for thermal resistance called the 'R' factor, where the higher the 'R' the better. Some products such as fibreglass insulation have the figure printed on the packaging. To give an example, fibreglass insulation (3'') is 2 whereas solid brickwork (4½'') is 0.17. The accompanying drawing shows how heat is lost from typical uninsulated houses.

Draughts are another big moan. In principle a house requires on average 1½ air changes/hour to keep the smells down. This to most people seems an amazingly high figure, but the truth is the non-draught-proofed traditional house probably has about 5-10 air changes an hour, with wind whistling through the sash windows and up the disused chimney. If all was well, with two air changes an hour, heating up the incoming fresh air would account for 20% of the total fuel bill.

Apart from double glazing, which is relatively expensive for what it saves, or not very cost effective, most home insulation is not expensive and fairly easy to install.

A quick list of checks for the house you are inspecting:
a      Is the roof space insulated?
b      Has the HW cylinder a comfy jacket?
c      Have the cavity walls been injected with cavity fill? If so ask for the guarantee.
d      Have the heating pipes been insulated?
e      Is the cold water rising main insulated?

WHERE THE HEAT GOES —

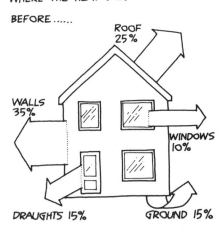

BEFORE ......
ROOF 25%
WALLS 35%
WINDOWS 10%
DRAUGHTS 15%
GROUND 15%

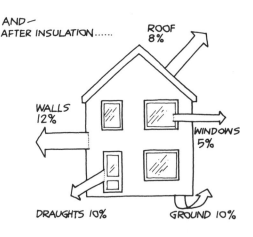

AND —
AFTER INSULATION ......
ROOF 8%
WALLS 12%
WINDOWS 5%
DRAUGHTS 10%
GROUND 10%

## 16 Will the outside need repainting soon?

As stated before, the less there is to paint the better. If the paint on woodwork is cracking and peeling, you will have to paint it soon. Check with the present owners when it was last done. With any luck they are the sort of people who believe the house fetches a better price if it has been recently decorated.

## 17 Kitchen units in good nick?

The other day I was in a well known London furniture shop in the kitchen department when I overheard a customer discussing the installation of some new kitchen fittings. My ears pricked up when I heard the estimated cost of £29,000. For some kitchen units! It's amazing the effect of the glossy magazines — kitchens seem to have replaced Rolls Royces for status. I expect this guy will only go in the kitchen once a week for a cup of coffee. Anyway he'll have it all done again next year to keep up with the fashion.

So before jumping to the conclusion that you can just slip in some nice new self-assembly kitchen fittings to replace the 1930 'Easiwork' units, remember that kitchens have everything happening in them from electrics to gas, from heating to water pipes, and as a result the cost of alterations is very high. The cheapest kitchen fittings, the knock up/fall down variety, cost about £300 for a set of units, so, if you are wise, remove thoughts of new ideal home dream kitchens and run through the following check list:

a     Is the cooker position big enough for your present cooker?
b     Can you get the fridge under the worktop?
c     Is there room for the washing machine and can you simply plumb it in?
d     What is the state of the kitchen units; are they gently rotting away under the sink?

7'6" MINIMUM OVER......

......50% OF......

......FLOOR AREA

WINDOW MINIMUM 1/10 OF FLOOR AREA

## 18 Is the house suitable for future modification?

You may find a house that will suit your present needs and pocket and think that you will be able to adapt the structure to provide additional bedrooms in the loft, together with extensions into the garden to accommodate your anticipated future wealth and six children. However, bear in mind the following constraints:

The major constraint to altering or extending is planning permission, which, if required, must be obtained or else the council has the legal right to come and remove the offending structure. If you intend to extend you will not require planning permission if the extension is under 15% of the original floor area (be sure to check that some of this hasn't been used already, for example, in conservatory extensions), as long as it is behind the original building line (i.e. the front of the house) and below the roof line. Then, as far as the planners are concerned, you can build your very own cruise missile launch pad, unless you are in a conservation area, or you are one of the privileged few living in a historic monument, in which case you can't do anything. So if you are thinking of a small extension, it doesn't do any harm to phone the planners and check.

Of course you may have something in mind that is totally impossible in terms of structure, for instance, building in the loft and removing all the struts that hold up the roof. This applies most to modern trussed roofs where there is little spare left to put anything, and insufficient headroom. By law a room must have a minimum headroom of 7'6" over at least 50% of the intended room area and a minimum window area of 10% of the overall floor area. If you are doubtful you can call in at the District Surveyor's or the Building Inspector's office and put your proposal forward and he should be able to give you some idea whether it will be accepted.

OK. Lastly, remember, if you think you are going to be able to get it done for 2/6d., that the current alterations and extensions building cost per sq. yd. of floor area is in the range of £400. So a small single-storey extension of 12'0" x 12'0" is £6,000, and then you will be lucky to find a builder who is reliable at doing this sort of work.

### 19 Nice wallpaper?

I bet you don't like the internal decorations. Nice house, shame about the decorations. Careful before your best friend persuades you that a complete redecoration can be done over a weekend. Remember that it takes at least two weeks of solid work for a team of decorators to do the average semi. It'll probably take you two nervous breakdowns and at least every weekend for six months.

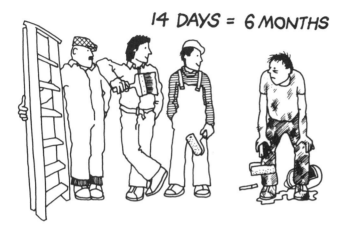

**14 DAYS = 6 MONTHS**

### 20 Quiet neighbours?

Most people only visit a house a couple of times before they purchase and generally at the most favourable times with a charming salesman or estate agent. Probably the most disturbing effect on your life style (walking around in your negligé) is loss of privacy by either your next-door neighbour peering over the fence or the children studying to become rock stars and sending 200 watts of power through the party walls. So check out the possibility of having to erect screens or improve the sound insulation to make life bearable.

| Top 20 Questions | Estimated cost | Estimated DIY time |
|---|---|---|
| 1   Is the house falling down? | | |
| 2   Are the outside walls bulging or leaning, or the chimney stacks leaning over? | | |
| 3   Are the floors collapsing? | | |
| 4   Is the roof collapsing? | | |
| 5   Is the roof leaking? | | |
| 6   Are the drains broken? | | |
| 7   Gutter problems? | | |
| 8   Is there dampness? | | |
| 9   Will the outside need constant maintenance? | | |
| 10   What is the condition of the windows and external doors? | | |
| 11   Are the ceilings falling down? | | |
| 12   Is the plumbing inadequate? | | |
| 13   Are the electrics out of date? | | |
| 14   Incompetent central heating system? | | |
| 15   Is it warm and cosy? | | |
| 16   Will the outside need repainting soon? | | |
| 17   Kitchen units in good nick? | | |
| 18   Is the house suitable for future modifications? | | |
| 19   Nice wallpaper? | | |
| 20   Quiet neighbours? | | |

Note: To summarize the survey of your ideal home, total up the cost of the repairs and improvements for the Top 20 Questions. Include both estimates for materials you'll require if you intend to do the work yourself and estimates from specialists such as plumbers and electricians. Where you intend supplying the labour make a generous allowance for the time required.

# MOVING
# EXPERIENCES

No matter how perfect and complete the home you've chosen, there will be plenty of things to do when you move in — cleaning, curtains, carpets, cookers, a shelf here and there. Homes are not like hotels and you can rarely just move in, hang up your coat, draw the curtains and settle down to a nice cup of tea in front of the fire.

This chapter deals with all the little things you'll be confronted with whether you like it or not. The sort of things you need to do before making that cup of tea, for example.

### Not so fast

If your dream house is not so perfect and complete, and you know it needs a lot more than a shelf here and there, **hang on**! If there are fairly major works to be carried out such as re-roofing, re-decorating or internal alterations, try and get them done before the family moves in. Building works of any kind soon take you and the whole place over; nervous breakdowns and divorces soon follow if you're trying to maintain normal relations under several inches of plaster dust.

If you need to employ a builder or roofer to carry out the essential repairs, refer to Chapter 8: Tradesmen, to ensure you don't lose your dream house altogether. Arrange for any major works to start as soon as 'completion' (legal acquisition) has taken place.

### Start compiling your maintenance manual

Slip down to the stationers now and buy yourself a nice large loose-leaf file and start filing maintenance manuals, operating and cleaning instructions for things like the central heating boiler and floor tiles. Provide a section for addresses, for example, where the sliding windows came from, who the plumbing and electrical contractors were, and so on. Put the guarantees in another section. Lastly, take, with the best possible camera available to you, photographs of the outside of the house when you move in as documentary evidence of the condition of the house and have them printed in foolscap size and witnessed. They will be invaluable should you have to claim on your insurances in the future, or if you have a dispute with adjoining owners.

.....ISN'T THIS NICE — THE FIRST MEAL IN OUR NEW KITCHEN......

# Water

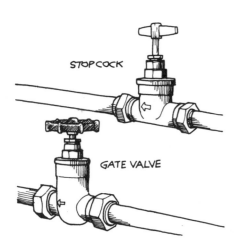

Stopcocks

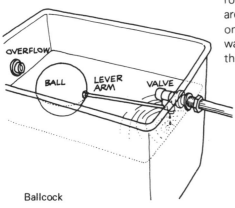

Ballcock

The system illustrated on the opposite page is the most common. Yours, unfortunately, may not be like it. The most common variations are: firstly, that there isn't a cold-water storage tank because the local Water Board doesn't require one; secondly, that you don't have a hot-water cylinder because there is gas or electric instantaneous water heating directly off the rising main. If you are moving into a new house you may find instead of a cold-water storage tank in the loft, a 'plumbing unit' with hot and cold water storage combined in a cupboard on the top floor.

### Basic knowledge of the system

Somewhere in the pavement near the front gate you will find the Water Board's stopcock which, they stress, is theirs — not yours. From this stopcock the water supply for your house is laid, preferably in a clay drain below the garden path up to the house. Sometimes there is a stopcock just inside your garden. Immediately inside the house is the main stopcock, which is yours and not theirs. From this stopcock a 'rising main', as it is termed, branches off to supply the kitchen sink with drinking water, to the cold-water storage tank in the loft, the feed and expansion tank for the central heating and in some cases to the washing machine. All these branches should have stopcocks next to the appliances like the stopcock you will find below the kitchen sink.

Water flowing into the storage tank is governed by the 'ball-cock' which is simply an airtight ball made of copper or nowadays plastic, that sits on the water's surface in the tank and is held in position with a lever arm which, as the tank fills, forces a stopper into the rising main. Just in case the ball springs a leak or the level arm jams, an overflow pipe is fitted to the tank above the normal water level. If you are up in the roof it's always fun to hold the ballcock down and make the tank overflow. Just to see it work — or not.

The 'down services', as they are termed by plumbers, are the pipework runs from the tank to the kitchen and bathroom. There are generally two pipes leaving the base of the cold-water storage tank: one to supply cold water to the hot-water cylinder and one to supply cold water to the bathroom and WC. The hot-water cylinder has a pipe popping out of the top which goes back to the cold-water storage tank so that, should the water in the hot-water cylinder get too hot, it has room to expand. Off this expansion pipe the hot water 'down services' are run to the bathroom and kitchen sink. You may find 'gate valves' on the down services next to the cold-water storage tank and the hot-water cylinder. A 'gate valve' has a red wheel top and does the same thing basically as a stopcock.

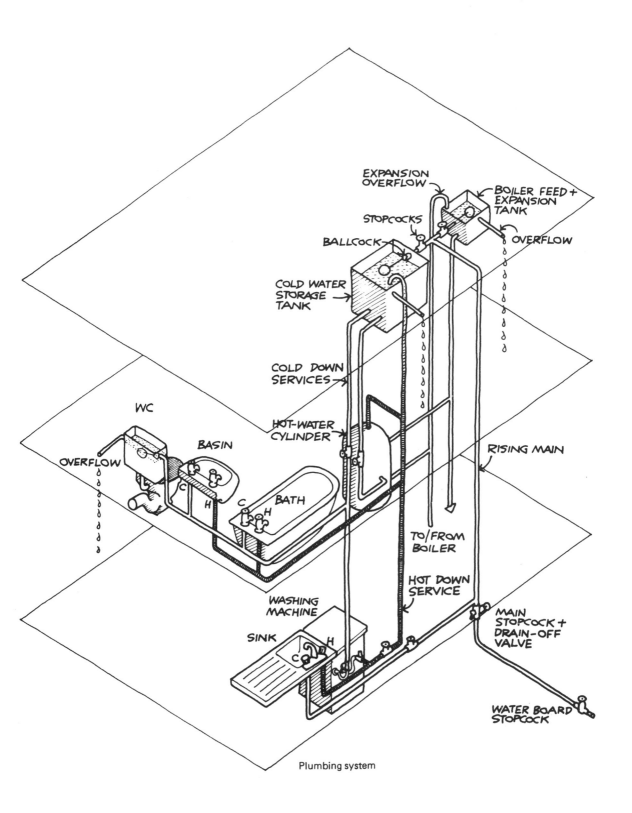

Plumbing system

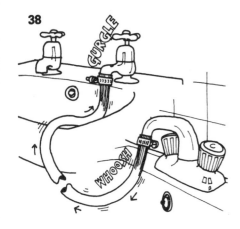

### Turning on

As you well know, you can't be everywhere at once, so to avoid flooding the house, know this method, which should also avoid airlocks. Know this method backwards and you'll also know how to get turned off — in emergencies, going away on holidays or just for something to do at weekends.

a      Turn off all sink and basin taps.

b      Turn off all stopcocks (B) and the cold-water storage tank (CWS) stopvalve (c) including the feed and expansion tank for the central heating system — if you've got one.

c      Turn on main stopcock (A).

d      Turn on stopcocks (B) and let CWS cistern fill up.

e      Turn on CWS cistern stopvalve (C).

f      Go round and try all taps, WC cistern.

If the water's been off for a while this procedure will generate a lot of gurgling, spluttering and coughing, but don't worry — it's only air being pushed out of the pipework by the water. Remember never to force a stopcock without being sure that you are going in the correct direction: clockwise for *off* and anti-clockwise for *on*. Always turn a stopcock back half a turn from being completely off or on, to avoid the stopcock jamming. If no water is coming past the Water Board's stopcock don't attempt to turn it on yourself. Ring the Water Board. You'll find them on your doorstep before you've drunk your tea (out of a flask).

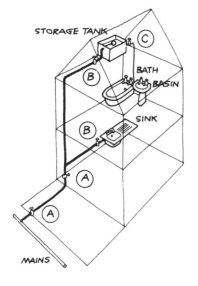

STORAGE TANK

BATH
BASIN

SINK

MAINS

### Problems

If you've turned on and can't get water out of the bathroom tap or kitchen hot tap, for example, it's probably an airlock — air trapped somewhere in the pipework and blocking the water flow. You should be able to budge this by connecting the offending tap to the kitchen sink cold tap with a garden hose suitably secured with a hose lock. Turn the offending tap on. Turn on the kitchen cold tap and the mains pressure should release the air locked in the pipe.

    Don't confuse air locks with 'water starving', which is the term used when one tap reduces the flow in another when both are turned on, and is caused by bad plumbing design. For instance when someone is running a bath there may only be a trickle of hot water in the kitchen sink. Normal plumbing systems have ¾'' down pipes serving the bath from both the cold-water storage tank and hot-water cylinder, with ½'' branches to sinks, basins and WC cisterns. Your plumber may have saved a bob or two — have a look.

If you've got leaking stopcocks and taps, or jamming ballcocks, have a look in Chapter 5: Techniques for the cure.

WHERE'S YER STOP COCK?

# Gas

Gasmen are awfully nervous nowadays about their installations going boof! Well there have been a large number of boofs recently. A typical gas system is illustrated opposite. Now your system will probably be different in that there will be pipework all closed in throughout the house. The Gas Board would encourage you to ensure that all pipework is well ventilated, so that pockets of gas don't build up from leaks.

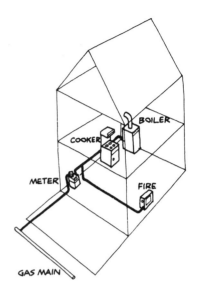

### Basic knowledge of the system

Not a lot to know. Pipe from street meets gas meter, from which the service runs to the appliances such as the gas cooker, gas boiler or gas fire. In old houses meters can be found in all sorts of odd and awkward places, not favoured by the modern gas man. In newer houses they are probably near an outside wall and more recently may be in a meter cupboard built into the external wall. Pipework by the Board is usually run in ½" to 1" diameter black painted steel or 'barrel' as they call it, to make it difficult for you to nail into. You may find some pipework running from the meter done in copper. This usually indicates that someone else other than the board has carried out the work. This is OK by the board but of course it is easy for you to nail into — and boof!

Before each appliance there should be a stopvalve on the pipe to shut off the supply. Boilers and fires are usually connected rigidly to the supply pipe, but cookers now have a flexible rubber hose connection. Make sure this is properly connected and not perished.

### Read the meter

Before using any gas, read the meter and keep a note of it to avoid paying for somebody else's gas. Just for interest, the white figures indicate hundreds of cu. ft. and the red figures ten cu. ft. and to work out the number of therms you use and pay for, simply work out the following formula.

$$\frac{\text{Calorific value}}{100} \times \frac{\text{Hundreds of cubic feet}}{} = \text{Therms}$$

The calorific value of natural gas is generally in the region of 1035 but check with your local gas showroom. There is no more town gas used in this country.

### Turning on

1. Turn off all appliances.
2. Turn on meter stopvalve.
3. Turn on individual appliance stopvalves as necessary.
4. Make sure pilot lights have been lit, e.g. cooker, boiler, etc. Be patient with pilot lights if you have difficulty in lighting them as you may have to wait some time for the gas to percolate through if the gas has been off for some time.

Make sure you know how individual appliances, such as fires and boilers, work before turning on and lighting, because we don't want you to start life in your new home with a bang.

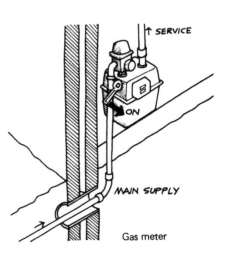

Gas meter

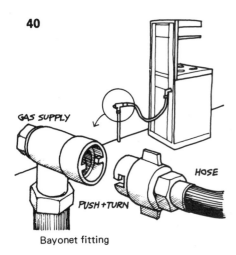

GAS SUPPLY

HOSE

PUSH + TURN

Bayonet fitting

### Fitting a cooker

If you need to fit a new cooker you'll probably have to get the Gas Board to install it. You might be lucky and find a 'bayonet fitting' where you want to put the cooker; it is just like a light bulb socket. As long as your cooker has a rubber hose with a suitable end fitting, you can simply plug in and get the dinner going.

### Safety tips

By the way, there's no point in putting your head in the gas oven any more if you can't pay the gas bills, as North Sea gas is non-toxic. If you do try, you'll only get sick and have to pay an even bigger gas bill.

However you can die slowly, if you wish, from carbon monoxide poisoning which is caused by the lack of proper ventilation or flues in rooms with gas burning appliances. A recent report has indicated that ten times as many people die from cabon monoxide poisoning as do from gas explosions. Carbon monoxide kills by suffocation, starving the brain and muscles of oxygen, and causing headaches and stomach ailments. Early warning signs of carbon monoxide build-up are discolouration and strange markings on the fire or boiler; a clear gas fire will suddenly turn brown or dingy. If in doubt, call the Gas Board round for an inspection.

If you are off on your hols don't forget to turn the gas off at the meter.

...REMEMBER WHEN YOU CONNECTED THE COOKER?........

# Electrics

### Basic knowledge of the system

**Supply ...** The mains supply to each house is brought in by the Electricity Board's cable to the 'mains head' which contains a sealed fuse and should never be tampered with. This fuse is designed to blow in case of fire, for example, preventing other houses in the neighbourhood being cut off from electricity.

Next to the head is the meter, also property of the Electricity Board. This is usually somewhere near an outside wall — by the front door, under the stairs. Newer flats or houses sometimes have an external meter cupboard built into the wall.

**... and demand** The domestic installation has several circuits going from the fuse-box, known to the Electricity Board as the 'consumer unit', which is usually located next to the meter (but doesn't have to be).

The consumer unit has a number of outlets or fuseways with a fuse unit or miniature circuit breaker (MCB) for each circuit. These prevent the circuits from carrying more current than they're supposed to. When this happens, the fuse blows and breaks the circuit, or, in the case of an MCB, switches itself off. Some houses have a 'trip switch' for the whole house; if circuits carry too much current, the trip will switch off all current. Just turn on; if it happens again, call an electrician.

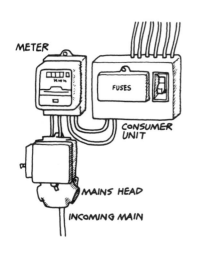

METER

FUSES

CONSUMER UNIT

MAINS HEAD

INCOMING MAIN

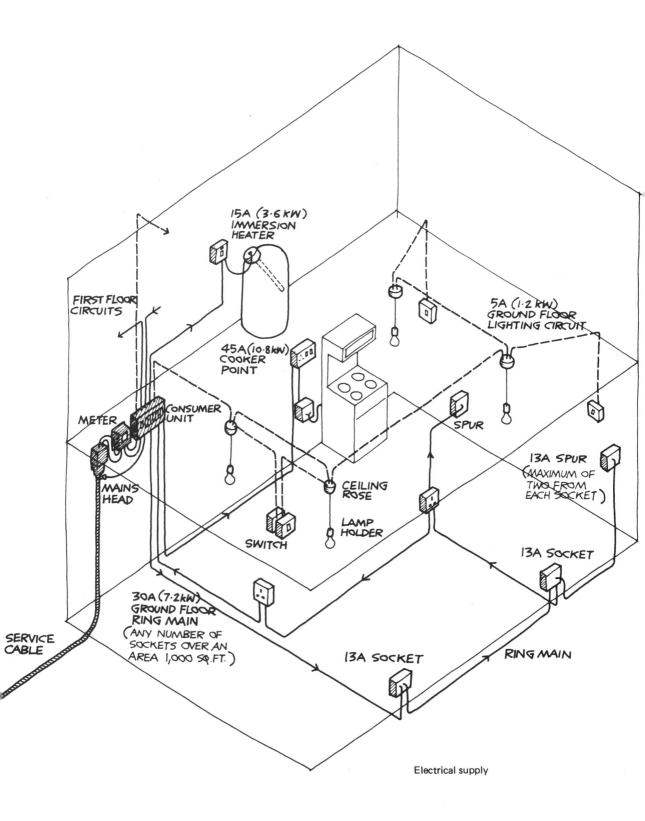

15A (3·6 kW) IMMERSION HEATER

FIRST FLOOR CIRCUITS

5A (1·2 kW) GROUND FLOOR LIGHTING CIRCUIT

45A (10·8 kW) COOKER POINT

METER

CONSUMER UNIT

SPUR

13A SPUR (MAXIMUM OF TWO FROM EACH SOCKET)

CEILING ROSE

MAINS HEAD

LAMP HOLDER

SWITCH

13A SOCKET

SERVICE CABLE

30A (7·2 kW) GROUND FLOOR RING MAIN (ANY NUMBER OF SOCKETS OVER AN AREA 1,000 SQ.FT.)

13A SOCKET

RING MAIN

Electrical supply

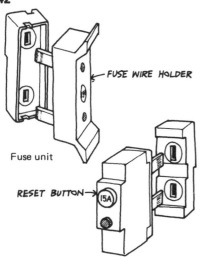

Fuse unit

Miniature circuit breaker (MCB)

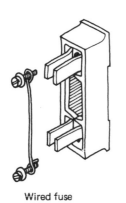

Wired fuse

Fuses or MCBs are rated to suit the circuit they control; domestic circuits are usually either for lighting with a 5-amp current rating, or for power ('ring-mains') with a 30-amp rating. Other circuits supply individual appliances, such as cookers, immersion heaters or night storage heaters and have current ratings to suit the kW rating of the appliances. For example: 15 amps for immersion heaters, 45 amps for cookers.

### Wiring

All modern domestic wiring uses grey or white PVC sheathed cable, mostly with two insulated cores (red and black) and an un-insulated earth conductor. Cable sizes are 2.5mm² for power and 1.0mm² for lighting (area of core cross-section). Anything not using this cable will be very old and needs immediate re-wiring.

### Lighting circuits

A lighting circuit consists of a number of lighting points connected to the circuit cable, which runs from a 5-amp fuseway in the consumer unit. The current flowing from the circuit to each lighting point is broken by the switch or switches. A 5-amp circuit can supply up to 12 light points to a maximum 100W — that is 1-2 kW total. Six or eight points is ideal so that some of the lights can be multi-bulb fittings or bulbs of 150W.

Your average sized house has one circuit for each floor; if the upstairs circuit fuse blows, the downstairs lights will stay on and vice versa.

### Power circuit

A power circuit or 'ring-main' runs around the house from a 30-amp fuseway, loops into socket outlets on the way and returns to the same fuseway — hence the 'ring'. This system has been used in all houses wired since 1947.

One circuit can have any number of 13-amp socket outlets along its length but it must not serve a floor area of more than 100 sq. metres or 1,000 sq. feet. Although average sized houses are less than

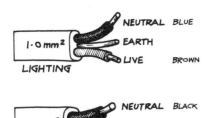

Two core, PVC sheathed cable

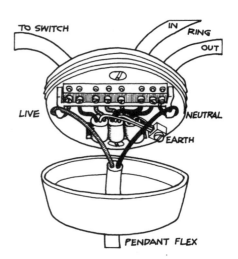

Ceiling rose lighting point

1,000 sq. feet, it is good practice to have more than one ring-main, usually one for each floor. This makes wiring easier and avoids all the power going off if one fuse blows.

Single branches can be taken from the ring-mains. These are called 'spurs'. A spur can supply up to 2 single sockets and the number of spurs must not be more than the number of sockets on the ring-main.

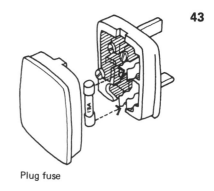

Plug fuse

### Earthing

The most important element in a wiring system is the earthing. Modern earthing systems are what's called 'protective multiple earthing'. The system earths metalwork, notably pipework, baths and kitchen sinks, directly to the main fuse-box and then to the board's earthing cable. Older earthing systems which used gas and water pipes for earthing are becoming obsolete as plastic pipes are replacing metal ones.

### Turning on

Before using any power, read the meter, and why not pop into your showroom and ask for the Electricity Board's *Home Energy Audit* for electrifying results? If the mains supply is connected you only need to turn on the main switch and off you go! Then go round and make sure all appliances such as cookers, fires, immersion heaters are turned off. Also make sure immersion heaters and instantaneous water heaters are full of water before turning on (i.e. that the water is on, and individual stopcocks are on).

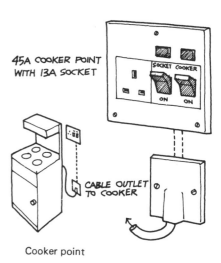

45A COOKER POINT WITH 13A SOCKET

CABLE OUTLET TO COOKER

Cooker point

### Confused?

You've turned on the mains but a socket outlet isn't working? First of all always check the fuse in the plug. It's probably blown (to mend, see Chapter 5: Techniques). If all the upstairs lights won't go on it's probably a mains fuse that's blown.

Mend the fuse (see Techniques again), or switch on the MCB and try again; if any main fuse keeps on blowing call an electrician.

### Fitting a cooker

Electric cookers use more power than the ordinary 13-amp socket can provide, so don't plug them into one. They need their own cooker point connected to a separate 45-amp circuit.

### Fuses

Before you get too far it's worth taking a look at the plugs on all your electrical appliances and checking that the fuses in the plugs are right for the job. No use having a small 3-amp table lamp with a 13-amp fuse — it could be set on fire by some fault and the fuse wouldn't blow and wouldn't cut off the current. Fuses are there for your safety. Go down to your local electrical shop or Electricity Board showroom and stock up with spare fuses. Then, of course you can put them away somewhere nice and safe until you need them and you won't be able to find them, will you?

### Safety tips

Be sure to avoid two pieces of equipment that you can obtain easily in most electrical shops: two- or three-way adaptors, and pendant sockets with multiple outlets. Both may overload the system or indicate that the house doesn't have sufficient sockets in the first place. Consider instead having additional wall sockets fitted.

NO!

Adaptors

**Fuse chart**

| Fuse rating | 3 amp | 5 amp | 13 amp | 15 amp | 20 amp | 30 amp | 45 amp |
|---|---|---|---|---|---|---|---|
| Colour code (cartridge fuses for plugs) | Red | White (or Black) | Brown | Blue | Yellow | Red | Green |
| MCBs | — | White (or Black) | — | Blue | Yellow | Red | Green |
| Fuse wire diameter (for wired fuses at fuse-box) | No wired fuses | 0.2 mm | No wired fuses | 0.5 mm | 0.6 mm | 0.85 mm | 1.25 mm |
| Maximum load | 720 W | 1.2 kW | 3 kW | 3.6 kW | 4.8 kW | 7.2 kW | 10.8 kW |
| Use (type of appliance or circuit) | Lamps up to 60 W B+w TVs | Lighting circuits Lamps over 60 W | Kettles Fan heaters Washing machines Colour TVs | Immersion heaters | | Power sockets Ring mains | Cookers |

# Central heating

### Basic knowledge of system

There are many variations of central heating, from electrical convectors to oil-fired central heating. The most common systems are what the trade call 'wet systems' — that is, where the heat is distributed by water through individual room radiators. The heating of the water can be either by gas, electricity, coal or, of course, oil. We've chosen to illustrate gas, as this is the most common.

### Gas central heating

The system on the opposite page has many variations and yours may of course be one, just to make life a little more difficult. The most common variation relates to the pumping of the water. In some systems only the central heating water is pumped, the water for the hot-water cylinder being fed by gravity pressure. Having said all that, the system on the opposite page works like this:

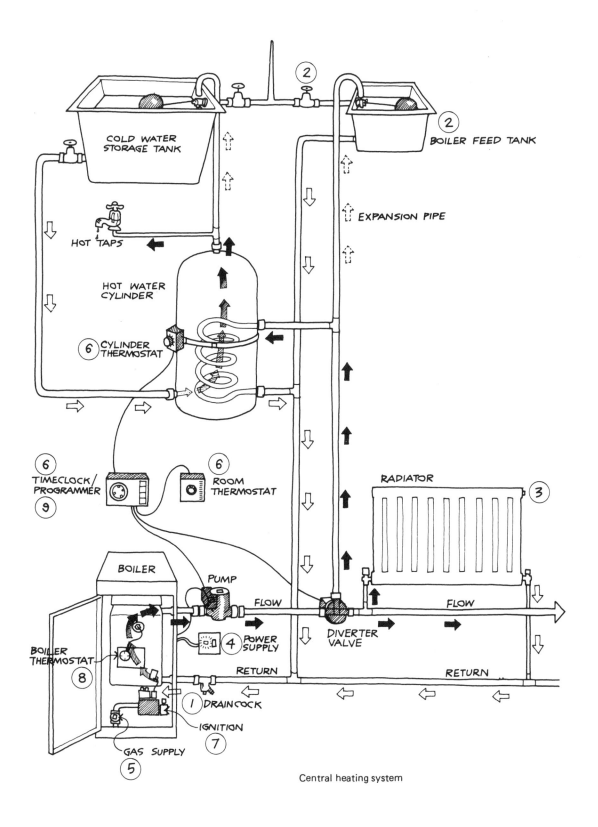

Central heating system

The gas burner in the 'boiler' heats up water in the 'heat exchanger' directly above, and the fumes pass through and up the flue, be it a conventional or balanced flue. The heat exchanger is basically a kettle full of water, as I said before, but with one difference. It is made of a continuous coil of pipework so that the heat can get to the greatest surface of water. The heat exchanger has the cold 'return' water coming in at the bottom and the hot 'flow' water going out of the top.

The next stage is the formation of two independent loops of pipework: one for the radiators, and one for the hot-water cylinder. The outgoing 'flow' and the incoming 'return' water divides into each circuit. So there you are — hot water feeding the radiators and the hot-water cylinder. By the way, the hot water from the boiler doesn't come out of the taps. The hot-water cylinder is fed from the cold-water storage tank; inside the cylinder is a pipework coil through which runs the hot water from the boiler — it's just like having a radiator inside the cylinder.

A pump is generally required to push water round, and this is located before the 'T' or the motorized valve so that it just pushes water regardless of which loop it's going down.

A time clock is provided so that you can have the system working at different times, such as in the morning and evening, and not in the daytime when you are out at work.

The only problem left is to stop the boiler heating up the 'flow' and 'return' water when either the radiators or the hot-water cylinder are hot enough. This is done with thermostats: a room thermostat located in a typical room and a hot-water cylinder thermostat. When either or both of these thermostats have reached the required temperature, they send an electrical current to the 'motorized' diverter valve to stop the water coming round the 'loops'. A 'motorized' diverter valve is placed at the 'T' on the flow and is a small motor which drives a sort of golf ball to block up one or the other loops, or if need be the incoming pipe, so that neither gets any water.

### Parts explained

#### The thermocouple

This is a safety device made from a simple piece of copper tubing that passes an electrical current to the gas valve by being heated up by the pilot light. This electrical current opens a valve in the gas valve, allowing gas to flow to the main burners. If the pilot light goes out for one reason or another, no electrical current passes down the thermocouple and gas cannot get into the burner. It is very easy to replace and has the good fortune of working if it's correctly installed, thereby preventing disasters created by your installation. To change a thermocouple, see Chapter 5: Techniques.

#### The pump

Most central heating systems use centrifugal pumps powered by ½-1 h.p. electric motors. A centrifugal pump is rather like a water wheel in reverse. The pump motor is switched on when either the central heating or the HW cylinder thermostats call for heat and is switched off when both thermostats have reached the required temperature.

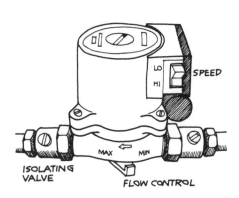

Typical pump

### Motorized valves

Motorized valves allow water to pass down selected routes. The simplest kind uses a 'T' in the pipework to allow hot water from the boiler to go either to the hot-water cylinder or to the radiators. The system is designed to give priority to the hot-water cylinder, which means that the radiators remain cold until the hot-water cylinder has reached the required temperature. The second variety is slightly complicated in that it divides the hot water from the boiler between the hot-water cylinder and the radiators so that the radiators and cylinder warm up simultaneously. With this system there would either be one or two valves — two being used in a large house.

### Radiator valves

There are three valves on a radiator: an airvent or vent plug at the top allows air to escape when the system is filled; a radiator ON/OFF valve and a Lockshield valve, which is practically the same as an ON/OFF valve but is used to balance the central heating system by reducing the flow of hot water into the radiators nearest the boiler so that radiators furthest away are not starved of heat.

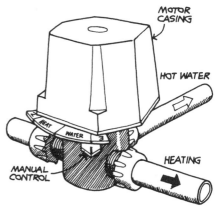

Motorized valve

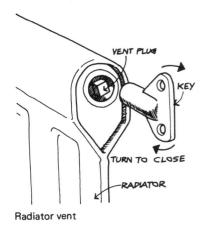

Radiator vent

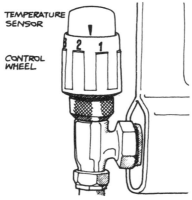

Thermostatic radiator valve

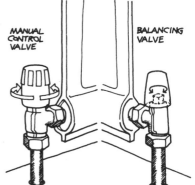

Radiator valves

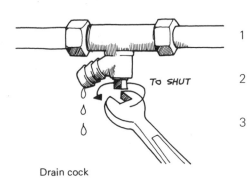

Drain cock

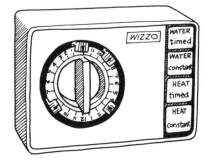

Time clock

## Turning on — step by step

1   Look for the drain-off cock(s) on the pipework and turn clockwise to 'shut' position if not already done.

2   Fill boiler feed tank by opening stopcock next to the tank. This will then fill boiler, radiators and pipework.

3   Bleed radiators to let out air trapped in the top of the radiators. Start with the lowest radiator in the house and work upwards. Undo the airvent at the top of the radiator with your radiator key (see diagram), which can be bought from ironmongers. Turn the key slowly to let the air out, until water begins to dribble out. Then close the vent quickly.
The hot-water cylinder may also need to be bled. Look for a brass screw-type fitting close to the cylinder on top of a short pipe. Using a screwdriver, gently undo this so that air escapes, until water begins to come out. Then quickly close the screw.

4   Switch on boiler electrical supply.

5   Turn on gas supply.

6   Set time clock to 'on' and set the thermostats on the hot water cylinder and room thermostat to the desired temperature. (Start with 110°F for the hot water, and 65°F for the room thermostat.)

7   Ignite boiler strictly in accordance with manufacturer's instructions, making sure that the boiler thermostat is 'off'.

8   Set boiler thermostat to recommended temperature, generally 180°F.

9   Adjust time clock to programme required.

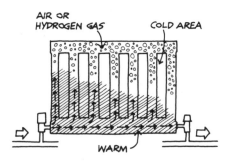

## A cold radiator?

If you've just started up, this is most likely due to air trapped in the radiator. Bleed the radiator until water starts squirting out.

# Walls

### Know your wall

So after a nice cuppa, how's about some nice shelving in the living room for the hi-fi? Considerable concentration is required or else we might go through an electric cable or water pipe.

First of all, check the possibility of any pipework lurking about. Can you see any radiators nearby or are you close to a kitchen or bathroom? Have a look at the plumbing diagram (p. 37) and try to work out where pipes might be running.

Also check for electrical cables buried below the plaster. If the house has been properly wired cables running in a wall will run vertically up and down from any light switch or power point (see electrical diagram, p. 41).

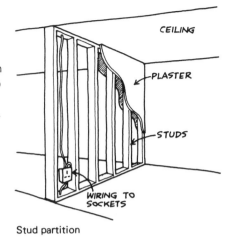

Stud partition

Now the difficult bit: how to establish what type of wall it is and what sort of fixing is required. Refer to Chapter 5: Techniques for fixings, having established what type of material you are fixing to. To establish the type of wall, firstly look at Chapter 1 for the three main types of house construction. As you may note, there are three main types of walls to fix into — solid brickwork or blockwork, stud partitions with plasterboard on them, or stud partitions with lath and plaster or expanded metal levelled with plaster, and third, solid laminated plasterboard partitions.

For starters, bash the wall with your hand. If the whole house shakes, it's more than likely plasterboard on studwork. If it shakes but with a dull sound, it's probably lath and plaster, or, if it's a new house, laminated plasterboard partition. And if it hurts your hand, it's probably solid. Another method for identifying internal partitions is to establish the thickness of the wall by taking dimensions at doorways.

| Overall thickness | Partition construction |
|---|---|
| 2½'' | Solid laminated plasterboard. |
| 4'' | 3'' stud partition with plasterboard. |
| 4'' | 3'' blockwork with plaster. |
| 5'' | 4'' stud partition with plasterboard. |
| 5'' | 3'' stud partition with lath and plaster. |
| | 4'' blockwork partition with plaster. |
| | 4'' stud partition with plasterboard. |
| 5½'' | 4½'' solid brickwork with plaster. |
| 7'' | 6'' blockwork with plaster. |
| 10'' | 9'' solid brickwork with plaster. |

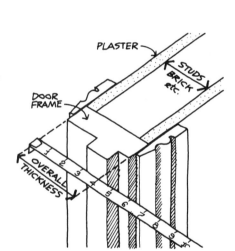

Wall thickness

# Home security 1

### (Resist those criminal tendencies)

It's no joke being burgled — the shock to your system is bad enough, let alone the cleaning up afterwards. It really could happen to you and often does. Any home is fair game — large or small, smart or scruffy — but the risk of being burgled can be greatly reduced by taking a few simple precautions.

Whether your place is new or old it's worth checking the security of all external doors and windows. It only needs a little effort on your part to deter your average domestic crook. First of all, fit a new lock to the front door when you move in. Most are fitted with the 'nightlatch' type of lock which isn't very effective. Change to a 'dead-lock' mortice type which can be locked from the inside as well as outside. Not only will you have a better lock but you'll know exactly who has all the keys.

Then have a look at other external doors, which are often poorly secured. Make sure a good deadlock is fitted and finish off with a bolt top and bottom. French windows should also be given the treatment with a lockable bolt top and bottom of each door.

On outward opening doors the hinges will be exposed to attack by would-be intruders. To finish the job properly, fit hinge bolts which will hold the door to the frame if the hinges are broken off.

Most burglars get in through windows because they are usually not fitted with locks or are simply left open. There are many kinds of window locks available and these should be fitted on all windows that can be reached from the ground or from flat roofs, porches, drain pipes, trees — you've heard of cat-burglars, haven't you?

Casement windows (the ones with hinges) should be fitted with locking devices which hold the catch in place or you could fit a new catch with a lockable handle. The stays can also be held closed with screw-down devices.

Sliding sash windows can be fitted with sash stops — which

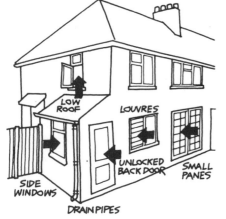

Danger spots

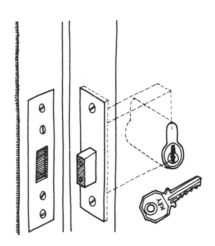

Mortise deadlock

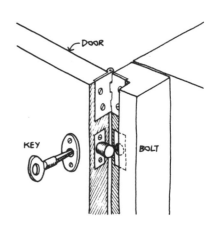

Hinge bolt

prevent the window being fully opened but allow some ventilation — or sash locks, or dual screws which fasten the two sashes together and prevent any opening at all. These are really for when you're away on hols or for windows not used very often. You don't want to feel that you're living in Fort Knox every time you need a bit of fresh air.

When you've got all this hardware fixed (see Chapter 5: Techniques for details) make sure you use it! If you leave your place unoccupied for any length of time, close and lock all windows and doors. For more ideas on keeping out the nasties just call your friendly neighbourhood Crime Prevention Officer down the nick. They're only too pleased to advise on all aspects of burglar-proofing.

'Evening all.

# Home security 2

### (Like a house on fire)

Burglary is bad enough, but a fire can be much worse. Every year in the UK there are 800 deaths caused by domestic fires due to overloaded electric sockets, faulty appliances, heaters and so on. Not to mention the countless injuries and the damage to property which results from all kinds of conflagrations, large or small.

Apart from making your home and its contents safe in the first place, it's a wise precaution to get a fire blanket and an extinguisher. There are several made for domestic use available in handy-sized containers. They are best kept together in a central and easily accessible place — on the wall in the kitchen, for example. It's a good idea to learn how and where to use them **before** you need to use them.

This time why not call the Fire Prevention Officer at the local fire station who can advise on extinguishers and all matters incendiary?

BLANKET..... OR FOAM

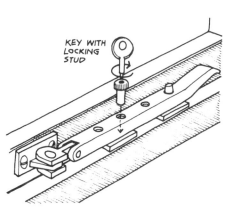
Casement windows: stays and handles

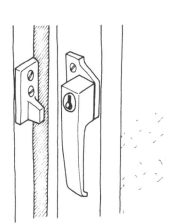

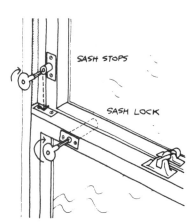
Sash windows

# 3

So there you are feeling justifiably relaxed, having purchased the ideal home, when you hear a dripping sound. Undoubtedly having dealt with this minor problem you will merrily discuss how fortunate you were to be at home when the dripping started. However, as most home owners are aware, disasters rarely happen to suit your programme. It is therefore wise to conclude that the minimum effort of regular maintenance can, as with cars (which we are more accustomed to maintain regularly), reduce the number of unexpected calamities.

In this chapter we propose an 'autumn maintenance programme' to cover electrics, plumbing, heating and drainage, and timber, and a 'five yearly maintenance programme' to cover external decorations, roofing and external walls.

## Autumn maintenance programme

### The drainage system

### Drainage systems explained
I doubt if there are any two identical drainage systems in this country. There are numerous combinations from district to district, using different materials and different methods of moving the waste away. You may not even be on main drainage. You may be one of the fortunate few blessed with septic tanks, the maintenance of which will probably have been impressed on you by the previous owners. The system on the opposite page is probably the most common and is generally typical of new housing.

### Underground drainage
Here we have a choice of two systems. One is where the rainwater is kept separate from the waste/soil water. The other is where both are combined underground at the manholes, and discharged to the main sewer in the street. I understand that in some areas you are not allowed to drain rainwater into the drainage system at all. It is intended that you form soakaways on your own property.

### A single-stack system
This is the modern form of drainage above ground where the WC, basin and bath are connected separately to one downpipe. To prevent suction breaking the traps, the wash-hand basins, baths, showers and WC are all within two metres of the downpipe.

### A two-pipe system
This is the same as the above, but the WC is taken separately to the manhole.

Traps

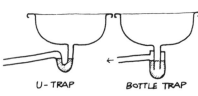

U-TRAP          BOTTLE TRAP

DOUBLE SYPHONIC     WASHDOWN

### A vented system

This applies to both the above systems when the fittings are farther than two metres away from the downpipe. Then, to prevent the traps being broken, a vent pipe is located close to each individual trap to let in air and prevent the suction building up.

### Traps explained

The purpose of a trap is very simple: to prevent pong coming from the main sewer into your house. A trap is formed with a U bend of pipes, in which water is trapped; between 1½" and 3" for baths, wash-hand basins and showers, and approximately 6" deep for WCs, rainwater gullies and yard gullies. Suction is formed between the trap and the discharged water; the larger the distance the greater the suction, so to prevent the water in the trap being sucked out, basins, baths, showers and WCs are all within 2 metres of the downpipe in a single-stack system.

There is one special trap which is intended to stop rats coming from the main sewer into your drainage system. This is the interceptor trap, and is located either at the edge of your property or in the last manhole before the main sewer. Too often when the drainage is blocked, the interceptor stopper is removed and this allows the rats to climb straight in without attempting to go through the trap. So in your maintenance, look for the stopper and tie a piece of polypropylene rope to it. Attach this to a hook at the top of the manhole and then you will be able to pull it and release a blockage.

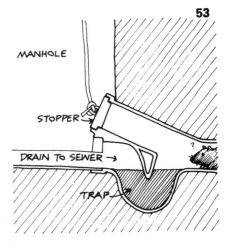

Interceptor trap

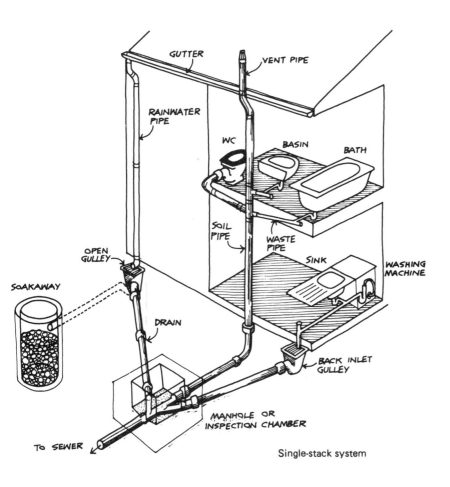

Single-stack system

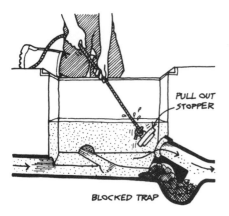

PULL OUT STOPPER

BLOCKED TRAP

# Drainage

### What's going to go wrong anyhow?

Ugh! Sewage — yes, blocked manholes and a £30 (approx) bill to clear it from the emergency plumber! But far worse is that water, which is the single most destructive force to any house, could start running down the outside of the house from defective pipes and gutters. Water, as you have gleaned, can cause dry rot, dampness, condensation, and bring down ceilings. Any sign of dampness should be dealt with forthwith. However, it is very difficult to know if a guttering system is working effectively unless you are prepared to stay outside on a rainy day.

### Each year carry out the following

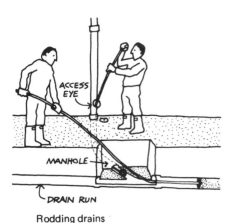

ACCESS EYE

MANHOLE

DRAIN RUN

Rodding drains

1    Clean out all gutters and hoppers and wash down.
2    Clean out all external gullies either with one of those new wet and dry vacuum cleaners or by hand. You will find a lot of sludge at the bottom of the trap.
3    Hose down the internal walls of manholes, checking that the rope that pulls up the interceptor trap still works. Before putting the manhole back, clean out the rim and put some grease in to ease lifting for next year's inspection.
4    Rod through all drain runs even if it means opening rodding points (access eyes).
5    Dismantle all internal traps to sinks, baths, basins, dishwashers and washing machines, and wash out congealed soap and hair — very common in baths and wash-hand basins.
6    Finally, when everything has been replaced, fill the bath, turn on all the taps, flush the WC, in order to flush out the system.

### To avoid blockages
Avoid putting tea-leaves, sanitary towels, babies' disposable nappies into the drainage system, or pouring down cans of old paint or bags of plaster, or washing cement away.

### Leaf guards
If you live in a forest, you may be interested in leaf guards made from plastic netting and simply clipped to the edge of the guttering (see Where to Find It).

### Leaking gutters
If you are unwilling to replace the guttering system because the only problem is leaking joints, you can seal the joints with a new form of mastic applied with the use of a gun. If, on the other hand, it is simply one section of, say, cast-irion guttering that has rusted away, remember to check if you can still obtain replacements. It is quite surprising how many building materials are still readily available. If your local builders' merchant cannot help, contact the Building Centre (see Where to Find It).

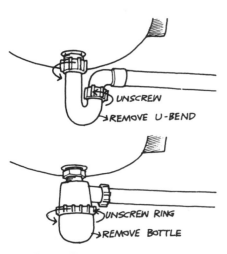

UNSCREW

REMOVE U-BEND

UNSCREW RING

REMOVE BOTTLE

Dismantling traps

# Timber

### What's going to go wrong anyhow?

OK so no-one's perfect. You knew before you bought the house that the previous owners had never looked after the place, and had allowed the gutters to overflow. However, you looked inside the house for signs of dry rot in the skirtings and much to the astonishment of the estate agent, did a jump test as suggested in Chapter 1. Now, after all that, there it is in the living room bay-window skirting.

By the way, don't assume that this section can be skipped because the house has been treated by a specialist and you are the proud possessor of a 20-year guarantee. Bear in mind that the guarantee is only valid if the house is properly maintained and that even if the company does accept liability, it only covers their work and not the associated builder's work.

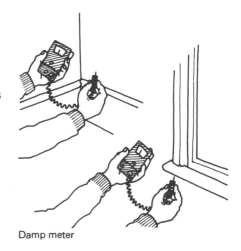

Damp meter

### Each year carry out the following

1    Inspect the whole house for dampness with your damp meter.
2    Ensure all airvents are in working order and clear if necessary.
3    Inspect as much structural timber as possible throughout the house, for instance, in roof and cellar spaces. Use a powerful torch or, better still, a portable fluorescent strip light.
4    Remove bath panel to look for dampness in flooring beneath bath trap.
5    Prod all timber sills to windows and doors, especially at the corners, to see whether the timber has gone soft.

### Dry rot explained

Assuming that the outbreak is minor because of your constant vigilance, there should be no need to evacuate the house if immediate action is taken — bearing in mind that true dry rot fungus, that is *merulius lachrymans*, can grow at the rate of 2" a day. Timber that has been saturated with water and therefore unable to sustain fungus may dry out till it contains 20-30% moisture, when it becomes ideal for the growth of the fungus, especially if it is drying out in the spring months.

The cycle of *merulius lachrymans* starts with the formation of very fine threadlike tubes of *hyphae* which form below, say, the timber ground floor — if the airvents are blocked or if the builder has used the sub-floor area as a skip. (Dry rot can't stand draughts.) The *hyphae* shrivel up on exposure to dry air and turn yellow on exposure to light, whereas in slightly drier areas, for instance behind skirtings, the *hyphae* form yellow or grey coloured rubbery sheets. The truly exciting aspect of dry rot fungus is the ability of *hyphae* to traverse any form of inorganic material to reach their food source — timber.

Finally, in a display of heroic victory, the formation of 'sporophores' or fruiting bodies. These majestic red or orange growths edged in lilac or white, sending forth to rich and pleasant pastures millions of rust coloured spores to start the cycle anew, would be the first sign to the non-vigilant home owner that he was failing in his regular yearly investigations.

Dry rot

There is another form of dry rot fungus called **poria vailanti**, the white pore fungus which requires higher moisture content and rarely forms fruiting bodies.

### Wet rot explained

Although similar to dry rot, wet rot does not spread, and requires saturated timber to survive. Once affected timber is removed, the problem ceases. Although timber with a moisture content greater than 80% cannot support dry rot, the fringes of wet rot areas are ideal for dry rot.

### Woodworm explained

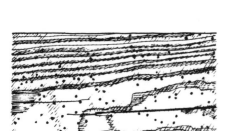

Woodworm

Woodworm is easily identified from the honeycomb effect caused by our little friend the common furniture beetle and her babes in the wood. You can kill 'em easily enough with poison obtainable from builders' merchants and manufactured by firms like Rentokil, Solignum, Protim and Sovereign. The poison can be applied either with a spray, or, more safely, as a paste.

It may be wise if you find extensive worm holes to spray other parts of the house such as the roof space. Treatment is best in the spring-time when the fresh batch of beetles are delivered. If the house has had timber treatment, check from the guarantee the areas of treatment.

Unfortunately when you notice the holes in the floorboards you are seeing the last events in the cycle. These are 'flight' holes, the escape routes of the adult beetles who are simply off in search of a mate after being in your floorboards, gathering strength, over the last three years. On mating, the adult will, shortly before dying, lay eggs which are invisible to the naked eye, in the cracks and joints of the timberwork. From here the baby beetles bore deep into the soft grains of tasty sapwoods in search of sustenance. After three years the grub forms a pupal chamber just below the surface and turns into a beetle of sufficient strength to bite a way to freedom.

### Death watch beetle (not explained)

If you are host to a death watch beetle, by simple deduction you are fairly wealthy, as this beetle prefers only the finest hardwoods, as found in more exclusive properties. So simply drift over to your personalized pearl-studded phone and ring Woods, Woods and Stone Partners — the family surveyors — and instruct them to sort it out.

SHRIEK!!

# Central heating

### What's going to go wrong anyhow?

Yes, obviously the system may fail to provide hot water or heating. This deals with the maintenance of the boiler and parts replacement.

If you want to establish what part is causing the system to malfunction, refer to Chapter 4: Help!

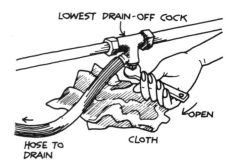

### Each year carry out the following

1   Switch the boiler off, both gas and electrics, and turn off the rising main stopcock to the feed and expansion tanks.

2   Inspect all radiator valves for leaks. The constant expansion and contraction can work the compression joints loose. If there are leaks, drain the system for repairs.

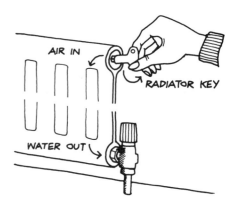

3   Locate the lowest drain-off cock and fix a hose to it. Run the hose out of doors to a gulley. Undo the square-headed nut to drain-off cock, making sure to have some cloths below to prevent drips falling on to the Afghan rug. Then go to the top radiator in the house and open the vent plug which will break air locks. Eventually open all the radiator vent plugs. In some systems there may be more than one drain-off cock on the lowest floor radiators. Inspect the central heating water as it flows into the gulley. It should not be sludgy black. If it is, it indicates corrosion within the system, making it all-important to add a rust inhibitor.

4   Now proceed to vacuum out the boiler — the part where the gas burns. You will need the boilermaker's manual to achieve this.

5   Inspect flue-ways for birds' nests and the like, and ensure that there are no obstructions to fresh air reaching the boiler. The Gas Board Regulations under the 1967 Gas Act require permanent fresh air vents to rooms or cupboards containing boilers. Balanced flue boilers need 2 sq. in. free ventilation for every 5,000 BTUs of boiler output; conventional flue boilers need twice this amount. There is no fresh air requirement for balanced flue boilers below 25,000 BTU output. Remember, if your home doesn't comply with the regulations and there is a fire, you may be held responsible and, even worse, be unable to claim on your insurance.

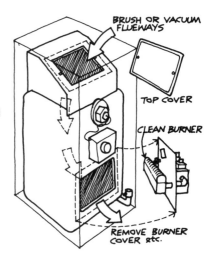

6   Reassemble boiler. Refill and add inhibitor.

NB  Only drain the system if necessary — corrosion inhibitor is expensive.

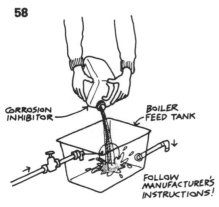

CORROSION INHIBITOR

BOILER FEED TANK

FOLLOW MANUFACTURER'S INSTRUCTIONS!

Corrosion inhibitor

### Radiators

Alarmingly enough, steel panel radiators have an anticipated life expectancy of only ten years *unless* some form of rust inhibitor is put in the water. The radiators may then start to leak at the seams. The leaks can be cured in two ways: by simply replacing the radiator, or by using a liquid sealant placed in the central heating water.

Replacing a radiator is quite simple. Refer to Chapter 5: Techniques.

### Inhibitors

Fresh clear water unfortunately is not the ideal medium for carrying heat around in a central heating system made of a mixture of different metals, as different metals can set up electrolytic action which accelerates corrosion. Fernox MB-1 is a corrosion proofer and water conditioner which reduces the effects of water. It is supplied in liquid form and poured into the header tank, in quantities recommended by the manufacturer.

### Hard water/de-scaling

You can easily tell if you live in a hard water area by looking inside the kitchen kettle. If it's anything like mine, you'll find a thick layer of brown plaster inside. This is a lime deposit. As you can appreciate, if this happens in your boiler, cylinder and pipework, you'll be needing more fuel to do the same job.

If you've recently taken over a heating system in your autumn maintenance plan, de-scale it thoroughly. Ask at your plumbers' merchant for Fernox DS-9 and follow the manufacturer's instructions. You will need a weekend to do it properly.

### Water treatment : prevention is better than cure

It is claimed by one manufacturer that Britain's householders pay out an extra £100 million as a result of scale formation which adds an extra £10 a year to a family's heating bills. Lime and calcium deposits block up heating pipes and kettles. The traditional method of treating hard water is to pass the incoming water through an ion resin to which the deposits cling and are then removed yearly by washing with sodium. Permutit is the largest supplier of water softeners and make a range of units costing between £300 to £500.

There is another method of treating water, which is to suspend the lime deposits in the incoming water by magnetic action . There are a number of manufacturers producing units on this basis at a cost of around £50 (see Where to Find It).

### Central heating maintenance contracts

Of course, if you are prepared to pay an annual premium of between £30 and £50, you don't have to take the slightest interest in central heating systems. People like the Gas Board, oil companies such as BP, and certain boiler manufacturers operate maintenance contracts which will insure you against parts failure, and provide a yearly maintenance check-up.

# Electrics

### What's going to go wrong anyhow?

Assuming that you have checked that the system is not out of date (see Chapter 1) there is not very much to go wrong. However, a broken plug or socket, a frayed wire or a wire pulled from a plug can lead to lethal electric shocks or fire. (Just to make you really worry, one in every three house fires is started by electrical faults.)

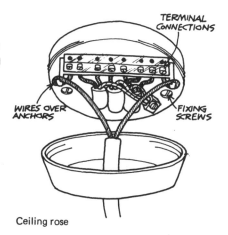

Ceiling rose

## So each year carry out the following

### *Turn off the consumer unit before starting*

1    Inspect all electrical sockets and switches for breakage, burning or looseness. If broken or burnt replace.

2    Inspect all ceiling roses and wall lights for exposure of individual cables.

3    Inspect all cables to electrical appliances and light fittings for frayed wires. If in doubt, unscrew plugs and sockets to ensure wires are not touching and are securely fixed to the relevant terminals. Just think, an earth wire can slip out and not impair the working of the appliance.

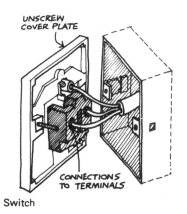

Switch

### Five-year maintenance

Regardless of the yearly checks by yourself, you should arrange with the Electricity Board or a qualified electrician to carry out a check, with the use of a 'megameter', every five years for leakage in the wiring, and inspect the earthing arrangements. Remember, better safe than sorry; it'll only take a couple of hours, and may save your life.

### Radio/TV interference

Another almost free service. Simply pop down to the Post Office and obtain standard form BRL 144 G. Send it in and there'll be a 'Telecom' van at your front door in a flash. You may not necessarily be the instigator of the interference. If your central heating boiler is not suppressed adequately you can cause interference to your TV or radio and those of the whole neighbourhood via the electric mains. The symptoms are unpleasant buzzing noises and flickering pictures. For a few bob 'Telecom' will fit a small compressor to the evil appliance. By the way, it's not always the fault of the manufacturers, as interference is a random event.

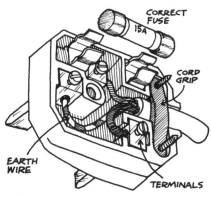

Plug

# Five-year maintenance programme

The most obvious element of long-term maintenance is having the outside of the house redecorated, a task regrettably highly suitable for 'doing it yourself'. However, before going out to buy the paint and arranging to hire/borrow some ladders, consider other parts of the external fabric that may need attention, such as the roof, the chimney stacks, the guttering system, which may have gone beyond yearly maintenance.

One of the most expensive items in carrying out repairs to the outside of a house is 'getting there', be it by scaffolding or ladders. Having decorated the house, you may decide that the roof should have been re-tiled, and you will find that the roofers will erect scaffolding that would have been very useful to you while you were painting top floor windows perched at the end of a ladder.

So read through the following checklists and draw up a small specification for the repairs needed. You may find a considerable amount, and may conclude that you should get somebody else to do it (refer to Chapter 8).

# Roofs

### What's going to go wrong anyhow?

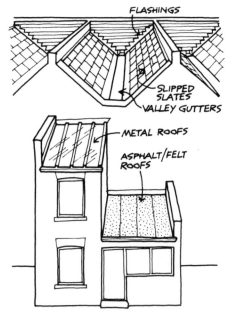

FLASHINGS

SLIPPED SLATES

VALLEY GUTTERS

METAL ROOFS

ASPHALT/FELT ROOFS

They are going to let the rain in. Some of the worst decisions concerning maintenance are made in connection with roof repairs. There's this home owner not a million miles from my front door who has spent a considerable amount of time over the last couple of years on cheap, quick solutions to his roof defects. It all started with the valley gutter leaking, so out came the bitumen which was sloshed about with gay abandon to no avail. Assumption was that the adjacent brickwork required repointing. Over the parapet on a piece of rope goes this 'man-and-boy' tradesman to carry out the pointing on the front elevation. The only trouble was he could only reach down six courses. Still the rain came in. Like a flash it came to them that the water was coming in at the edge of the slates, so they pointed round each slate; no good; only one thing left for it, black jack the whole roof. Well, last summer the sun beamed down and the black jack cracked and curled up. Nothing's happened since.

If the roof covering is coming to the end of its natural life, be sure to cure the problem in one foul swoop and provide a new covering that will last for at least thirty years. We include in this section temporary repairs to get you out of trouble while you sort out paying for a new roof covering (see Ch. 10).

**Every five years carry out the following**

1    Inspect all flashings to see if they've come loose or started corroding.

2    Inspect all valley gutters for ponding.

3    Inspect pitched roofs for broken or slipped slates.

4    Inspect metal roofs for corrosion.

5    Inspect asphalt roofing for blistering and cracking, especially at the edges.

6    Inspect felt roofing for cracking, blistering and adhesion.

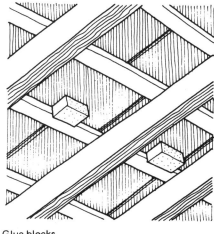

Glue blocks

# Temporary repairs

### Slipped slates

Hang on a tingle, someone's come up with these glue blocks that you can stick on the back of the slate from inside the roof space (see Where to Find It).

However, it's not always easy to reach slates from underneath, so to learn the old method is still worthwhile. As you are aware, slates are held in position with nails which, when slating is carried out, are covered by the following slate. Therefore it is not possible to re-nail a slate as originally intended. So a 'tingle' is used to hold a slate in position. This is simply a piece of 1'' wide copper/aluminium or lead strip which is nailed to the roof batten that is exposed when the slipped slate is removed, and leaves the joint of the slates below open. The copper strip is nailed to the batten so that its length runs down the roof. The slate is pushed back in its original position and the exposed length of copper folded over at the bottom to form a hook. Obviously if the slate is broken, there is no reason why you can't slip in another.

By the way, if you've got a nail in the way, this can be removed with a slate ripper. I have one, never been used, which I am prepared to sell at half today's current price.

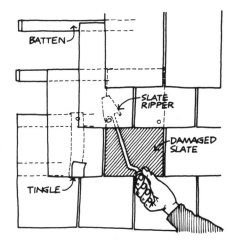

### Sylglas

OK so that dealt with pitched roof coverings. What about flat roof coverings and flashings?

Flashing can either fall out or corrode. If they fall out, replace in same position, using lead wedges to hold them. Lead wedges are simply folded strips of lead, which can be bought from any builders' merchant. Then, to prevent water seeping down behind, make good the pointing, using 1 part cement to 3 parts sand (i.e. mortar). Refer to Chapter 5 for the finer points of pointing. If they corrode, stick something on the hole — patch and repair. And what could be better than 'Sylglas', which is 4'' wide thin strips of aluminium with bitumen on the back.

Similarly 'Sylglas' can be used to stick up holes on flat roofs too, or for those in dormer roofs or in valley gutters.

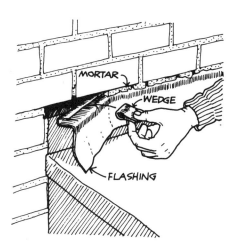

### Asphalt roofs

Asphalt roofs fail by blistering, sagging, and becoming brittle from old age.

Blistering is the building term for air pockets forming under the asphalt, puffing it up. The blisters can be simply cured by puncturing and warm with a blow torch. You'll probably find asphalt sagging at the edges where it's been carried up the wall, where the sun has softened it, and where it has dropped because of its own weight. The only makeshift job is the use of 'Sylglas'.

When asphalt has come to the end of its life, it becomes brittle and cannot be softened to make good, and the only temporary treatment is to paint it with some bituminous paint which will then become, although very thin, your rainproof protection.

At all costs redecorate asphalt every five years with solar reflectant paint: that is white Sandtex or something similar. As you probably know, black colours attract heat, whereas white surfaces reflect. Don't bother if you have white granite chippings.

# External decorations

### What's going to go wrong anyhow?

Divorce at the very least over which colours to choose. However, the primary object of external decorations is protection, an objective that even some professional decorators find hard to achieve.

### Every five years carry out the following

1   Establish the level of decoration required. That is either a complete strip down or simply a clean and a new top coat.

2   Clean down and sand metalwork, ensuring removal of all rust, and redecorate.

3   Clean down all woodwork including gutter boards, scrape off loose paint, sand and redecorate.

4   Wash down painted render, scrape off loose and flaky paint and redecorate if you've strength.

5   On completion, re-do sealants around window frames.

### Time factors

The reason why decorations are an ideal DIY task is because they are labour intensive and it's soon to be your labour. So fully understand and estimate how long it's going to take before starting, or else you may just lose interest after the first window. For instance, a typical window, say 4'0'' sq., would take at least a day to strip down and prepare (if necessary), with an hour a coat for painting subject to good weather. So in our opinion, the average semi with three bedrooms would take between three and four weeks solid work or ten weekends to complete.

# External walls

### What's going to go wrong anyhow?

Hmmm! Is that crack getting bigger or is it just my imagination? Only occasionally, such as in 1976, do fractures or movements happen quickly enough for us to be sure that something is wrong. Bulging brickwork or leaning chimney stacks take time to develop. A regular eye may well pick up developments soon enough to take adequate precautionary steps to prevent costly repairs.

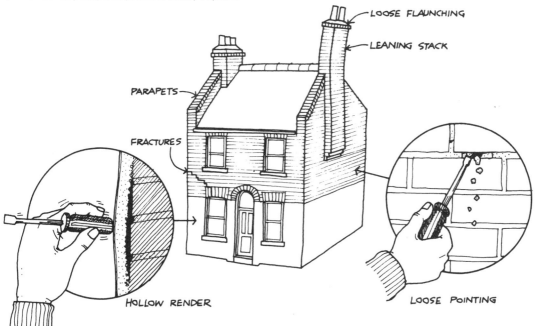

HOLLOW RENDER

LOOSE POINTING

### Every five years carry out the following

1   Look over window and door openings for fractures.

2   Inspect for loose pointing.

3   Inspect chimney stacks for loose flaunching (the mortar surrounding the base of a chimney pot .)

4   Inspect parapets and copings for stability.

5   Tap rendering for hollowness, especially after a severe frosty winter.

### Tell-tales

If you are not sure if a crack is getting larger but are getting worried, you can allay your fears by fitting over the crack a piece of microscope glass glued either side with Araldite glue. If it breaks, the house is, as feared, on the move. If so, call your surveyor.

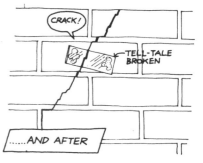

BEFORE......

CRACK!

......AND AFTER

| | Unpainted surfaces | Painted and in reasonable condition | Painted but flaking and clogged up |
|---|---|---|---|
| Softwood<br>White wood | Sand down and clean<br>Primer coat<br>Undercoat<br>Gloss coat | Wash down<br>Touch up blisters or<br>cracks with undercoat<br>twice<br>Gloss coat | Burn off<br>Sand down and clean<br>Primer coat<br>Undercoat<br>Gloss coat |
| Hardwoods<br>Either | Sand down and clean<br>Oil | Re-oil | Clean off with stripper<br>Oil |
| Or | Sand down and clean<br>Aluminium primer<br>Undercoat<br>Gloss | Wash down<br>Touch up blisters or<br>cracks with primer twice<br>Gloss coat | Burn off<br>Sand down and clean<br>Aluminium primer<br>Undercoat<br>Gloss |
| Metalwork<br>(Cast iron and steel<br>not aluminium) | Sand down and clean<br>Red oxide primer<br>2 coats gloss | Wash down<br>Remove rust with rust<br>remover<br>Touch up with primer | Burn off<br>Wire brush down<br>Red oxide primer<br>2 coats gloss |
| Render | Don't | Wash down<br>Touch up with alkali<br>resisting primer<br>Gloss | Burn off<br>Alkali resisting primer<br>Undercoat<br>Gloss coat |
| Brickwork | Don't | Leave it | Strip off for good |

# HELP! AND ANXIETY     4

## There's a smell of gas

| Symptom | Possible cause | Quick cure | Proper job |
|---|---|---|---|
| Smell comes from appliance. | You left it on unlit. | Turn it off. Don't re-light for 15 mins at least and open windows. | — |
| Smell comes from appliance with pilot. | Pilot light blown out. | Turn it off. Don't re-light for 15 mins at least and open windows. | — |
| Smell from flue. | Leaking carbon monoxide. | To maintain flue, see Ch 3. Open windows. | — |

**IF SYMPTOMS PERSIST TURN OFF GAS AT METER AND RING GAS BOARD EMERGENCY NUMBER IN TELEPHONE DIRECTORY (OR RING DIRECTORY ENQUIRIES)**

## Water is leaking

| Symptom | Possible cause | Quick cure | Proper job |
|---|---|---|---|
| Tank in attic over-overflowing. | Ballcock jammed or leaking. Overflow blocked or non-existent. | Turn off main stopcock; make hole in ceiling to let water drain. Put bucket beneath. Run all taps & turn off heating. | Repair ballcock. Unblock overflow or install one (see Ch. 5) |
| Pipe burst. | It froze or someone put a nail through a central heating pipe. | As above & drain central heating if a central heating pipe affected (see Ch. 3). Wrap burst pipe with cloth or better still, plastic padding available from DIY shops. | Replace damaged section of pipe (see Ch. 5) and insulate pipe if in roof space or exposed to frost. |
| Roof leaking. | Flashing, tile or slate has blown off or covering sprung a leak. | Put bucket in loft. Cover hole with something sticky (see Ch. 3) or replace slate, tile or flashing. | Perhaps replace roof covering (see Ch. 3). |

| Symptom | Possible cause | Quick cure | Proper job |
|---|---|---|---|
| Gutters or downpipes leaking | a They're blocked. | Get up & clear them. | Install leaf guard. |
| | b Joints leaking. | If cast iron, seal with mastic; if plastic, clip back together. | Dismantle & replace. |
| | c Gutter pulling away from eaves board. | Replace rusty screws with sheradized screws. | Replace eaves board if rotten. |
| Skylight leaking. | a Glass broken. | Staple sheet of polythene over opening. | Reglaze. |
| | b Gap between glass & frame. | Staple sheet of polythene over opening. | Allow frame to dry out; when dry, paint frame & reputty. |
| | c Flashing leaking. | Use Sylglass (see Ch. 3). | New flashing. |

# No hot water or central heating
## A (Gas central heating)

| Symptom | Possible cause | Quick cure | Proper job |
|---|---|---|---|
| Pilot light won't come on and no gas comes out of any appliance. | You haven't paid the gas bill; you haven't turned on the meter. | Pay it. Turn it on. | |
| Pilot light won't come on and yet gas comes out of other appliances. | Boiler gas cock off. | Turn it on (see Ch. 2). | |
| Pilot light lights but won't stay on. | It's windy. | Close windows or doors. | |
| | Pilot set too low. | Turn it up (see manufacturer's instructions) | |
| | Thermocouple faulty. | Change it (see Ch. 5). | |
| Pilot light won't come on at all. | Gas valve faulty. | | Contact manufacturer for specialist advice. Do not attempt to replace yourself. |

| Symptom | Possible cause | Quick cure | Proper job |
|---|---|---|---|
| Boiler won't ignite. | Power off? | Turn on. | |
| | Fuse blown? | Replace fuse. | |
| | Turn programme to constant. If it comes on, time clock faulty. | | Install new time clock. |
| Boiler won't ignite when programme on constant. | Either<br>a Hot-water thermostat faulty (check by turning on full). | | Get heating engineer to replace. |
| | b Room thermostat faulty (check by turning on full). | | Get heating engineer to replace. |
| | c Boiler thermostat faulty (check by turning on full). | Call Gas Board. | Get heating engineer to replace. |
| Boiler ignites but goes out quickly. | Pump failure — if the pump is not vibrating, it has failed. | Open air vent (if you have one); put pan under to catch water; insert screwdriver to spindle; rotate to clear blockage. | See Chapter 5 for replacement, or call Gas Board. |
| | Diverter valve failure — if it works when you've opened valve manually, then valve has failed. | Open valve manually. | Contact manufacturer for technical advice; drain down system and replace if motor burnt out. |
| | Flue blockage. | Clear out birds' nests in flue. | |

**B: Immersion heater**

| Symptom | Possible cause | Quick cure | Proper job |
|---|---|---|---|
| No hot water. | a Fuse blown. | Replace fuse. If still no hot water . . . | |
| | b Immersion may be burnt out. | Replace it. | |
| | c If gradual loss of heat in water, the cylinder may be scaled up. | Use de-scaler in hot-water cylinder (see Ch. 3) | |

**Refer to Chapter 2 Turning on Central Heating for explanation of different parts of equipment**

## C: Oil-fired boiler not working

| Symptom | Possible cause | Quick cure | Proper job |
|---|---|---|---|
| Boiler won't fire. | No oil. | Order some. | |
| | Oil cock off at tank following delivery. | Turn on. | |
| | Leak or muck in oil line or clogged oil filter. | | Call heating engineer & ensure sludge cock drained before next oil delivery. |
| | No power. | Turn on or replace fuse. | |
| | Reset button tripped. | Reset. | If it trips again, call heating engineer. |
| | Trip lever on oil control valve tripped. | Reset. | |
| | Photo-electric cell window dirty. | Clean. | Boiler requires servicing (min. service once a year). |
| | If none of these call heating engineer. | | |

# Water is pouring out of the overflow

**Refer to Chapter 2 if in doubt about stopcocks and gate valves**

| Symptom | Possible cause | Quick cure | Proper job |
|---|---|---|---|
| Cold water storage tank overflowing. | a  Ballcock jamming. | | |
| | b  Float of ballcock fallen off or leaking. | Turn off rising main stop cock now. | Refer to Ch. 5 for ballcock repairs or replacement. |
| Feed and expansion tank overflowing. | c  Ballcock set too high (or overflow too low). | | |
| WC cistern overflowing. | | Try flushing loo to see if this clears it. If not, turn off down service gate valve now and repair ballcock. | |

| Symptom | Possible cause | Quick cure | Proper job |
|---|---|---|---|
| Sink or basin. | Trap blocked. | Put plug in, block over-flow and bucket out waste. Try using plunger to clear. Otherwise place bucket under trap, undo and clear blockage. | |
| Manhole or outside gulley. | Grating or drain blocked. | Prevent anyone using WC. Put plugs in all fittings. Lift gulley grating or manhole cover or closest access eye and clear by rodding (use bamboo cane or drain rod obtainable from hire shop or wet and dry vacuum cleaner. | |
| Interceptor trap. | Interceptor blocked. | Pull interceptor chain or as above (see Ch. 3 drainage explained). | |
| WC | Trap blocked. | Bucket out waste if you can bear it. Clear by using large plunger (from hardware stores) or wrapping a wet towel around a brush handle to form plunger. Take care not to break the china-ware! | |

**You are not maintaining your drainage. Carry out long-term maintenance (see Ch. 3).**

# Water is not coming out of the tap/loo

| Symptom | Possible cause | Quick cure | Proper job |
|---|---|---|---|
| Lack of water. | a Mains off? Check with Water Board if all taps without water. | Patience. | |
| | b Air lock. | Attach hose with clips to mains tap & offend-ing tap; turn both on full. | |
| | c Water starvation because of poor plumbing (i.e. pipes too small). | Turn off any other other taps that are being used. | Re-plumb with appropriate size of pipe (see Ch. 2). |

# Electrics not working

| Symptom | Possible cause | Quick cure | Proper job |
|---|---|---|---|
| Everything in the house has gone out. | Electricity failure (if everyone else's lights have gone out too). | Patience. | |
| | Trip switch for house has switched off (if you have one). | Turn it on. | Call electrician to check wiring if no obvious cause. |
| One appliance not working. | Its fuse has blown. | Replace fuse (see Ch. 5). | |
| Several lights or appliances not working. | Circuit fuse blown at fuseboard. | Replace fuse at fuseboard (see Ch. 5) or reset MCB. | |
| Fuse at fuseboard blows again when replaced. | Too many appliances on one circuit (try turning some off). | Disconnect some. | Install more points on separate circuit. |
| | Cooker or night storage heaters on ordinary ring main. | Disconnect cooker or night storage heaters. | Install new circuit for cooker or night storage heaters. |
| | Wire has slipped out of plug and is causing shorting. | Re-wire plug. | |
| | Someone is swinging on chandelier. | Persuade them to come down. | |
| | Wiring is old and worn out. | — | Re-wire the house. |
| | Power is leaking through the earthing cables because something's shorting. Turn off all appliances in house. Mend fuse. Turn on power. If meter is recording, electricity is leaking. | Call Electricity Board. | |

# House smells musty and damp and there's black mould on the walls

| Symptom | Possible cause | Check | Cure |
|---|---|---|---|
| Peeling & discoloured wallpaper; salts on plaster; damp meter readings in lowest floor. | Rising damp. | Is earth banked above above DPC? If so . . . | Remove it. |
| | | Is there a DPC? If not . . . | Install one. Re-plaster. |
| | | Lack of ventilation. | Improve it. |
| Damp round window & door openings. | Falling damp (see Ch. 1); only in cavity walls. | Have you got weep holes to let out moisture? If not . . . | Install some. |
| General damp or one whole wall damp. | Penetrating damp; only in houses without cavity walls. | Are gutters overflowing? If so . . . | Clear them out or repair if necessary. |
| | | Is pointing no longer waterproof? If so . . . | Re-point (see Ch. 5) or seal with silicone wall treatment. |
| Black mould, steamed up windows, discoloured decorations at ceiling level. | Condensation. | Are you using wet form of heating (e.g. paraffin or gas)? If so . . . | Change heating or provide extractor fan or ducted cooker hood. |
| | | Lack of ventilation? If so . . . | Provide extractor fan. |
| Salts on plaster. | Hygroscopic plaster. | Have you got Carlite plaster on solid wall? (is plaster pink all the way through?) If so . . . | Re-plaster with either sand/lime/cement render or plaster that's not hemi-hydrate. |
| Curling skirtings; floor soggy; cuboidal cracks in woodwork; windows rattle when you walk on floor. | Dry rot. Wet rot. | Is there damp? If so . . . | Get rid of it. |
| | | Are there white strands in roof or floor spaces? If so . . . | Call timber treatment specialist. Or evacuate. |

# There's a crack in the wall and it's getting bigger

| Symptom | Possible cause | Check | Cure |
|---------|----------------|-------|------|
| Hairline cracking in walls. | Building materials shrinking as they dry out. | Has house been recently constructed or re-plastered? Have you recently installed central heating? | No cure. Use Polyfilla to fill cracks. |
| House settling. | Ground movement. | Are other houses in district doing same? (ask local Building Inspector). Is house in mining area or on hill? If so . . . | Contact surveyor & insurance company. |
| Settlement cracks through doors & windows. | Clay shrinkage under house. | Is house built on clay? Are there trees or a river nearby. If so . . . | Contact surveyor; insurance company underpinning specialist. |
| House lopsided; windows & doors out of square; walls out of plumb. | Design failure. | If identical houses nearby, are they the same? If so . . . | Contact surveyor, insurance company. |
| Fracturing round windows. | Structural decay. | Dry rot or decaying concrete lintels. | Contact timber treatment specialist or surveyor. |
| General cracking. | Vibration. | Underground trains? Pile driving on adjacent building site? Motorway? Railway? Earthquake? | Contact assumed offender. |
| Internal walls slipping. | Alterations. | Have load-bearing walls been removed? | Prop structure up immediately. Contact surveyor. |

# TECHNIQUES

## To replace tap washers

### Pillar tap

1. Turn off water supply, open tap and drain.
2. Remove cover by unscrewing by hand or with a wrench (protecting the cover with cloth).
3. Gently unscrew headgear with spanner.
4. Remove jumper and washer.
5. Grip jumper with pliers and unscrew retaining nut to remove washer.
6. Replace washer with brand-name facing downwards, and reassemble.
7. Check your nuts and turn on water supply.

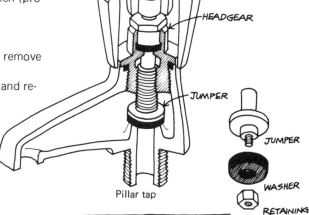

Pillar tap

### Supatap

1. No need to turn off water supply.
2. Undo locking nut above handle.
3. Remove handle/nozzle by turning in ON direction (water will flow at first but be stopped by check valve).
4. Knock sharply against work top to release jumper and anti-splash device.
5. Ease out combined washer/jumper.
6. Replace washer/jumper and reassemble.

### Washers

½" for sink taps
¾" for bath taps
Rubber washers for cold taps only
Fibre washers for hot or cold
Special type for supataps

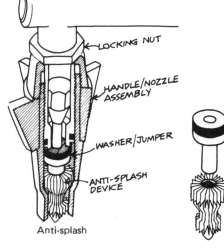

Anti-splash

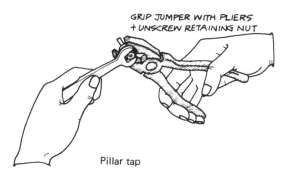

GRIP JUMPER WITH PLIERS + UNSCREW RETAINING NUT

Pillar tap

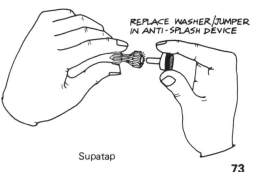

REPLACE WASHER/JUMPER IN ANTI-SPLASH DEVICE

Supatap

# To join pipes

### I. ABS plastic (solvent welded)

This is used for internal waste pipes from sinks, basins and baths, and is coloured white. Pipe and fittings (joints, bends, etc.) are joined with a solvent cement which melts the surfaces together. The joint cannot be taken apart.

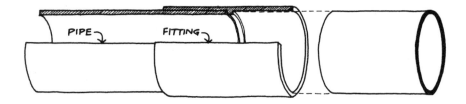

1. Cut pipe with hacksaw to required length.
2. File end smooth with file or sandpaper.
3. Test fit pipe end into fitting.
4. Clean dirt and grease from outside of pipe end and inside of fitting; ensure surfaces completely dry.
5. If joint fitting is to be fixed at an angle, set at required angle while dry and mark guide line for reference.
6. Smear even coating of solvent cement to pipe end surface.
7. Immediately push pipe into fitting and ensure fully inserted.
8. Hold in position for 15 seconds.
9. Do not use pipework for 12 hours (to let bond set).

**Note**

Use only solvent cement recommended for ABS pipes.

Jointing must be done as soon as solvent is applied — it sets very quickly.

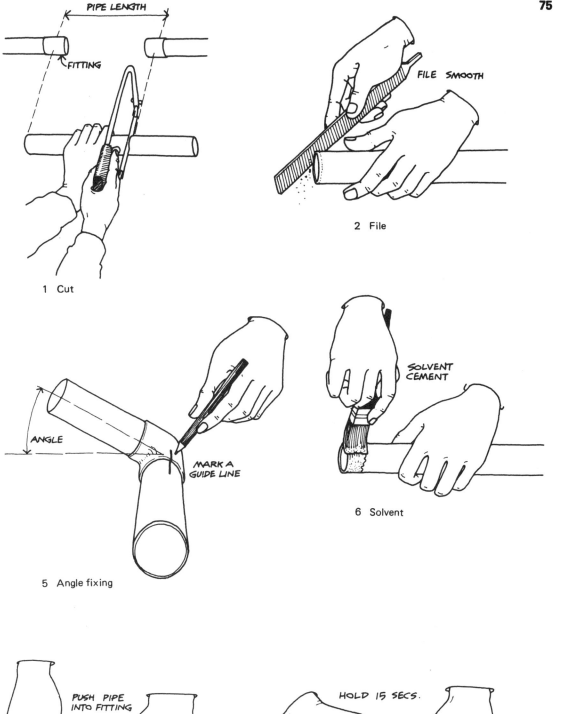

PIPE LENGTH

FITTING

1 Cut

FILE SMOOTH

2 File

ANGLE

MARK A
GUIDE LINE

5 Angle fixing

SOLVENT
CEMENT

6 Solvent

PUSH PIPE
INTO FITTING

7 Insert pipe

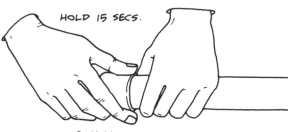

HOLD 15 SECS.

8 Hold

## II. Copper capillary (pre-soldered)

Capillary joints are cheaper than compression joints, but a bit more fiddly; you can use either on any copper pipe. A ring of solder already supplied in the fitting (joint, etc.) is melted and fills the gap between the pipe and mouth of the fitting by capillary action.

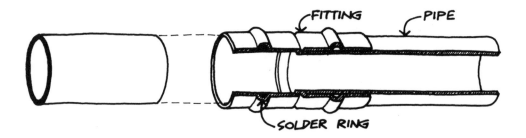

1. Cut pipe with hacksaw (if possible using a vice, protecting pipe with cloth).
2. Smooth pipe end with file, clean pipe and fitting ends with wire wool or fine sandpaper.
3. Test fit pipe end into fitting.
4. Smear 'flux' on inside of fitting and outside of pipe.
5. Test fit and remove excess flux.
6. Refit pipe, heat one end of fitting with blowlamp until solder appears at mouth of fitting.
7. Continue a few seconds longer and repeat at other end of fitting.
8. Clean off excess solder before cooled.

**Note**

Prepare and insert all lengths to be joined at one fitting so all are ready to solder together.

Ensure pipe ends are dry or solder melts unevenly.

Use flux recommended by manufacturer of fitting.

If one end of fitting cannot be heated at same time as other end, insert piece of unfluxed pipe and protect solder ring with wet cloth.

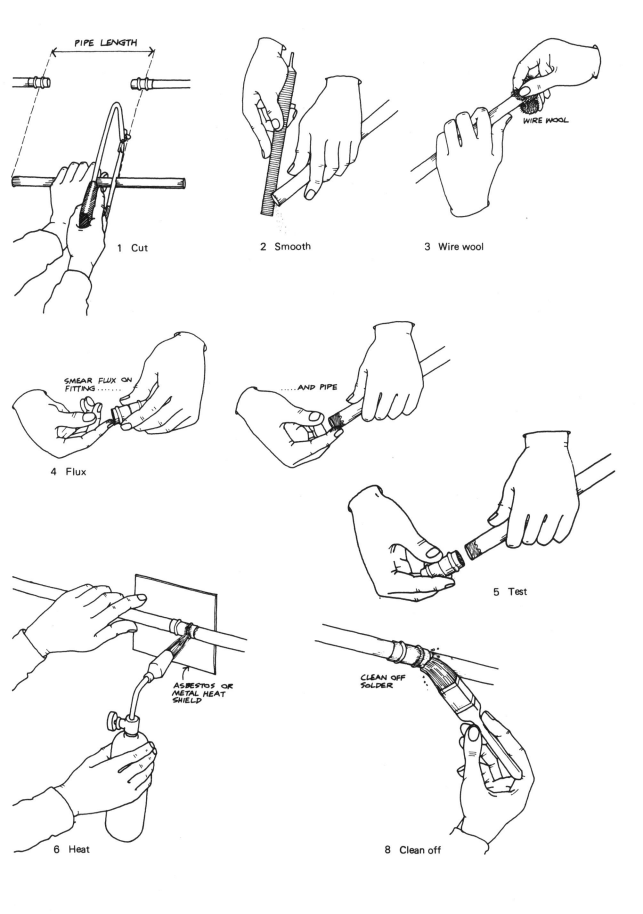

PIPE LENGTH

1 Cut

2 Smooth

3 Wire wool

WIRE WOOL

SMEAR FLUX ON FITTING.......

4 Flux

.....AND PIPE

5 Test

ASBESTOS OR METAL HEAT SHIELD

6 Heat

CLEAN OFF SOLDER

8 Clean off

## III. Copper compression (non-manipulative type)

Avoid the manipulative type, as special tools are needed. In compression joints a shaped metal ring, or olive, is wedged between the pipe and fitting with a coupling nut. Only use if you enjoy nuts and olives.

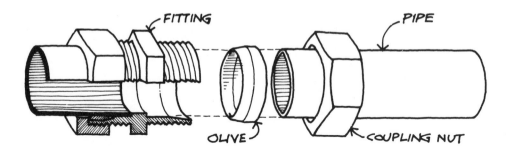

1.  Cut pipe with hacksaw — use vice if possible, protecting pipe with cloth.
2.  Smooth pipe end with file and clean with wire wool.
3.  Test fit pipe end into fitting.
4.  Fit nut and olive over pipe end, as shown in illustration.
5.  Insert pipe end into fitting, ensuring it's tight against shoulder inside.
6.  Smear round mouth of fitting with Boss White or jointing paste, just in case your joint isn't tight (not essential).
7.  Push olive into place and tighten coupling nut by hand.
8.  Fit all other pipes into fitting.
9.  Tighten coupling nuts with spanner. Use second spanner to grip fitting if necessary.

**Note**

Have some spare olives in case of damage.

Use correct size of spanner and do not overtighten.

Correctly prepared joints should not leak — if they do, tighten again with spanner.

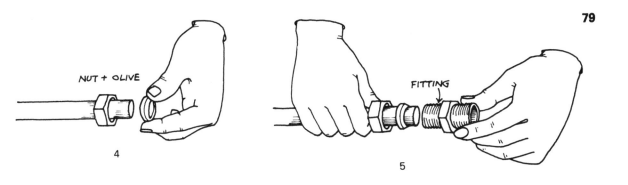

NUT + OLIVE

4

FITTING

5

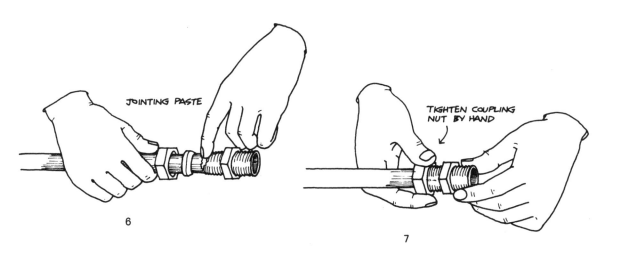

JOINTING PASTE

6

TIGHTEN COUPLING
NUT BY HAND

7

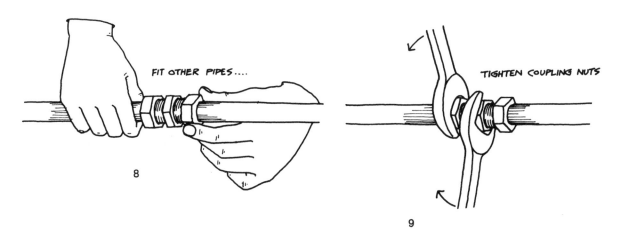

FIT OTHER PIPES....

8

TIGHTEN COUPLING NUTS

9

# To replace ball valves

Shown here is a traditional and commonly used ball valve of the 'Portsmouth pattern' to British Standard 1212.

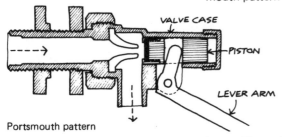

Portsmouth pattern

1. Turn off water supply to tank.
2. Remove split pin holding lever arm and remove arm.
3. Unscrew cap at end of valve case.
4. Insert end of screwdriver into slot and slide out piston.
5. Unscrew piston end cap and replace washer.
6. Smear piston with light grease (e.g. Vaseline).
7. Reassemble and turn on water supply.

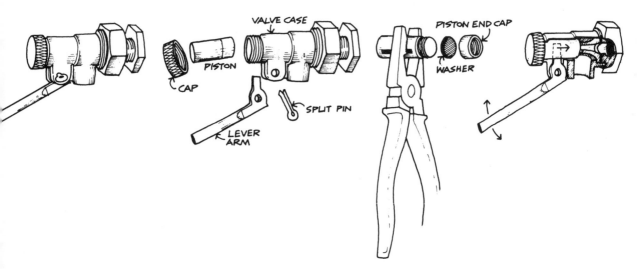

The other type of ball cock is the 'Croydon pattern', found on older cisterns. The piston is attached to the lever arm; to replace washer, ignore items 3 and 4 above.

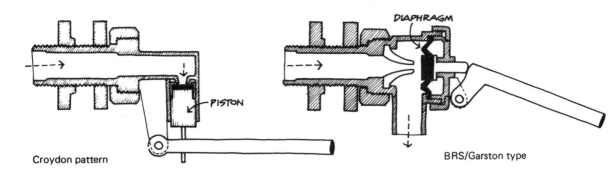

Croydon pattern

BRS/Garston type

# To replace radiators and valves

1. Drain down system and close radiator valves.
2. Protect floor under radiator from water spillage.
3. Unscrew nuts to heating pipes at each end of radiator with spanner, leaving nuts and olives on pipes.
4. Lift radiator off support brackets, and lay face down.
5. Bung up pipe ends with cloth to keep out dirt.

5 Bung pipes

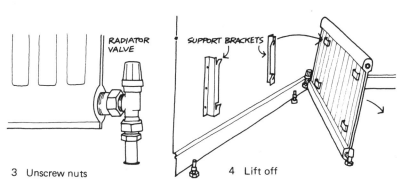

3 Unscrew nuts

4 Lift off

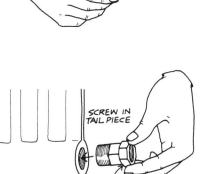

### To fit a new radiator

Ensure new radiator matches old in length between tappings and diameter of tappings. Otherwise pipework and valves must be altered.

1. Undo coupling nut between valve body and tailpiece and remove valve body.
2. Unscrew tailpipe from radiator tapping with radiator spanner and clean screw threads.
3. Seal screw thread of tailpiece with PTFE tape.
4. Screw tailpiece into new radiator (with coupling nut in place) until tight.
5. Lift radiator onto fixing brackets and ensure firm support.

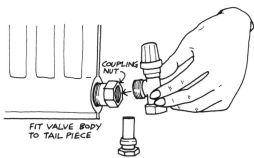

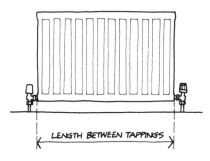

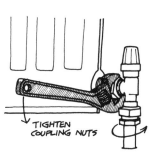

### To fit a new valve

1. Tailpiece is fitted into radiator as described in 3 and 4 above. Ensure coupling nut is in place.
2. Smear end of tailpiece with jointing paste.
3. Fit valve body to tailpiece and hand tighten coupling.
4. Ensure nut and olive are in place on heating pipe, and olive is undamaged.
5. Smear end of pipe with jointing paste.
6. Push pipe end into valve body and hand tighten nut. Check valve is correctly aligned.
7. Tighten coupling nuts with spanner.

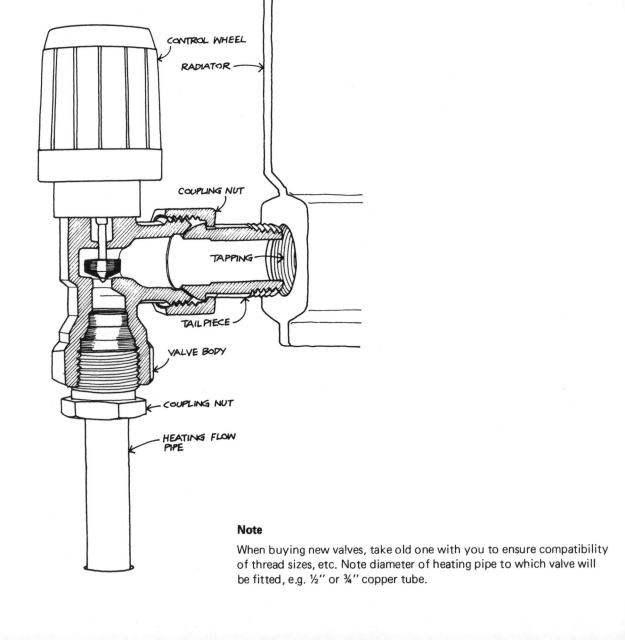

### Note

When buying new valves, take old one with you to ensure compatibility of thread sizes, etc. Note diameter of heating pipe to which valve will be fitted, e.g. ½" or ¾" copper tube.

# To fit new central heating pumps

1. If pump has isolating valves either side, screw shut with screw-driver. (This closes water supply to pump.)
2. If no isolating valves, drain down heating system.
3. Turn off electrical supply.
4. Unscrew couplings either side of pump body with spanner, and remove pump.
5. Remove electrical terminal box and locate block.
6. Mark wires live, neutral and earth for re-fixing to new pump.
7. Prepare new pump for fixing: flush with water to remove dirt, check direction of flow (arrow on casing) and open terminal box cover.
8. Place in position and reconnect couplings. Tighten with spanner.
9. Re-connect wiring to terminal block and fit cover.
10. Ensure pump spindle rotates freely as instructed by manufacturer.
11. Open isolating valves either side with screwdriver.
12. Turn on power and test joints. Tighten if necessary.

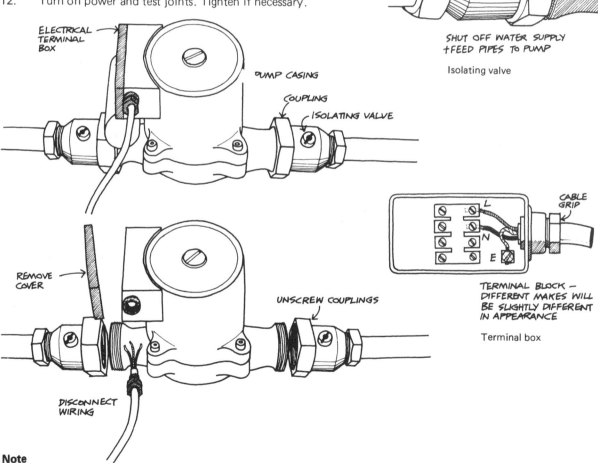

SHUT OFF WATER SUPPLY +FEED PIPES TO PUMP

Isolating valve

TERMINAL BLOCK — DIFFERENT MAKES WILL BE SLIGHTLY DIFFERENT IN APPEARANCE

Terminal box

**Note**

When buying a replacement pump, look for manufacturer's name on old pump and order by reference number.

# To replace thermocouples

The thermocouple runs from the burner chamber of the boiler to the gas control valve (the box on the front with the push buttons). It has a temperature sensitive probe at one end, which fits into the chamber near the pilot light window. The other end is an electrical connection to the gas control valve. Both ends are held in place by simple lock-nuts, screwed into a threaded hole.

1.  Buy a new thermocouple, which will come complete with the lock-nuts already in place. To order, look inside the boiler (or manual) and find the manufacturer's name, the name of the boiler and also the model number and output, e.g. RS50, CF30, etc.
2.  Turn off electrical supply, turn boiler thermostat to OFF and press the red gas control button to cut off gas. Allow boiler to cool.
3.  Undo nuts at each end of thermocouple, then withdraw probe from burner chamber and other end from gas control valve.
4.  Take new thermocouple and bend copper wire roughly to fit connections (use old one as a guide).
5.  Push plain end into terminal of gas control valve. Slip nut into place and tighten. Use small adjustable spanner or pliers.
6.  Insert probe into burner chamber and slip nut into place and tighten.
7.  Re-light boiler (see manual).

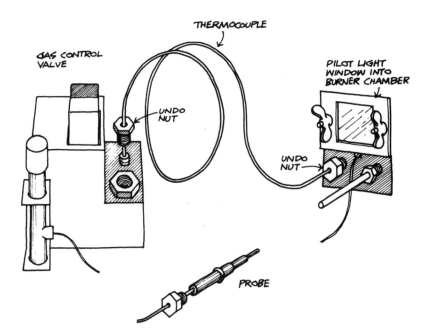

# To replace fuses

### Consumer unit fuses

### Wired fuse type
1. Turn off mains switch and remove fuse cover.
2. Locate blown fuse by removing fuse holders and looking for burnt or broken wire.
3. Unscrew retaining screws.
4. Remove broken fuse wire and clean fuse holder.
5. Wind new wire (clockwise) round retaining screw.
6. Run loosely to other screw, wind round and cut.
7. Refix retaining screws and tighten.
8. Replace fuse holder in fusebox.
9. Close fuse cover and turn on mains switch.

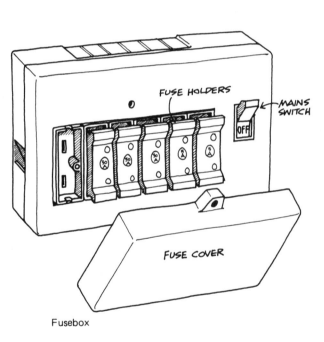

Fusebox

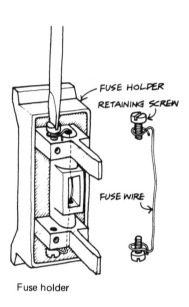

Fuse holder

### Note

Always use fuse wire of correct rating:

|  |  |
|---|---|
| 5 amp | lighting |
| 15 amp | power |
| 30 amp | ring main |
| 45 amp | cooker |

If fuse continues to blow, call an electrician.

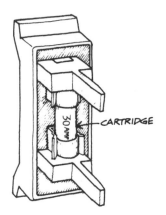

Cartridge fuse

### Cartridge fuse

Instead of a fuse wire, a cartridge fuse is simply replaced in the same way as the fuse in a plug. Always replace with a new cartridge of the correct rating.

### To replace a fuse in a plug

1. Remove plug cover.
2. Ease cartridge out from clips.
3. Press new fuse into clips.
4. Check cable is securely held in cord grip and replace cover.

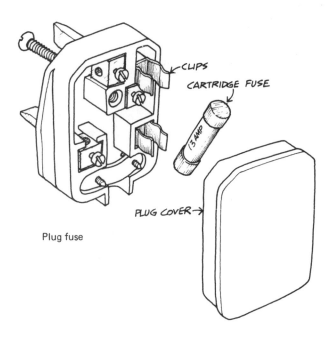

Plug fuse

### Note

Use only a fuse of the correct rating:

      3 amp    lights, radios, electric blankets
   13 amp    heaters, vacuum cleaners.

Throw away old cartridges and remember to buy spares.

# To fit plugs

You will need a small screwdriver, and a sharp knife for stripping the insulation (a wire-stripper is ideal for this job).

1. Cut back outer sheath of cable about 2'' – do not cut through insulation of core wires.
2. Remove plug cover, loosen cord grip screws.
3. Fit cable into plug and cut wires to reach terminals with ½'' to spare. Ensure live, earth and neutral are going to correct terminals.
4. Trim ½'' insulation from end of wires with wire-stripper or sharp knife – don't cut into wire!
5. Twist wire ends and double back.
6. Push flex under cord grip into plug. Undo terminal screws or clamps.
7. Insert ends of wire into terminal holes and tighten screws or clamps.
8. Tighten cord grip over cable sheath (not wires) and fix plug cover.

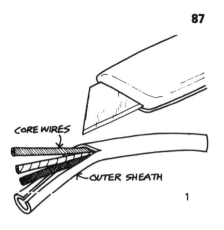

CORE WIRES

OUTER SHEATH

1

WIRE STRIPPER

4

4

5

5

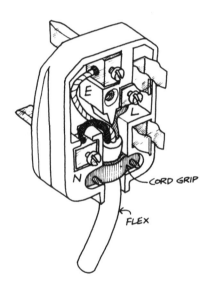

E

L

N

CORD GRIP

FLEX

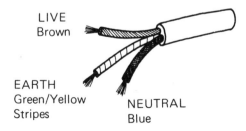

LIVE
Brown

EARTH
Green/Yellow
Stripes

NEUTRAL
Blue

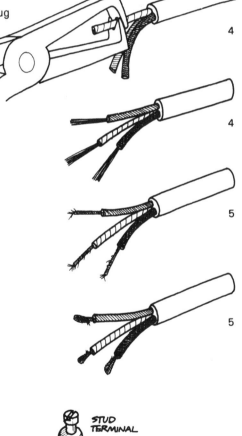

STUD
TERMINAL

PILLAR
TERMINAL

7

**Note**

Make sure plug is fitted with correct fuse for the appliance fitted to it.

# To fit new ceiling roses

### Are there lupins in your roses?

First identify what kind of lighting circuit you have — a modern 'loop-in' circuit or a 'junction-box' circuit?

**Loop-in circuit**: the main cable loops in and out of the ceiling roses, from which a light flex and switch cable run.

**Junction-box circuit**: the main cable runs from one junction-box to another, from which individual cables branch out to ceiling roses and switches.

Turn off at the consumer unit and take the cover off an existing ceiling rose. If it's a loop-in circuit it will have 3 cables coming in (one in, one out and one to the switch) with a total of 9 terminal connections, as well as the flex to the light.

If it's a junction-box circuit the ceiling rose will have one cable coming in with only 3 terminal connections, as well as the flex to the light.

### Connecting to a loop-in circuit

A cable for a new light can be connected to an existing loop-in ceiling rose and run to a new junction box, from which cables run to the new ceiling-rose and switch.

Decide position of new light and select the nearest existing ceiling rose. Check it's a loop-in type. The new extension can be connected here.

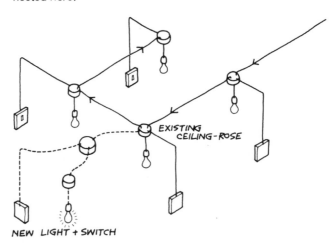

EXISTING CEILING-ROSE

NEW LIGHT + SWITCH

## Connecting to a junction-box circuit

A cable for a new light can be connected to an existing junction box and run to a new junction box, from which cables run to the new ceiling rose and switch.

Decide position of new light and find the nearest existing junction box on the lighting circuit. This may not be easy if within a floor-space. Trace back a cable from an existing ceiling rose until you come to a junction box. Turn off at the mains and inspect it. If it's in good condition and the terminals will take a new cable (it should have 4 terminal blocks) the new extension can be connected here.

If you're at all unsure consult an electrician.

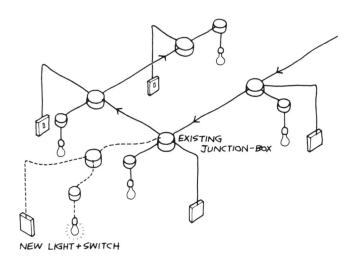

EXISTING JUNCTION-BOX

NEW LIGHT + SWITCH

## Bits and pieces

You will need to buy:

1. Cable: 1.00 mm² 2 core + earth/PVC sheathed. Measure the length needed to connect switch, new rose and junction box to existing circuit. Add 10% for waste, bends, etc.
2. Flex: 0.75 mm² 2 core/PVC sheathed. Between ceiling rose and lampholder.
3. Junction-box for lighting circuits (4 terminals).
4. Ceiling rose: terminals: 2 + earth.
5. Switch: 5 amp one-way plateswitch with surface or flush mounting-box (NB use ceiling switches in bathrooms).
6. Pendant lampholder.
7. Plastic cable clips for 1.0 mm² cable (one per foot run of cable).
8. Some short lengths of 2" x 1" timber for battens and wood-screws for fixing. (1½"/no. 8 screws.)

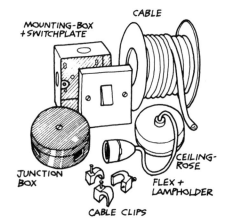

CABLE
MOUNTING-BOX + SWITCHPLATE
JUNCTION BOX
CEILING-ROSE
FLEX + LAMPHOLDER
CABLE CLIPS

Essential tools for electrical work: insulated electrical screwdriver; pliers — for cutting and twisting wires; sharp knife (or wire stripper) for stripping insulation from wires. See 'Fitting a Plug' for preparation of cable ends.

**Fixing the new light**

1. Locate position of connection to existing circuit (loop-in ceiling rose or junction-box).
2. Decide positions of new junction-box, ceiling rose and switch-plate. Junction-box is best fixed halfway between new ceiling-rose and point where cable drops to switch.
3. Decide route of cable between these points and provide access to floorspace or roof space above (see 'Lifting Floorboards'). In roof spaces you may have to lift insulation quilt.
4. Where cable needs to run through a floor joist (keep to a minimum), drill a ¾'' diameter hole on the joist centre line. Drilling off-centre or cutting notches weakens the joist.
5. Where cable runs from ceiling down to switch on:
   **Solid walls.** Cut a chase or groove ¾'' wide in plaster and chisel recess in masonry for switch mounting-box (if fitted flush). Use bolster chisel and club hammer.
   **Timber stud walls.** Cut hole in plaster for switch mounting box (if flush) and drop a weighted string from above to draw cable through.
   **Alternatively.** Use plastic mini-ducts fixed to wall surface (see 'Wall Fixings') and run cable to surface-mounted switch and box.

Wiring diagram

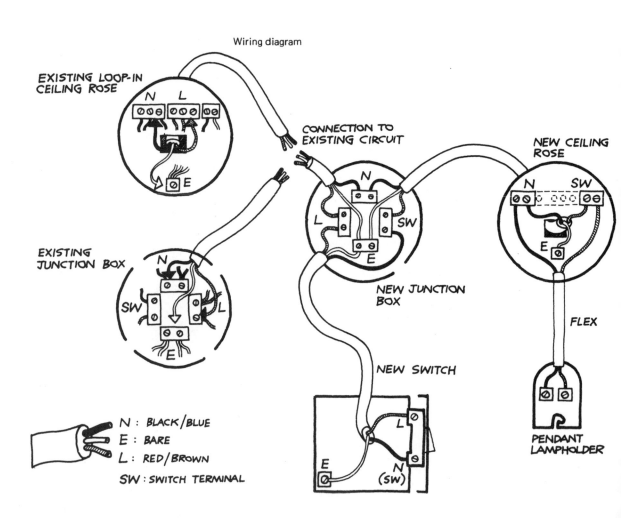

EXISTING LOOP-IN CEILING ROSE

CONNECTION TO EXISTING CIRCUIT

NEW CEILING ROSE

EXISTING JUNCTION BOX

NEW JUNCTION BOX

NEW SWITCH

FLEX

PENDANT LAMPHOLDER

N : BLACK/BLUE
E : BARE
L : RED/BROWN
SW : SWITCH TERMINAL

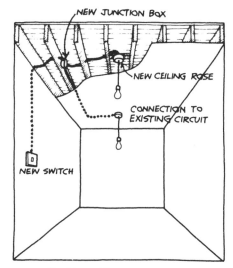

NEW JUNCTION BOX

NEW CEILING ROSE

CONNECTION TO EXISTING CIRCUIT

NEW SWITCH

Decide positions

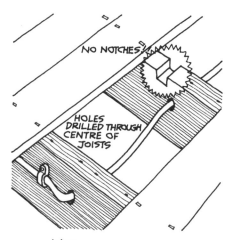

NO NOTCHES

HOLES DRILLED THROUGH CENTRE OF JOISTS

Joists

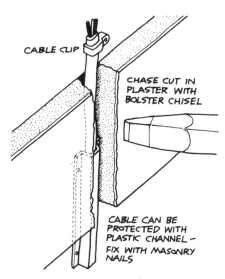

CABLE CLIP

CHASE CUT IN PLASTER WITH BOLSTER CHISEL

CABLE CAN BE PROTECTED WITH PLASTIC CHANNEL – FIX WITH MASONRY NAILS

Solid walls

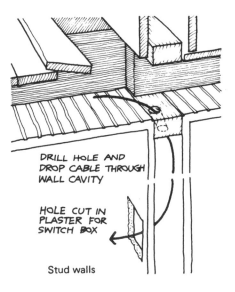

DRILL HOLE AND DROP CABLE THROUGH WALL CAVITY

HOLE CUT IN PLASTER FOR SWITCH BOX

Stud walls

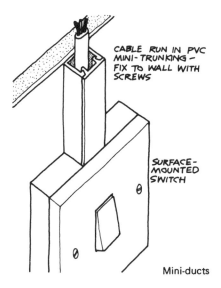

CABLE RUN IN PVC MINI-TRUNKING – FIX TO WALL WITH SCREWS

SURFACE-MOUNTED SWITCH

Mini-ducts

6. Fix battens to support junction-box, and ceiling rose/switch-box if necessary. Drill hole for cable to pass through into back of box/ceiling rose, etc.

7. Fix new junction-box, ceiling rose and switch in position. Ensure switchplate is level and square.

8. Run 1.0 mm$^2$ cable lengths in floor space or roof space above ceiling between points to be connected, and down wall to switch.

9. Cut lengths as required, with some to spare at ends. Push through back of ceiling rose and switch-box, and prepare all cable ends for terminal connections.

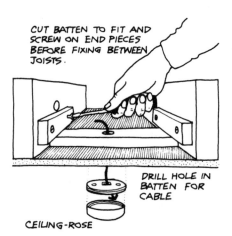

CUT BATTEN TO FIT AND SCREW ON END PIECES BEFORE FIXING BETWEEN JOISTS.

DRILL HOLE IN BATTEN FOR CABLE

CEILING-ROSE

Fix battens

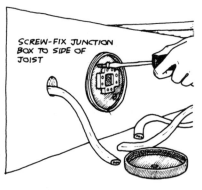

SCREW-FIX JUNCTION BOX TO SIDE OF JOIST

Junction-box

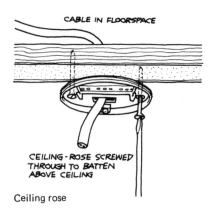

CABLE IN FLOORSPACE

CEILING-ROSE SCREWED THROUGH TO BATTEN ABOVE CEILING

Ceiling rose

MOUNTING-BOX SCREWED TO MASONRY OR TIMBER

RECESS CUT IN MASONRY (OR NOTCH IN TIMBER) TO SUIT DEPTH OF BOX

Switch

10. TURN OFF AT MAINS. Open up existing loop-in rose or junction-box and loosen terminals. If connection to loop-in ceiling-rose, push new cable down through ceiling with 3 others and prepare end for connection.

11. Connect cable ends to terminals of new switchplate, ceiling-rose and junction-box. Check that neutral, live and earth wires are correctly connected. With 2 core + earth cable, they are:

       Neutral  — BLACK insulation
       Live      — RED insulation
       Earth    — Bare copper

12. Make the connection to the existing circuit.

**Loop-in ceiling rose**

a    Connect the live/RED wire to one of the 3 centre terminals.

b    Connect the neutral/BLACK wire to one of the 3 neutral terminals.

c    Connect the earth wire to the single earth terminal.

**Junction-box**

a    This should have 4 terminal blocks:

b    Live — with red wires into it.

c    Neutral — with black wires into it.

d    Earth — with bare copper wires into it.

e    Switch — should be one red, one black.

Connect the live/RED wire to one of the live terminals.

Connect the neutral/BLACK wire to one of the neutral terminals.

Connect the earth wire to one of the earth terminals.

13. Lastly connect 0.75 mm² 2-core flex to new ceiling rose. With 2-core flex, the wires are:

       Neutral/BLUE insulation
       Live/BROWN insulation

Connect the neutral/BLUE wire to the neutral terminal block with black wire in.

Connect the live/BROWN wire to the switch terminal with red wire in.

Do not connect to the centre terminal block or the earth terminal.

14. Fit the pendant lampholder to the flex, one wire into each terminal.

15. Make sure all wires are securely fixed and all covers screwed down, then TURN ON AT MAINS.

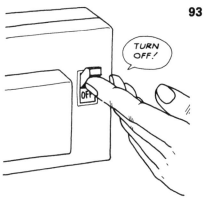

TURN OFF!

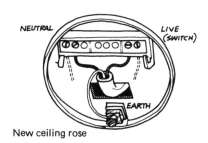

CABLE IN WALL

SWITCHPLATE

EARTH

MOUNTING BOX

Switch

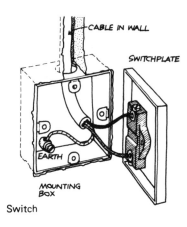

NEUTRAL

LIVE (SWITCH)

EARTH

New ceiling rose

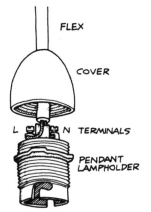

FLEX

COVER

L    N   TERMINALS

PENDANT LAMPHOLDER

BAYONET FIXING SHOWN    Pendant lamp-holder

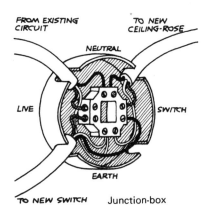

FROM EXISTING CIRCUIT

TO NEW CEILING-ROSE

NEUTRAL

LIVE

SWITCH

EARTH

TO NEW SWITCH    Junction-box

# To fit new spur socket outlets

If you have a ring-main circuit (see Ch. 2) you can extend a 13 amp spur socket from any point on the circuit, as long as the total number of spurs does not exceed the number of existing points on the ring-main. If a socket is on the ring-main it will have 2 cables coming in the back; if it is on a spur, it will only have 1. DO NOT use spur socket outlets for anything over 13 amps or 3kW — cooker points, night storage heaters, and some immersion heaters, for instance — these all need a separate supply from the consumer unit. Also, it is better not to use a spur socket outlet for a fixed appliance of 3kW or less (electric fire, gas boiler, washing machine, etc.); rather use a switched connection unit with a pilot-light and a flex outlet to the appliance.

The new spur cable can be run from the existing point either chased into the wall (safer) or on the surface. The new outlet can be fitted flush (recessed into the wall), or surface mounted if the new cable is surface-run.

**Warning!** DO NOT fit spur outlets in bathrooms or within 6 ft. (1,800 mm.) of a water fitting.

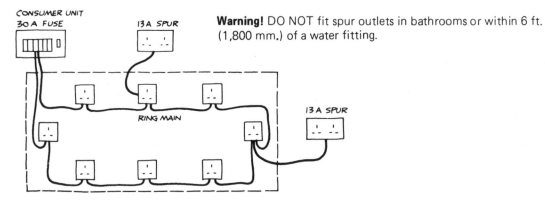

MAXIMUM NO. OF SPUR OUTLETS EQUALS NO. OF EXISTING SOCKETS ON RING MAIN

### Bits and pieces

You will need:

1. Cable: 2.5mm$^2$ 2 core + earth/PVC sheathed (grey or white). Enough to run from existing point to new outlet position plus an extra 12" (300 mm.) for cutting.
2. Spur outlet — either:
   13 amp switched socket outlet (double or single)
        or:
   13 amp switched connection unit with pilot light and flex outlet
        and:
   Mounting-box for flush or surface mounting.
3. Plastic cable clips for 2 mm.$^2$ cable (one per foot run of cable).

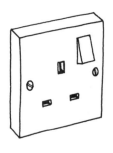

13 AMP SWITCHED SOCKET OUTLET (SINGLE SHOWN)

13 AMP SWITCHED CONNECTION UNIT WITH FLEX OUTLET

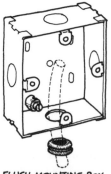

FLUSH MOUNTING-BOX WITH GROMMET FOR CABLE ENTRY HOLE

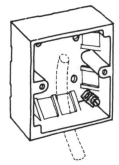

SURFACE MOUNTING-BOX WITH 'KNOCK-OUTS' FOR CABLE ENTRY

1. Decide position of new spur outlet and locate nearest convenient point on existing ring-circuit.
2. Decide route of cable between these two points and prepare for fixing — chasing into wall, fixed to surface or run under floor. (See To Fix a New Ceiling Rose, items 4 + 5). Prepare recess in wall for mounting-box.
3. Run cable between two points and fix in position, leaving spare loose ends.

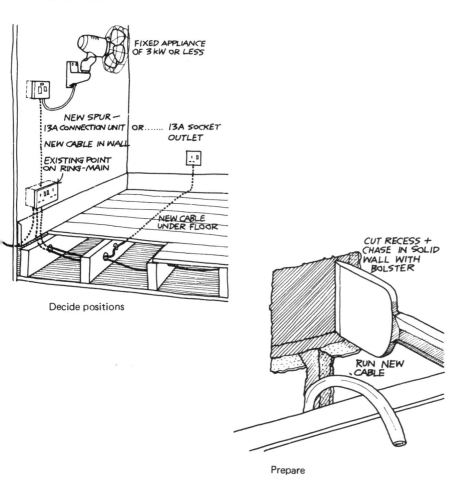

Decide positions

Prepare

Run cable

4. Break open knockout-hole in mounting-box of new spur outlet then fix.
5. Draw cable end through hole in mounting-box.
6. Prepare cable end to new outlet. Double over wire ends and connect to terminals. Check that neutral, live and earth wires are correctly connected. With 2 core and earth cable, they are:

      Neutral  — BLACK insulation
      Live     — RED insulation
      Earth    — Bare copper

7. *Turn off at mains*. Unscrew switch-plate of existing point and pull away from mounting-box.
8. Break open knock-out hole in mounting box then draw new cable through.
9. Prepare cable end as before, then proceed to join wires of new cable to corresponding wires of existing cable.
10. First undo Neutral (BLACK) terminal, remove existing wires, then twist Neutral (BLACK) wire of new cable around them with pliers. Fit back into terminal and tighten screw.
Repeat this with the Live (RED) and Earth (bare copper) wires.
11. Make sure all cable is securely fixed and outlet covers are screwed down, then *turn on at mains*.
12. If fitting a fixed appliance connection-unit: turn off at mains, remove cover, push appliance flex through outlet hole. Prepare ends and connect to terminals as shown. Fix cover and turn on at mains.

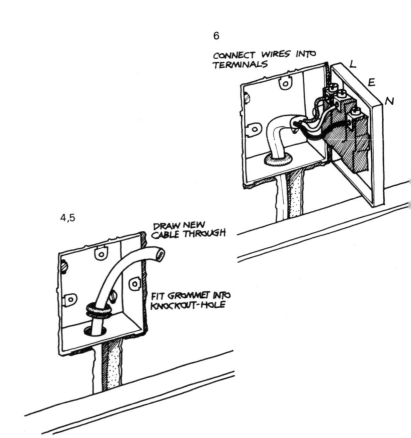

6

CONNECT WIRES INTO TERMINALS

L

E

N

4,5

DRAW NEW CABLE THROUGH

FIT GROMMET INTO KNOCKOUT-HOLE

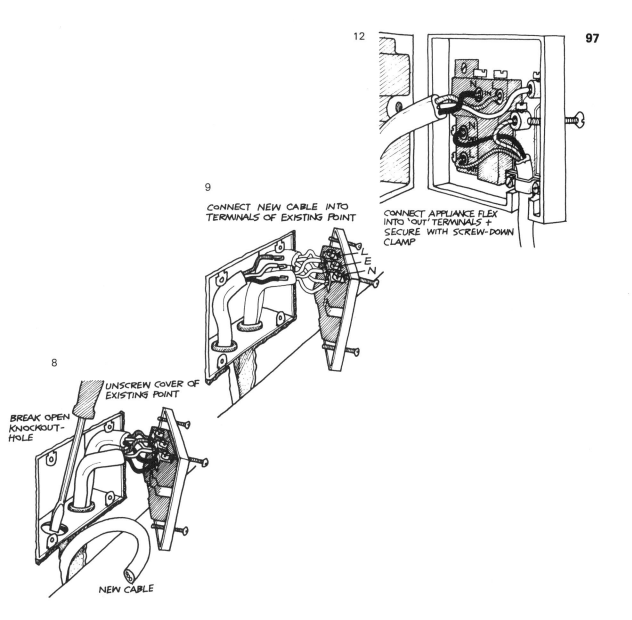

12

CONNECT APPLIANCE FLEX
INTO 'OUT' TERMINALS +
SECURE WITH SCREW-DOWN
CLAMP

9

CONNECT NEW CABLE INTO
TERMINALS OF EXISTING POINT

L
E
N

8

UNSCREW COVER OF
EXISTING POINT

BREAK OPEN
KNOCKOUT-
HOLE

NEW CABLE

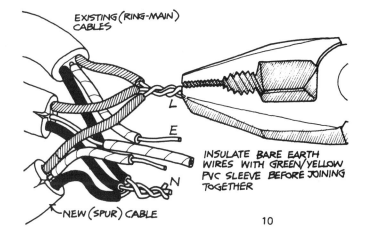

EXISTING (RING-MAIN)
CABLES

L

E

INSULATE BARE EARTH
WIRES WITH GREEN/YELLOW
PVC SLEEVE BEFORE JOINING
TOGETHER

N

NEW (SPUR) CABLE

10

# To hang and trim doors

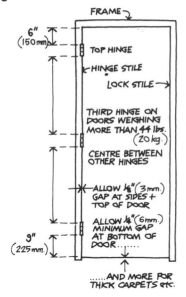

FRAME

6" (150mm)

TOP HINGE

HINGE STILE

LOCK STILE

THIRD HINGE ON DOORS WEIGHING MORE THAN 44 lbs. (20 kg.)

CENTRE BETWEEN OTHER HINGES

ALLOW ⅛" (3mm.) GAP AT SIDES + TOP OF DOOR

ALLOW ¼" (6mm.) MINIMUM GAP AT BOTTOM OF DOOR.......

9" (225mm.)

......AND MORE FOR THICK CARPETS etc.

1. Before starting, get some small timber wedges or bits of 1/8" thick hardboard for packing.
2. Put door against frame, with packing under to lift clear of floor. Allow ¼" clearance to floor (or more if you have fitted carpets).
3. Mark line of frame on to door (with someone holding door against frame and you on other side). Allow 1/8" clearance around top and sides.
4. Stand door on edge and cut or plane to fit, testing size as you go. Plane from corners inwards. Use saw if removing more than 1/8".
5. If floor slopes up from door opening, allow for this in line of bottom edge. Bevel lock stile slightly to allow easy closing.
6. When planed to fit, wedge door into frame and mark hinge positions.

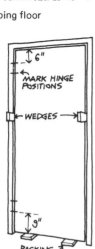

BOTTOM EDGE CUT TO SLOPE

FLOOR SLOPES UP

5  Sloping floor

PLANE FROM CORNERS TOWARD CENTRE

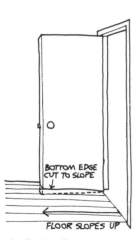

6"

MARK HINGE POSITIONS

WEDGES

9"

PACKING

6  Hinge positions

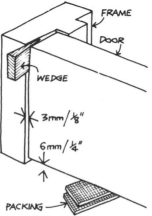

FRAME

DOOR

WEDGE

3mm/⅛"

6mm/¼"

PACKING

6  Wedges and packing

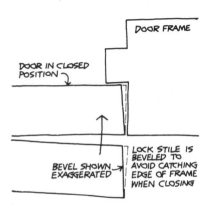

DOOR FRAME

DOOR IN CLOSED POSITION

BEVEL SHOWN EXAGGERATED

LOCK STILE IS BEVELED TO AVOID CATCHING EDGE OF FRAME WHEN CLOSING

5  Bevel lock stile

7. Stand door on edge. Trace hinge plate onto door edge with sharp knife and pencil line.
8. Cut round outline with chisel to depth of hinge plate. Hold chisel vertically and tap with hammer.
9. Shave out recess with flat chisel cuts from end to end.
10. Ensure hinge plate is flush with door edge and fix with two screws.

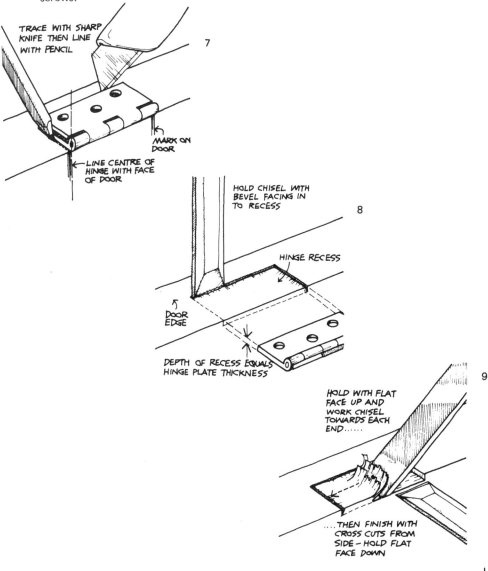

TRACE WITH SHARP KNIFE THEN LINE WITH PENCIL

7

MARK ON DOOR

LINE CENTRE OF HINGE WITH FACE OF DOOR

HOLD CHISEL WITH BEVEL FACING IN TO RECESS

8

HINGE RECESS

DOOR EDGE

DEPTH OF RECESS EQUALS HINGE PLATE THICKNESS

9

HOLD WITH FLAT FACE UP AND WORK CHISEL TOWARDS EACH END......

....THEN FINISH WITH CROSS CUTS FROM SIDE – HOLD FLAT FACE DOWN

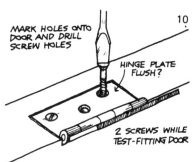

10

MARK HOLES ONTO DOOR AND DRILL SCREW HOLES

HINGE PLATE FLUSH?

2 SCREWS WHILE TEST-FITTING DOOR

## Note

This is not a job to be rushed. Marking out, planing and chiselling all need to be done very methodically and evenly.

Use minimum 1¼″ (32 mm.) wood screws for fixing door hinges. Heavy, solid doors will need 3 hinges: position the middle one centrally.

**100**

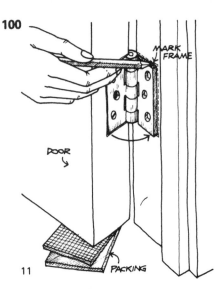

11

11. Put hinge stile on door against frame. Open hinges against frame and trace position onto frame.
12. Cut recesses for hinge plates into frame as 8, 9 above. Test fit to ensure hinge plate does not project above surface of frame.
13. Prop door against frame and fix hinges to frame with one screw only.
14. Test door opening and closing and correct any faults. Adjust alignment of door hinges by deepening frame recesses or packing out with thin card.
15. Finally fit remaining screws and tighten.

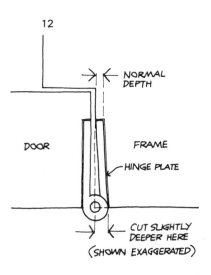

12

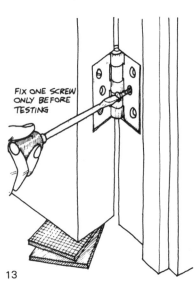

13

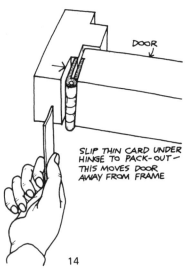

14

# To fit new door locks

I. Mortise type

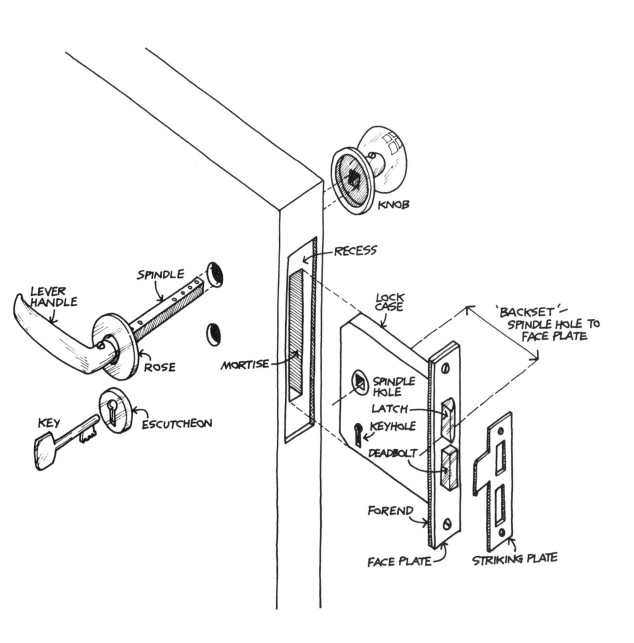

KNOB

RECESS

SPINDLE

LEVER HANDLE

ROSE

MORTISE

LOCK CASE

'BACKSET'
SPINDLE HOLE TO
FACE PLATE

SPINDLE HOLE

LATCH

KEY

KEYHOLE

ESCUTCHEON

DEADBOLT

FOREND

FACE PLATE

STRIKING PLATE

1. Mark centre line of door and top and bottom of lock case.
2. Hold lock case against door and mark centres of spindle hole and key hole.
3. Use brace and auger bit to drill spindle and keyholes.
4. Use brace and auger bit (see Chapter 6) to bore mortise for lock case. Diameter of bit to be width of lock case plus approx. 2mm.
5. Use chisel to form clean, square mortise.
6. Test-fit lock case and chisel mortise clean if necessary. Mark outline of forend or face plate on door.
7. Chisel around outline to depth of face plate, then chisel out recess carefully in up and down directions. Test fit lock and adjust recess if necessary.

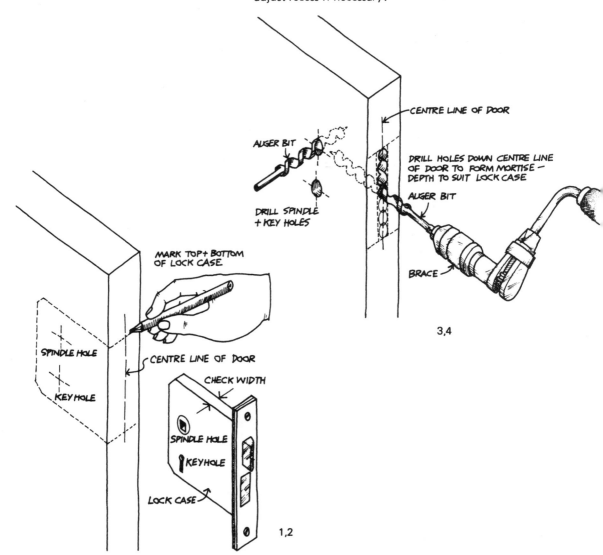

CENTRE LINE OF DOOR

AUGER BIT

DRILL HOLES DOWN CENTRE LINE OF DOOR TO FORM MORTISE — DEPTH TO SUIT LOCK CASE

AUGER BIT

DRILL SPINDLE + KEY HOLES

BRACE

3,4

MARK TOP + BOTTOM OF LOCK CASE

SPINDLE HOLE

KEY HOLE

CENTRE LINE OF DOOR

CHECK WIDTH

SPINDLE HOLE

KEYHOLE

LOCK CASE

1,2

**Note**

Ensure door is firmly fixed before working on it. Wedge from both sides if door is hung.

When drilling mortise, keep drill bit on centre line of door. Mark bit with depth of lock case — use tape or rubber band.

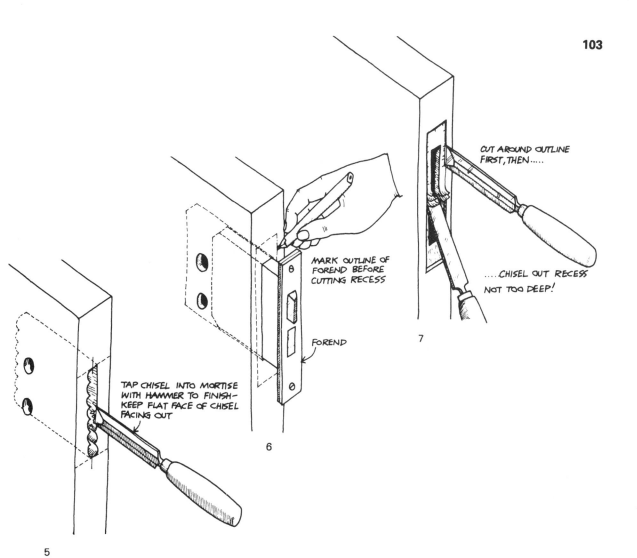

TAP CHISEL INTO MORTISE WITH HAMMER TO FINISH—KEEP FLAT FACE OF CHISEL FACING OUT

5

MARK OUTLINE OF FOREND BEFORE CUTTING RECESS

FOREND

6

CUT AROUND OUTLINE FIRST, THEN.....

.....CHISEL OUT RECESS NOT TOO DEEP!

7

8. Fit lock case, screw forend to door. Slide spindle through lock and fit hand/rose/escutcheons, etc.
9. Mark level of latch on face of door. Close door and transfer level to frame. Measure latch position from face of door and mark outline of recess on frame.
10. Hold striking plate against frame in required position and mark outline and position of recess for deadlock.
11. Chisel or drill recesses for latch and deadlock. Carefully chisel recess for striking plate as for face plate in 7.
12. Test fit, then screw to frame.

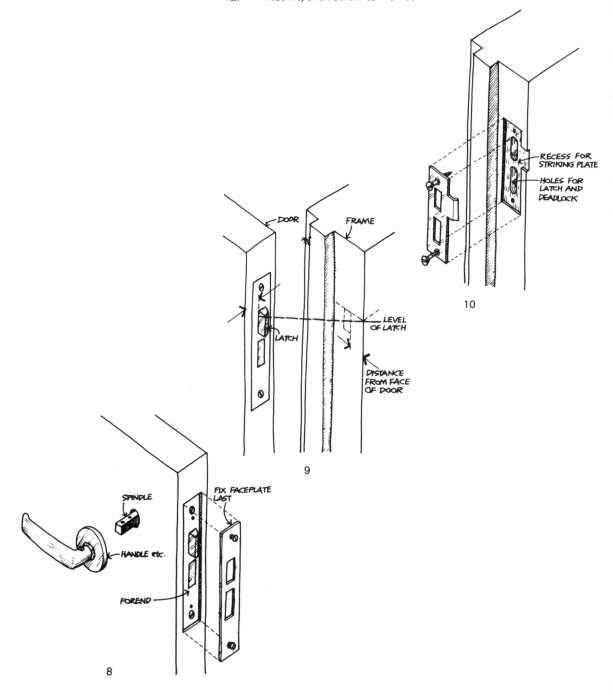

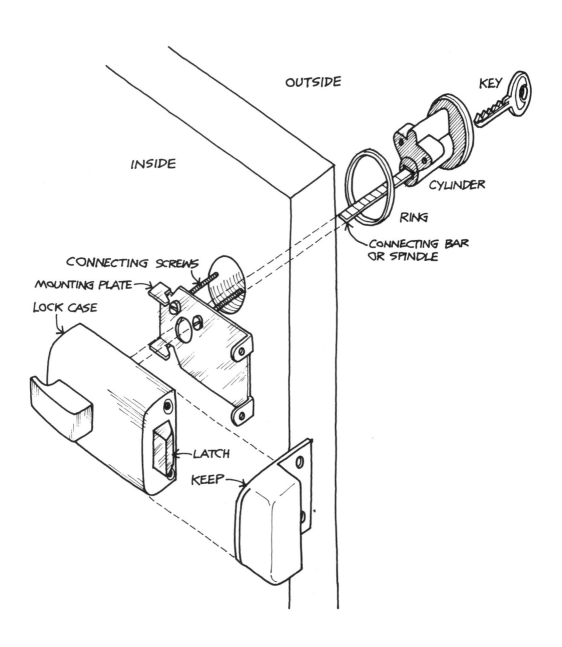

Manufacturer will usually supply paper template with lock for marking out holes on door.

1.  Mark cylinder hole centre on door face and drill hole to size required (usually 1¼" diameter.) Use a brace and centre bit (see Ch. 6).

2.  Cut connecting screws to suit door thickness. Fit connecting screws through mounting plate into cylinder and tighten. Screw mounting plate to door face.

3.  Fit lock case to mounting plate, ensuring spindle is correctly inserted into mechanism. Adjust spindle length if necessary. Fix lock case with screws provided.

4.  Fit keep (or striking plate) over latch, close door and mark outline onto frame. Chisel recess in frame for keep and screw into frame with minimum 1¼" (32 mm.) long wood screws.

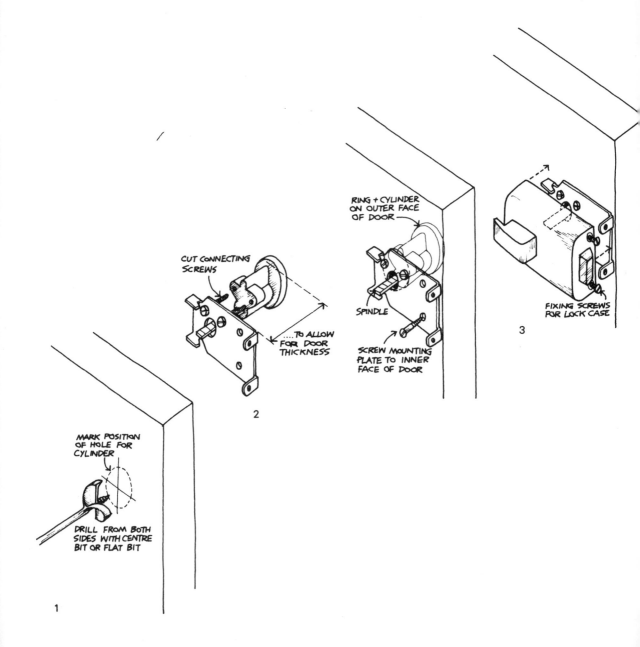

CUT CONNECTING SCREWS

....TO ALLOW FOR DOOR THICKNESS

2

RING + CYLINDER ON OUTER FACE OF DOOR

SPINDLE

SCREW MOUNTING PLATE TO INNER FACE OF DOOR

FIXING SCREWS FOR LOCK CASE

3

MARK POSITION OF HOLE FOR CYLINDER

DRILL FROM BOTH SIDES WITH CENTRE BIT OR FLAT BIT

1

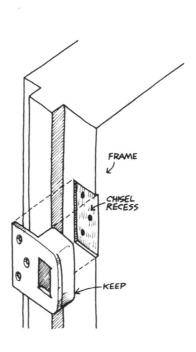

FRAME

CHISEL RECESS

KEEP

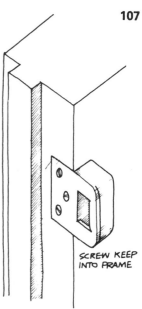

SCREW KEEP INTO FRAME

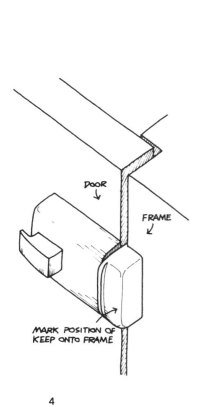

DOOR

FRAME

MARK POSITION OF KEEP ONTO FRAME

4

# To lift and replace floorboards

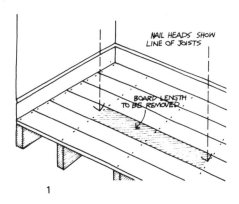

NAIL HEADS SHOW LINE OF JOISTS

BOARD LENGTH TO BE REMOVED.

1

Your floorboards will either be plain-edged or tongue-and-groove ('T & G' to the trade). When drilling or cutting through floorboards watch out for cables and pipework under. Turn off the electricity at the consumer unit .

**To take out a length of floorboard for access or repair**

**I. Plain-edged boards**

1. Identify the length to be removed and locate the nearest joist to each end. The joists are revealed by the rows of nail heads.
2. Find the inside edge of the joists at one end. Use a kitchen knife between the boards, or guess: joists are 1½"-2" wide.
3. Measure out ½" from the joist edge and draw a line across the board. Drill 3 or 4 1/8" diameter holes along the line to start a saw cut.
4. Saw through the board with a padsaw or small tenon saw, cutting at a slight angle to leave a chamfered edge.
5. Use a bolster to lever up the board edge. Slip a small batten of timber under the board and work this along to the other end to be cut.
6. At the other end, with the board lifted up over two battens, cut the board exactly over the centre of the joist. First remove any old nails from the board.

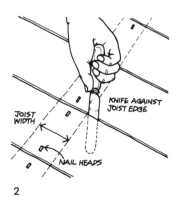

JOIST WIDTH

KNIFE AGAINST JOIST EDGE

NAIL HEADS

2

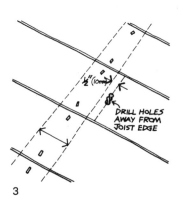

½" (10mm)

DRILL HOLES AWAY FROM JOIST EDGE

3

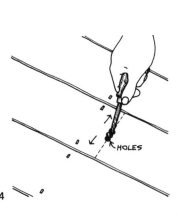

HOLES

4

### To replace

1. Where the first cut was made, fix a timber batten 2″ x 1¼″ to the side of the joist with no. 8/50 mm. wood screws. This supports the new board end.
2. Cut new board to length required, with one end chamfered as in 4 above.
3. Clean dirt from top of joists, remove old nails, test fit and nail down with floor-brads (see Ch. 7).

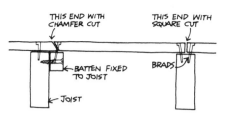

To replace

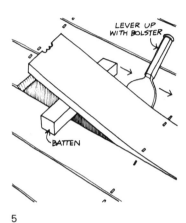

5

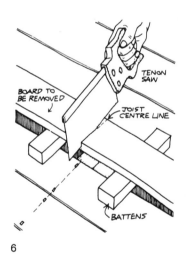

6

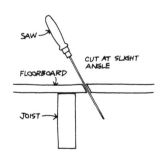

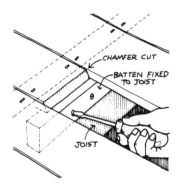

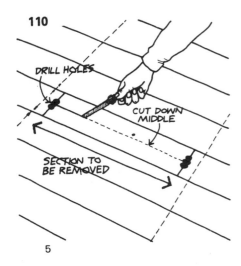

DRILL HOLES

CUT DOWN MIDDLE

SECTION TO BE REMOVED

5

## II. Tongue-and-groove boards

Not quite so easy because the edges are jointed. Follow steps 1 — 4 for plain-edged boards, and then:

5.      Having cut each end of the section to be removed, split or cut it down the middle lengthways, and lever out the two pieces.

### To replace

1.      Fix timber support battens at each end as for plain-edged boards.
2.      Cut new board to length required, with chamfered ends. Ensure tongue and groove are on the correct sides.
3.      Chisel off lower edge of groove.
4.      Test fit and nail down to the battens.

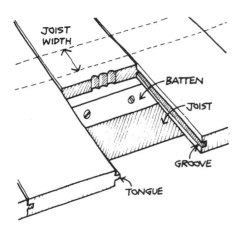

JOIST WIDTH

BATTEN

JOIST

GROOVE

TONGUE

Fix batten

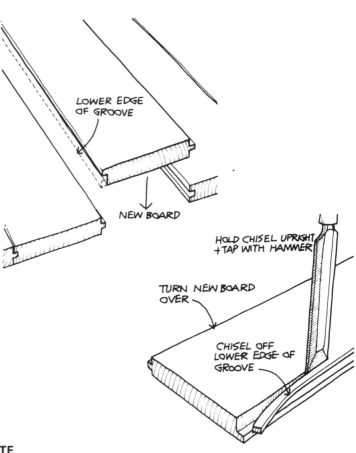

LOWER EDGE OF GROOVE

NEW BOARD

HOLD CHISEL UPRIGHT + TAP WITH HAMMER

TURN NEW BOARD OVER

CHISEL OFF LOWER EDGE OF GROOVE

## NOTE

Metric size floorboards are slightly thinner than old imperial size boards. If you can't get old boards to match, pack the new board up at each end with strips of card or wood veneer.

# To paint walls and ceilings

**Emulsion**

**Preparation**

**Emulsion paint**: wash with water and sugar soap. Scrape away flaking areas and prime with one coat emulsion.

**Old wallpaper**: ensure it is stuck to the wall, otherwise, strip it. Heavy patterns may show through so try a test patch first.

**Cracks**: if plaster is basically sound, fill with a patent filler. If plaster loose and crumbly, you may need to cut out and re-plaster.

**Porous/flaky surfaces**: clean down and paint with a sealer/primer paint.

**Black mould**: treat with a fungicidal wash, but also cure the cause (e.g. condensation, damp walls). Then use a fungicidal paint.

**Fittings**: remove or protect switch covers, ceiling roses, light shades, and, of course, the Picasso.

**Equipment**
1. 3'' (75 mm.) or 4'' (100 mm.) brush for corners, edges and small areas.
2. Roller (or paint pad) for large areas.
3. Paint tray.
4. Stepladders (ones that can hold a paint tray on top).
5. Damp cloth.
6. Radiator roller for behind radiators.
7. Paint to finish the job.

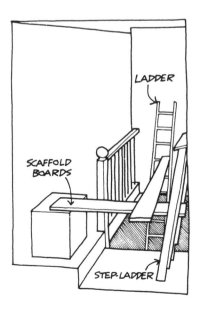

Access to stairwell

## Painting

1. Order of work should be: ceiling, walls, woodwork.
2. Paint around edges of ceiling and cornices with well filled brush. Feather out paint from edge.
3. Fill paint tray to $\frac{1}{3}$ full, dip in roller, run up and down to spread paint evenly. Do not overload.
4. Work from one side of room (preferably window side) across, in patches of criss-cross strokes.
5. Re-load roller when dry and start new patch. Try to maintain single coat at a time.
6. Finish off each patch by lightly rollering over in one direction (parallel to one wall) to even out paint.
7. Paint corners and edges of walls with brush. Feather out paint.
8. Work from top of wall to bottom, in bands of criss-cross patches.
9. Never leave a wall or ceiling half-finished or you will notice the join.
10. Wash roller thoroughly with water when the job is finished, or if you are stopping work for more than half an hour. Wipe any paint splashes before they dry with damp cloth.
11. Allow each coat to dry for 4 hours minimum before applying next coat.

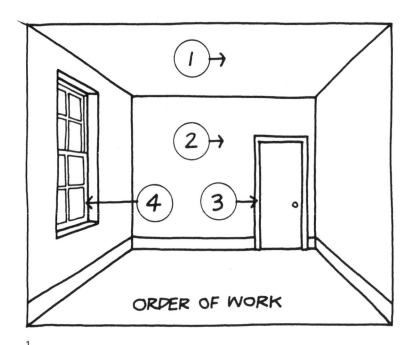

1

PAINT TRAY

3

### Note

If painting a different colour, apply a first coat thinned with water as an undercoat. Add water as directed on the can, usually 1 part water to 8 parts paint.

If using more than one can, mix them together in plastic bucket before use, to even out any colour differences. Stir well before painting.

Clear the room of furniture and protect shelves, carpets, etc., with dust sheets or old copies of *Yorkshire Post*, etc.

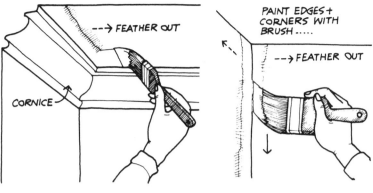

2 Ceiling and cornice          7 Corner

4

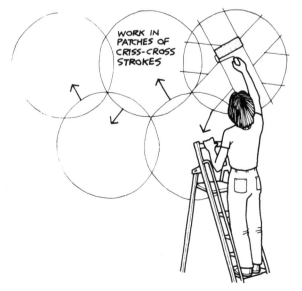

# To paint woodwork

**Gloss or eggshell paint**

**Surface preparation**

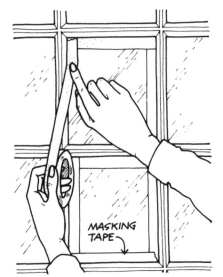

**New wood**: sandpaper smooth. Paint 'knotting' (or Shellac) over knots to seal resin. Apply wood primer as first coat (aluminium wood primer for hardwoods) and allow to dry for 12 hours minimum.

**Painted wood**: wash with water and sugar soap. If oil-based paint, rub down, lightly, with fine sandpaper and wipe over with damp cloth. Apply wood primer to any bare patches. Remove cracked or peeling paint by burning off.

**Cracks**: fill cracks and holes with filler.

**Damp wood** (e.g. leaking sills and window frames): Paint will not adhere for any length of time so cure the dampness and stop the rot! Allow timber to dry before painting or use aluminium wood primer.

**Doors and windows**: if possible remove handles and other fittings which have to be painted around. Protect glass around edges with 'masking tape'.

MASKING TAPE

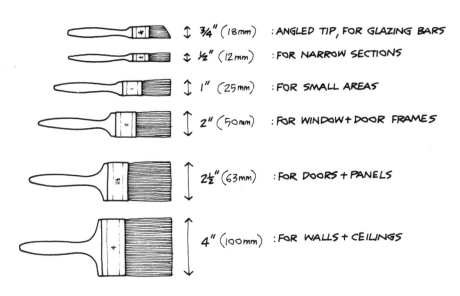

$\updownarrow$ ¾" (18mm)  : ANGLED TIP, FOR GLAZING BARS

$\updownarrow$ ½" (12mm)  : FOR NARROW SECTIONS

$\updownarrow$ 1" (25mm)  : FOR SMALL AREAS

$\updownarrow$ 2" (50mm)  : FOR WINDOW + DOOR FRAMES

$\updownarrow$ 2½" (63mm)  : FOR DOORS + PANELS

$\updownarrow$ 4" (100mm)  : FOR WALLS + CEILINGS

**Equipment**
1. Right brushes for job.
2. White spirit and jam-jars for brush cleaning.
3. Rags for accidents and brush cleaning.
4. Old newspaper.
5. Stepladder.
6. Undercoat and minimum one coat gloss paint.
7. Stick for stirring and screwdriver to open paint cans.

## Painting

1. Paint prepared surfaces with undercoat to suit top coat. Apply thinly and evenly and allow to dry 24 hours.
2. Apply top coat evenly. Do not overload brush or paint will run.
3. Paint with a series of cross strokes on flat areas, brushing and smoothing out across the panel.
4. Complete a whole area or section at a time.
5. On panels, work from the edges in towards the middle.
6. Brush over drips or runs with dry cross strokes as they happen. Do not allow to harden.
7. If drips or runs have hardened, let them dry, then sand down and re-paint.

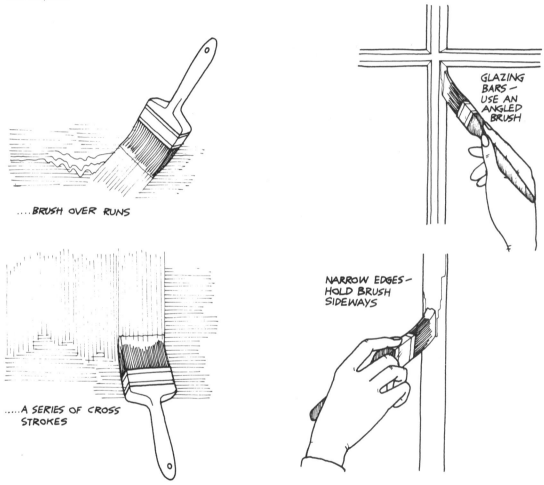

....BRUSH OVER RUNS

.....A SERIES OF CROSS STROKES

GLAZING BARS — USE AN ANGLED BRUSH

NARROW EDGES — HOLD BRUSH SIDEWAYS

## Note

Use all new brushes for undercoating first to get rid of loose bristles.

Prepare new cheap brushes by soaking in linseed oil for a day to soften bristles.

Ensure old brushes are thoroughly cleaned of old paint.

Stir oil-based paints before painting and regularly during painting.

Keep a stirrer in the can.

8.  Panel doors: paint edges same colour as inside of frame (unless you want to be perverse).

9.  Flush doors: paint edges first, then paint a series of squares across and down the door. Paint each square up and down, and sideways. Do the one next to it, then finish off with light vertical brush strokes to avoid runs.

10. Windows: paint the glazing bars with an angled brush; paint the edges to the glass first then finish off the rest with even strokes along the bar.

11. Sash windows: pull bottom sash up and top sash down and
    a   paint stile
    b   bars and stiles as far as possible
    c   lower edge of bottom sash
    d   Inside top of frame
    e   3" of inside frame.
        Nearly close window sashes
    f.  Inside of frame
    g   Top of top sash
    h   Top of bottom sash
    i   Sides of bottom sash
    j   Bottom of bottom sash

Casement window

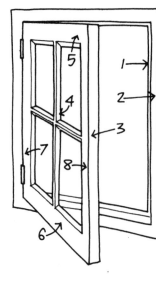

Flush door

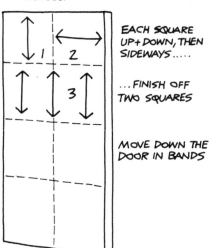

EACH SQUARE UP + DOWN, THEN SIDEWAYS.....

...FINISH OFF TWO SQUARES

MOVE DOWN THE DOOR IN BANDS

Panel door

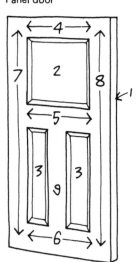

### Note

Before painting the inside of sash window frames, check they will still close. If you can't slide a piece of thin card (Corn Flakes packet) between window and frame, the old paint needs burning off.

If you have to close windows before paint is dry, put matches between window and frame to prevent sticking.

Maintain an order of work throughout. If using more than one paint type or colour, plan your painting programme so you can go through the whole job with one paint at a time, one after the other.

Sash window

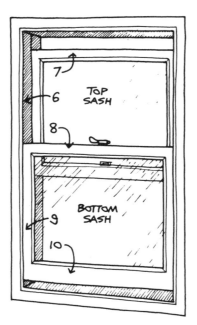

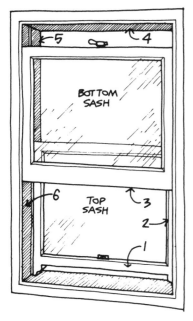

### Cleaning and storing brushes

1. After use, squeeze out remaining paint against edge of can, then with old newspaper clean metal band and handle.

2. Storing during lunch break or overnight: suspend brush in jar of water as shown. If no hole in brush, drill one. Before using, shake off excess water and wipe with rag or newspaper.

3. Cleaning: work brush around in a jar of white spirit until all paint is removed. Wash in warm water and detergent and rinse.

4. Store brushes carefully so that bristles are kept in shape.

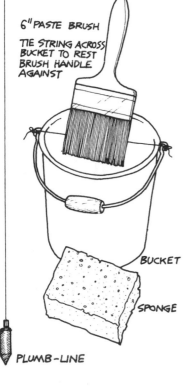

12" PAPERHANGERS SCISSORS

TOP FOLDS OVER

APPROX. 6 FT.

21"

LEGS FOLD FLAT

PASTING TABLE

PAPERING BRUSH

6" PASTE BRUSH

TIE STRING ACROSS BUCKET TO REST BRUSH HANDLE AGAINST

BUCKET

SPONGE

PLUMB-LINE

# To wallpaper

## Surface preparation

### Painted plaster

1. Wash down and scrape off flaky paint.
2. Fill cracks and holes with filler.
3. Treat wall with size to seal the surface: use glue-size powder and water mix, or a thin coat of cellulose paste.
4. Apply lining paper if surface is uneven.

### New plaster

1. Paint with emulsion until plaster dries out.
2. Allow 2 weeks for lightweight plaster (e.g. Carlite) and 6 months for sand/cement render to dry. When dry, treat with size.

### Plasterboard

If unpainted, paint with sealer/primer and apply lining paper.

### Old wallpaper

Best to strip old papered surfaces.
Loosen paper with water and sponge or steam-stripper, scrape off with stripping knife. Then prepare as for painted plaster.

### Skirtings

Fill cracks between wall and skirtings.

### Note

Be careful when stripping wallpaper off plasterboard not to remove the outer paper skin of the plasterboard. If nervous, simply paper over old wallpaper.

Whatever the surface, always use lining paper for a quality job. It comes in different 'weights', or thicknesses — use heavy weight for uneven surfaces and lighter weights for smooth walls.

### Equipment

1. Pasting table — same width as paper roll (21''/530 mm.).
2. Trimming knife and long scissors.
3. Paste brush.
4. Papering brush.
5. Plastic bucket for paste.
6. Spirit level for setting vertical line (or plumb-line).
7. Sponge.
8. Paste (adhesive).

### Note

Cellulose pastes are suitable for most papers of light to medium weight. Check with wallpaper supplier for suitable paste.

## How much paper?

Rolls are usually 11 yd long by 21″ wide (10 metres by 530 mm.). Some are printed with a blank margin, or selvedge, which has to be cut off and reduces the width to about 20″/500 mm. (get it cut in the shop).

1. Measure the height of wall to be covered and add 6″ (152 mm.) (for trimming).
2. Measure the total length of wall around the room.
3. Multiply height by length and subtract areas of windows and doors to give total area of wallpaper (in square feet or metres).

A standard 11 yd x 21″ roll covers approx. 55 sq. ft, so divide total wallpaper area by 55 to give number of rolls required (if you measure in metres, add 0.15 m to height covered and divide total by 5).

For large patterned wallpapers, add 10% to number of rolls required, allowing for wastage in matching-up edges.

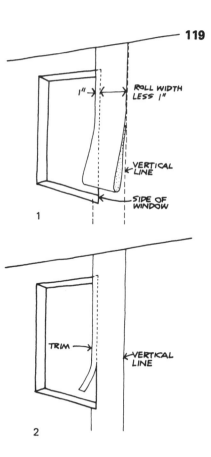

1

2

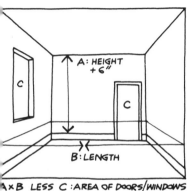

A: HEIGHT +6″

C

C

B: LENGTH

A×B LESS C : AREA OF DOORS/WINDOWS

How much paper?

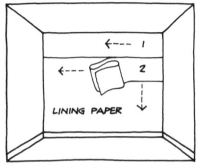

LINING PAPER

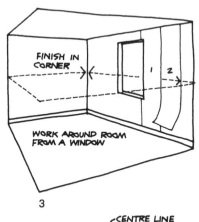

FINISH IN CORNER

WORK AROUND ROOM FROM A WINDOW

3

### Setting out

1. Start from a window. Measure out from side of window one roll width less 1″ (25 mm.), to allow for crooked window, and mark a vertical line with spirit level or plumb-line.
2. Hang first length with one edge against vertical line, the other trimmed around the opening.
3. Work away from window and around room, finishing in a corner.
4. Paper chimney-breasts and similar areas from centre outwards. Measure centre-point, measure out a half-roll width and mark a vertical line as starting point.

## Note

Hang lining paper ***horizontally***, not vertically, so joints will not coincide with top paper. Work from one end of room to the other and from top of wall downwards.

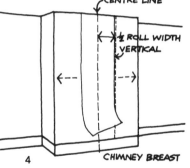

CENTRE LINE

½ ROLL WIDTH VERTICAL

4

CHIMNEY BREAST

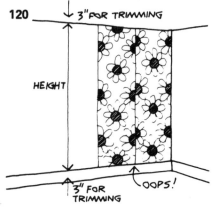

**HEIGHT**

3" FOR TRIMMING

OOPS!

Patterned paper

PASTE....

**Basic stick-up**

1. Cut enough lengths to do the whole room. Add 6" (152 mm.) for trimming top and bottom. Make sure lengths of large-patterned paper match up at edges.
2. Mix sufficient paste in bucket (not too thin).
3. Lay paper length on table, brush on paste from centre outwards to edges. Do one half, fold over and move up table to paste other half.
4. Double fold, hang over arm and carry to wall.
5. Unfold one end and place against top of wall with 3" to spare. Line edge against vertical line and brush paper down from top to bottom.
6. If paper is out of line, gently lift from wall, slide top of paper with palm of hand to adjust, then try again.
7. Brush paper into angle with ceiling and against skirting and crease a line with back of scissors.
8. Lift top and bottom of paper away and cut with scissors. Brush edges smooth.
9. Paste, fold and place next length. Unfold and slide edge against previous length to give a butt joint.
10. Continue around the room, preferably one person cutting/pasting and one person sticking.

FOLD OVER —
+ MOVE UP.....

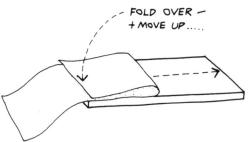

.....PASTE OTHER HALF....

.....AND FOLD OVER

DOUBLE FOLD......

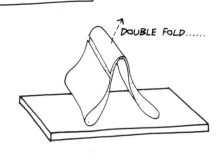

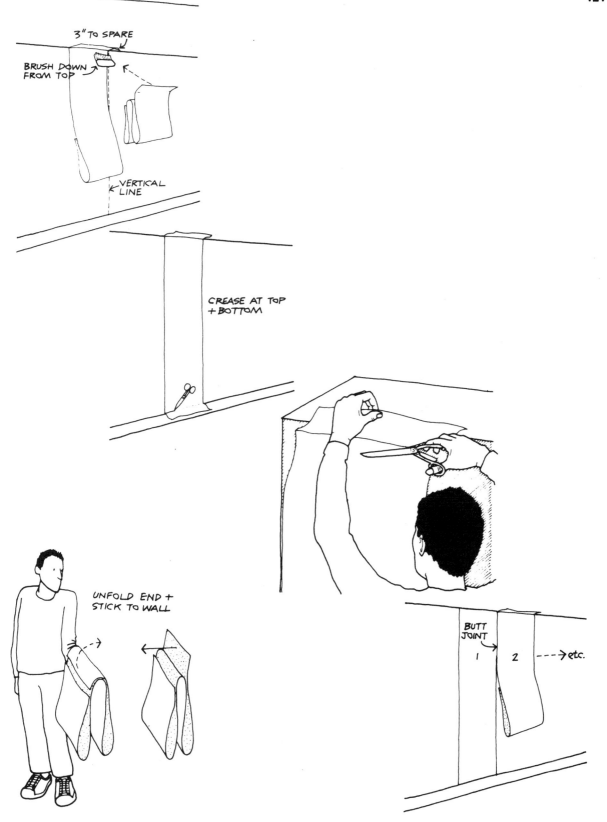

3" TO SPARE

BRUSH DOWN
FROM TOP

VERTICAL
LINE

CREASE AT TOP
+ BOTTOM

UNFOLD END +
STICK TO WALL

BUTT
JOINT

1    2    - - -> etc.

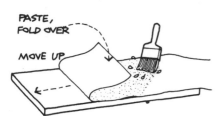

PASTE,
FOLD OVER

MOVE UP

## Concertina fold

For very long lengths (e.g. lining paper) use a concertina fold after pasting and support folded paper with an old roll of paper, cardboard tube etc. Paste down one fold at a time.

PASTE, THEN...

....CONCERTINA FOLD
AND MOVE UP
UNTIL PASTING
IS COMPLETE

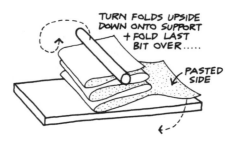

TURN FOLDS UPSIDE
DOWN ONTO SUPPORT
+ FOLD LAST
BIT OVER.....

PASTED
SIDE

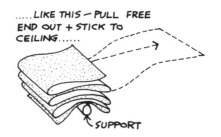

.....LIKE THIS — PULL FREE
END OUT + STICK TO
CEILING......

SUPPORT

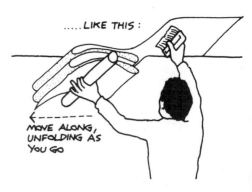

.....LIKE THIS :

MOVE ALONG,
UNFOLDING AS
YOU GO

### Tricky bits

1. Window recesses: cut strips to width of recess plus 1'' (25 mm.) to go around corner. Paper recesses first then overlap with lengths trimmed around opening.
2. Window and door openings: unfold paper loosely over frame, lightly trace outline with back of scissors, pull away and cut. Wipe paste from woodwork with damp sponge.
3. Corners: do not take the full roll width around corners. Trim paper width to give a ½'' (12 mm.) return on inside corners or 1'' (25 mm.) on outside corners. Overlap this return with next sheet.

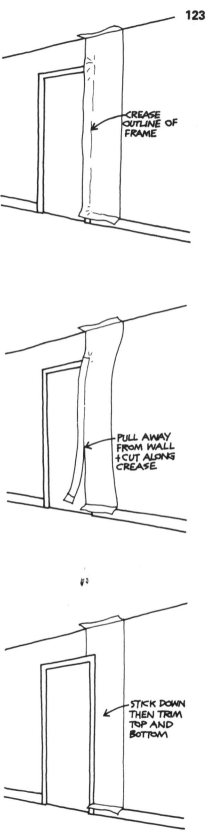

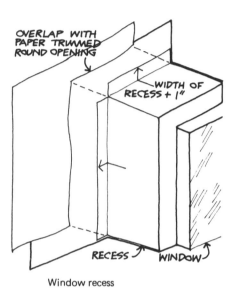

Window recess

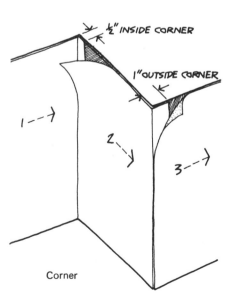

Corner

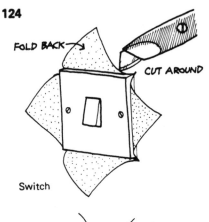

FOLD BACK

CUT AROUND

Switch

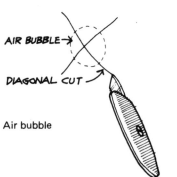

AIR BUBBLE →

DIAGONAL CUT

Air bubble

4. Switches: hang paper over switch, then make diagonal cuts to corners of switch-plate. Fold back, crease around switch, cut, then smooth down with brush.

5. Air bubbles: make a cross-cut over the bubble with sharp knife. Lift flaps of paper, brush a thin coat of paste and press back flaps. Press down with dry cloth or paper roller.

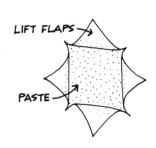

LIFT FLAPS →

PASTE →

PRESS BACK + SMOOTH

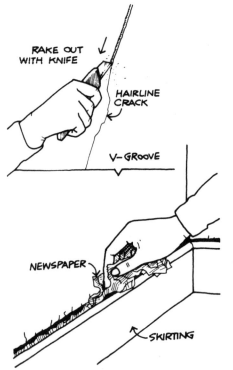

RAKE OUT WITH KNIFE

HAIRLINE CRACK

V-GROOVE

NEWSPAPER

SKIRTING

# To fill cracks

A peaceful pastime, this — the lull before the storm of vinyls and emulsions. And a very necessary preparation for a good paint job, so take your time and enjoy yourself.

### Plaster surfaces

1. Remove loose plaster from the edges of cracks or holes. Not too forcefully, or you'll have no plaster left.
2. Hairline (very thin) cracks are best widened to form a key for the filler. Run an old cutting knife along the crack to form a V-shaped groove.
3. Loose patches more than 2-3'' square really need replastering.

### Woodwork

1. Cracks in woodwork: clean out with knife, brush out dust and paint with wood primer before filling.
2. Gaps in woodwork (e.g. between architraves and frames): make sure the sections are securely fixed, nailed, etc., and will not move or warp.
3. Gaps between skirtings and walls: if very large (over ¼'') stuff old newspaper into gap to provide a base for filler.

## Preparation

1. Mix in a plastic tub if possible (e.g. an old freezer container) — when filler dries hard it can be easily removed by flexing the container.
2. Mix as directed on the packet. Use a drier, stiffer mix for larger holes and patches and a wetter, creamier mix for narrow cracks.
3. Dampen larger cracks and patches before filling.
4. Use broad-blade filling knife or scraper. Keep blade edge clean and free of old, dry filler.

## Filling

1. Fill cracks slightly more than necessary, then sand down smooth when dry. Some ready-mixed and resin-based fillers set very hard and are difficult to sand so smooth off with knife when applying.
2. Fill larger cracks/holes in two or three stages — each time apply as much filler as will stick without running or dripping. Let each coat dry before applying the next. Finish off with a thin skim coat.
3. Take a little at a time onto the blade edge and spread a thin layer across the crack or hole.
4. Clean blade edge on side of container then smooth off in opposite direction/along line of crack.
5. Clean off excess filler around crack or hole with blade.

## Sanding smooth

1. When filler has dried hard, sand smooth with a piece of fine glasspaper wrapped around a sanding block. Sand lightly in a circular motion.
2. Generally do not use an electric drill sander as this may damage surrounding areas of plaster.

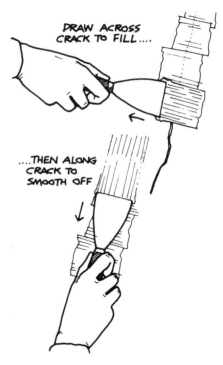

DRAW ACROSS CRACK TO FILL....

....THEN ALONG CRACK TO SMOOTH OFF

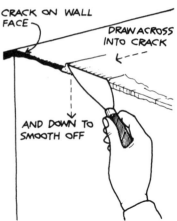

CRACK ON WALL FACE

DRAW ACROSS INTO CRACK

AND DOWN TO SMOOTH OFF

Sanding

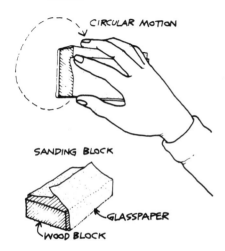

CIRCULAR MOTION

SANDING BLOCK

GLASSPAPER

WOOD BLOCK

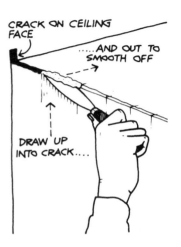

CRACK ON CEILING FACE

....AND OUT TO SMOOTH OFF

DRAW UP INTO CRACK....

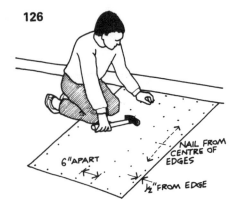

NAIL FROM CENTRE OF EDGES

6" APART

½" FROM EDGE

# To line floors

Always line floorboards with hardboard before tiling or carpeting, to give a firm, smooth base. Plywood can also be used: it is less liable to shrinkage or expansion due to moisture, but is more expensive. If you want to improve the appearance of a rough boarded floor without tiling or carpeting, cover it with large square 'tiles' of hardboard and seal with polyurethane varnish (or paint). Buy the hardboard cut to size in 2 ft (600 mm.) squares — one 4 ft x 8 ft sheet gives 8 squares. Try laying them in a diagonal pattern to avoid floorboards showing through.

### Conditioning

Hardboard is susceptible to moisture, so condition the boards to the room they will be laid in. Leave in the room exposed to the air for 48 hours. In damp rooms sprinkle the back (rough side) of the boards with water from a watering can and leave back to back for 2 - 3 days.

### Materials

Use hardboard or plywood 3 mm. thick in sheets of 4 ft x 3 ft size, which are easier to handle. Make a plan of the room and work out how many sheets are needed.

Apart from a hammer and a panel saw (and something to cut the boards on — an old table is ideal) you will need plenty of hardboard pins, 15 - 18 mm. long (see Ch. 7). Also floor brads or oval wire nails for nailing down old floorboards.

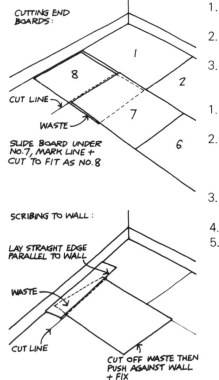

NAIL THIS SIDE FIRST

| 1 | 2 | 3 | 4 |
| 8 | 7 | 6 | 5 |
| 9 | 10 | 11 | 12 |
| 15 | 14 | 13 | |
| 16 | 17 | 18 | |

OFFCUT

CUT AROUND PROJECTIONS

USE OFFCUTS FOR ODD CORNERS

CUTTING END BOARDS:

8    1

CUT LINE    2

WASTE    7

6

SLIDE BOARD UNDER NO.7, MARK LINE + CUT TO FIT AS NO.8

SCRIBING TO WALL:

LAY STRAIGHT EDGE PARALLEL TO WALL

WASTE

CUT LINE

CUT OFF WASTE THEN PUSH AGAINST WALL + FIX

### Preparation

1. Do everything you have to do under the floorboards before you start, e.g. plumbing, re-wiring, timber treatment, insulation.
2. Nail down loose floorboards with floor brads (32 mm.); replace split, holed or damaged boards.
3. Hammer down any protruding nails in old floorboards.

### Fixing

1. As lining for tiles or carpet: lay hardboard rough side UP. As finished surface: lay hardboard smooth side up and seal.
2. Nail each sheet down with 15 - 18mm. hardboard pins, 6" (152 mm.) apart round the edges and over the face of the board. Nail ½" (12 mm.) from the edges and start from the centre.
3. Start laying against a straight wall, beginning in one corner. Continue the next row with cross joints staggered.
4. Scribe ends to wall if necessary (see drawing).
5. Leave odd corners, around fireplaces, etc., until last and fill these spaces with off-cuts.

# To fit floor tiles

This particularly includes vinyl and cork tiles, although the laying procedure applies to ceramic and clay tiles too. Before anything else, get yourself some nice kneepads!

### Surface preparation

**Solid concrete** Make sure concrete floors are damp-proofed or the tiles will float away.

**Timber boards** Before you lay tiles, do any work you want to do under the floorboards (e.g. central heating, wiring, insulation). Ensure boards are securely nailed and flat. Cover with 3 mm. hardboard (or plywood if you've money to spare). See Techniques.

**Old tiles** To remove loose/damaged tiles, warm surface with low-heat blow torch and lift with sharp paint-scraper. Remove stubborn adhesive with white spirit (open windows!). Replace with new tile. Throughly clean grease and dirt off. Check your doors will open OK.

**Uneven surface** Level with latex screed applied with a flat trowel. Sticky and tricky.

### Tools
You will need: sharp cutting knife, chalk line (string and chalk), and 4 nails, notched adhesive spreader (usually supplied with adhesive; ask for some spares).

## Note

Remember your floor level will rise by approx. ¼''. Check that your doors will open.

Different boxes of tiles will be slightly different in colour or texture, so mix them all up (shuffle the pack) before starting.

### Setting out
Important if you want to avoid narrow strips of tile round the edges and want a good job. If you don't, forget it.

### Assuming a square room:
1. Fix a nail in the floor at the centres of 2 opposite walls. Tightly tie a string between. Loosely lay tiles out from the string to the walls.
2. If there's a gap less than ½ a tile width, adjust the string sideways.
3. Rub chalk onto the string and 'snap' a chalk line onto the floor.
4. Loosely lay more tiles along this line, forming a right angle, and repeat the procedure.
5. Fix another string along the first row of tiles, making sure it forms a right angle with the other.
6. Chalk the second string and snap a line on the floor.
7. Now you have two lines to set out from. Leave the nails in place (just in case) and remove the strings.

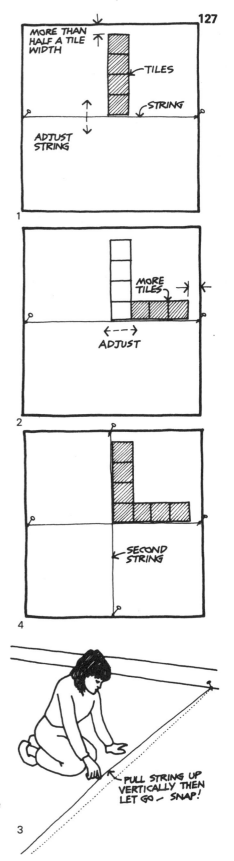

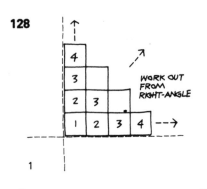

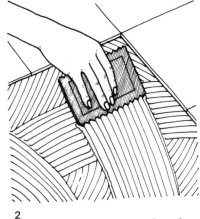

### Laying

1. Work out from the right angle in 2 directions.
2. Spread the adhesive as you go, applying enough for 3 or 4 tiles at a time. Always spread a little further than the tiles you are laying.
3. Press each tile firmly with the palm of your hand, and slide tightly against the next.
4. Tile the other quarters of the room, covering as much of the room as possible with whole tiles. Leave the margins and other cut tiles until last.

### Cutting

1. Margin tiles: put the margin tile on the last whole tile. Put a spare tile on top and slide it against the skirting. Score a line and cut the margin tile.
2. Shaping: to cut around projections or door frames, make a paper template or pattern. Trace this on to the tile and carefully cut. Better still, buy a template-former, which is pushed against the projection to reproduce the pattern.

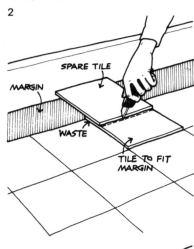

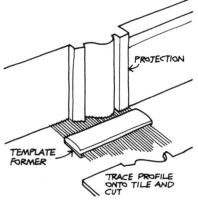

### Note

Use adhesives as recommended by manufacturer or supplier of tile.

Polish or seal the floor as soon as it's finished, especially cork. On vinyl use a water-based emulsion polish (ask for manufacturer's advice). Treat cork with 2 coats polyurethane varnish, 3 if possible.

If vinyl tiles curl up after laying, warm over gently with blow torch and press down with foot.

# To fix ceramic wall tiles

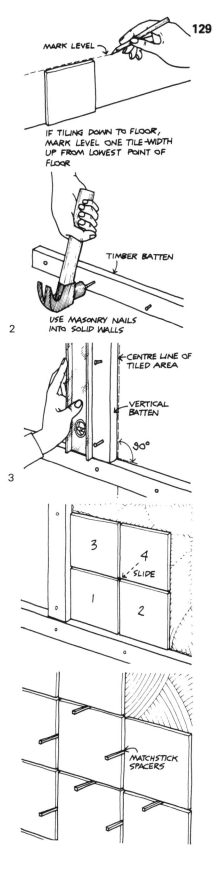

### Surface preparation
Surfaces must be dry, flat and firm.

**Old plaster** Ensure it is not damp; remove and fill loose areas; if porous or flaky, treat with primer recommended by adhesive manufacturer.

**New plaster** Allow to dry for 4 weeks.

**Paint** Scrape off loose, flaky areas.

**Timber boards/plasterboard** Fix securely to prevent movement or warping. Remove dust.

**Old ceramic tiles** Ensure firmly fixed and perfectly flat. Fill holes with adhesive.

**Bare brickwork** Will need rendering or plastering smooth, so find a plasterer.

### Tools
You will need: notched adhesive spreader, tile cutter, pincers, squeegee or sponge (for grouting), spirit level and timber battens (straight ones).

### Note
Remember to use Bullnose edge tiles for corners and edges.

If possible, use tiles with spacer lugs.

### Fixing
1. Determine level of lowest tile or lowest tile but one if going down to floor. Mark on wall.
2. Draw line against spirit level. Fix timber batten (approx. 2" x ¾") with nails to wall, and check level.
3. Place vertical batten on centre line of area to be tiled. Check with spirit level and nail to wall.
4. Starting from angle of battens, spread adhesive with notched spreader in 1 ft square sections.
5. Apply tiles, working out from angle. Press each tile into adhesive slightly out of position and slide against next tile.
6. If tiles have no spacer lugs around edges, use bits of matchstick instead.
7. Check for level with spirit level every 3 rows.
8. After tiling along both battens, remove battens and finish rest of wall.
9. Tiles at ends, round windows or basins, etc., will have to be cut. Do these last.
10. Wait 24 hours before grouting to allow adhesive to set.

MARK LEVEL

IF TILING DOWN TO FLOOR, MARK LEVEL ONE TILE-WIDTH UP FROM LOWEST POINT OF FLOOR

TIMBER BATTEN

USE MASONRY NAILS INTO SOLID WALLS

2

CENTRE LINE OF TILED AREA

VERTICAL BATTEN

90°

3

SLIDE

MATCHSTICK SPACERS

**130**

PIECE TO BE REMOVED

2

## Cutting tiles

1. Measure outline to be cut and mark with felt-tip pen.
2. Place tile on flat surface, glazed surface up, and score line with tile cutter against straight edge.
3. If cutting off a straight, wide strip, hold tile and break over a hard edge.
4. Otherwise use pincers to nibble away the waste in small pieces. Have a practice run first.
5. Smooth cut edges with fine file or carborundum stone.

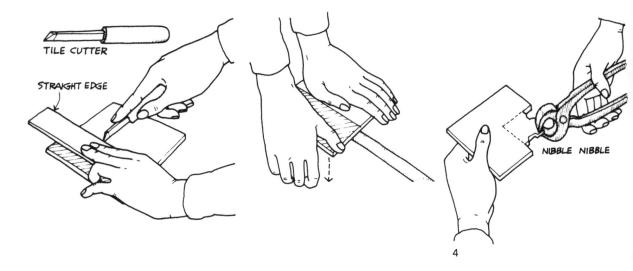

TILE CUTTER

STRAIGHT EDGE

NIBBLE NIBBLE

4

## Cutting quadrant tiles

1. Cut from back with hacksaw to halfway.
2. Tap sharply over hard edge to break.

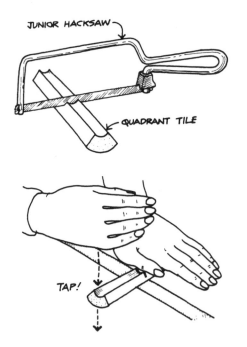

JUNIOR HACKSAW

QUADRANT TILE

TAP!

**Tiling upside down (e.g. at the top of windows)**

1. Cut a flexible strip of plywood/hardboard of the required length, and 3 bits of timber as props.
2. Fix the first tile, position the strip and wedge in the first prop.
3. Fix the second tile and fit the second prop. Work this along to halfway.
4. Work the third prop along from halfway to the end.

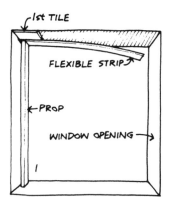 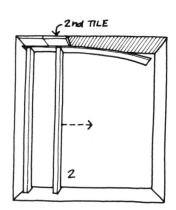 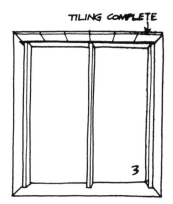

**Grouting**

After the hard work, the relaxation.

1. Mix enough grout to cover the tiled area. A stiff, creamy consistency is needed, not a wet and runny one.
2. Use a clean sponge or squeegee to spread grout over the tiles, filling joints as you go. Avoid leaving too much grout on tile surface.
3. When grout has set (but not hardened), wipe excess grout from tile with a damp cloth. Grout and wipe 1 sq. yd at a time.
4. For a proper job, smooth over the joints with a rounded point.
5. Finally, when grout is dry, polish over with a dry, soft cloth.

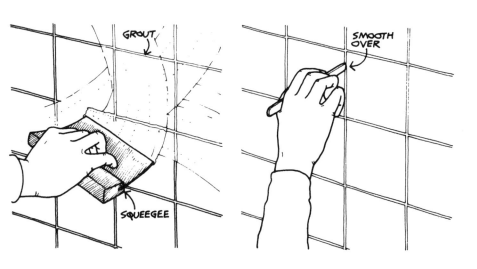

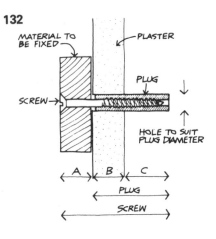

MATERIAL TO BE FIXED
PLASTER
SCREW
PLUG
HOLE TO SUIT PLUG DIAMETER

A — B — C
PLUG
SCREW

A : THICKNESS OF FIXED ITEM
B : PLASTER THICKNESS — USUALLY ½"–1" (13–25mm)
C : FIXING INTO WALL — ENSURE MINIMUM ½" (13mm)

# To fix things into walls

You will be fixing into two basic kinds of wall: solid masonry (brick or blockwork) with plaster, and timber studs with either plasterboard or plaster and laths. Knock a wall with your knuckles, and, if it hurts, chances are it's brick.

The size and type of fixing will depend on the load carried. As a guide:

| | |
|---|---|
| light loads | wardrobe shelves/bathroom fittings |
| medium loads | medicine cabinets/kitchen shelf for pots and pans/ paperback books/mirrors |
| heavy loads | TV or stereo/kitchen worktop/radiators |

### I. Solid walls

Use a plug and screw fixing, fibrous plugging material or an expanding bolt for structural loads. They both work on the principle of the fixing expanding inside a pre-drilled hole.

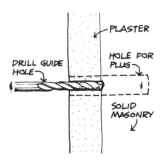

PLASTER
HOLE FOR PLUG
DRILL GUIDE HOLE
SOLID MASONRY

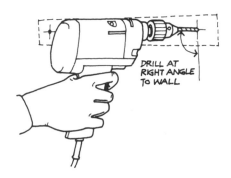

MARK HOLES ON WALL

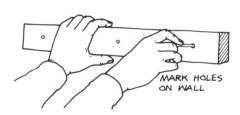

DRILL AT RIGHT ANGLE TO WALL

### Plug and screw

1. Any kind of woodscrew can be used. Select size and length according to material to be fixed, depth of plaster and weight of load.
2. Select size and length of plug to suit screw. Buy plugs and screws together in shop.
3. Select drill bit to match diameter of plug. Use special 'masonry bit'.
4. Place material to be fixed against wall and mark screw holes. (Drill holes in the timber you are fixing to the wall first.) Use nail if pencil is too big.
5. Using old 1/8" diameter bit, drill pilot or guide holes through plaster to solid masonry.
6. Using masonry bit of correct size, drill holes to required depth. Drill at right angles to wall. Scrape or blow out dust (close eyes!).
7. Test fit plugs in holes. Ensure they do not project above wall surface.
8. Fit screws into material to be fixed, so point is just through.
9. Place material against wall, push screw points into centre of plugs and screw in.
10. Screw each screw in turn until all are driven home, then tighten.

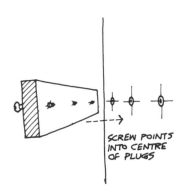

SCREW POINTS INTO CENTRE OF PLUGS

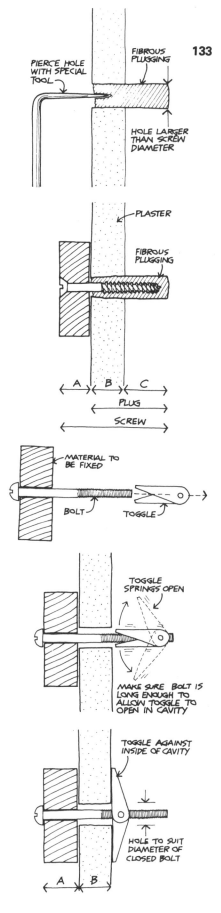

### Fibrous plugging material

1. Select masonry drill bit slightly larger than diameter of screw (see Ch. 6).
2. Drill hole to suit screw length.
3. Take enough plugging material to fill the hole, moisten and roll into a plug.
4. Insert into hole and push in with tool provided.
5. Pierce hole into centre of plug with pointed end of tool to make a guide for screw.
6. Put screw through item to be fixed, insert into plug and tighten.

### II. Hollow walls

Use a 'toggle' type of fixing, or an 'umbrella' or collapsible anchor type of expanding plug, which remains in place if the screw is removed. Both work by screwing into a device which opens up behind the plasterboard as the screw or bolt is tightened.

It is advisable to use these only for light loads. For heavier loads the fixing should be done directly into the studs or via a batten or timber plate fixed into the studs. Find the studs by drilling across the wall with a 1/16'' bit at about 2'' intervals until you come to something solid. Studs can be anything between 15'' and 24'' apart.

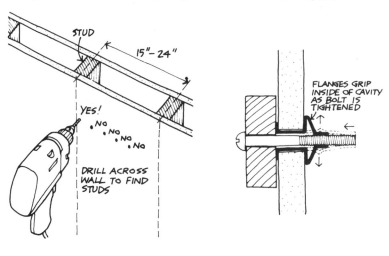

### Fixing

1. Place material to be fixed against wall and mark fixing holes with pencil or nail.
2. Toggle bolts or collapsible anchors come with bolt supplied. Remove toggle, place bolt through material to be fixed, and replace toggle loosely.
3. Using masonry or wood bit, drill hole in plaster to diameter of closed toggle or anchor. This will be larger than the bolt diameter.
4. Place material to be fixed against wall. Close toggles and push into cavity through holes. Push bolt in as far as possible to allow toggles to spring open.
5. Tighten screw. Pull material away from wall slightly so that toggles grip against inside of cavity. Do not overtighten.

### Note

If toggle bolts are removed, the toggle will fall into the cavity and a new fixing will be needed.

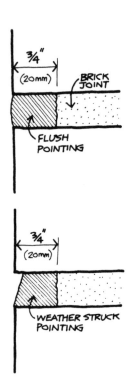

3/4" (20mm)

BRICK JOINT

FLUSH POINTING

3/4" (20mm)

WEATHER STRUCK POINTING

# To repair brickwork

Shown here are two types of pointing: the flush-joint or the weather-struck joint. The flush-joint is easier but the weather-struck joint is better for weathering the rain. There are others but we'll leave those to the professionals.

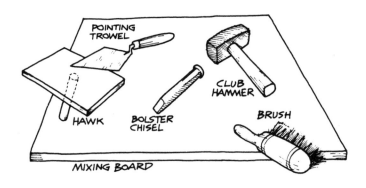

POINTING TROWEL

CLUB HAMMER

HAWK

BOLSTER CHISEL

BRUSH

MIXING BOARD

### Essential tools

Bolster chisel; club hammer; board for mixing mortar; hawk (mortar-board) for holding mortar; pointing trowel (smaller than bricklaying trowel); old brush.

### Mortar mix

Use Portland cement, hydrated lime powder and clean washed builder's sand (all available from builders' merchants). With too much cement, or no lime, the mortar is susceptible to cracking. Always make sure there is lime in the mix to produce a less rigid, more 'flexible' joint. For general re-pointing use a 1:1:6 mix (1 part cement/1 part lime/6 parts sand).

### Mixing

Cement:lime:sand mortar is prepared in two stages: first 1 measure of lime and 6 of sand are mixed into 'coarse stuff' before the cement is added. Blend together dry, then add water and mix to a stiff consistency. (The volume of coarse stuff (lime and sand) equals the volume of sand because the lime fills the spaces between the grains of sand without increasing the overall volume.) Then combine 1 measure of cement with the coarse stuff on the board and mix gradually with water into a workable consistency.

Use mortar within 2 hours of mixing. If it begins to dry or harden, throw it away, don't add more water.

### Pointing in the right direction

Avoid re-pointing (and any concrete work) during winter when frost is likely. Protect finished work from rain with polythene sheet, etc.

If re-pointing large areas, start from top left-hand corner and work across and down the wall to keep work clean.

Provide a suitable platform; try and work at chest height.

Put enough mortar on the hawk to cover one square yard at a time.

START FROM TOP LEFT-HAND CORNER ......

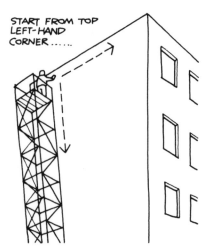

## Method

1. Using 3/8'' wide bolster chisel and club hammer, chip out old mortar to a depth of ¾''. Rake clean and brush out dust with a stiff brush.
2. Mix sufficient quantity of mortar.
3. Dampen the raked-out joints with clean water and old distemper brush. Do not saturate bricks. (This prevents water being sucked out of mortar mix.)
4. Trowel some mixed mortar onto the hawk and form into a flat 'cake'.
5. Slice back edge of trowel into mortar and lift out a wedge of mortar sufficient to fill the joint. (Practise this before you start pointing.)
6. Press mortar wedge into raked-out joint with back of trowel, vertical joints first then horizontal joints.
7. For a flush joint, finish mortar flush with bricks. Wait until mortar has dried a little, then rub in one direction with a cloth.
8. For a weather-struck joint, recess mortar at top of horizontal joint with edge of trowel then draw down to finish flush with brickwork at bottom of joint. Similarly recess left hand side of vertical joint and draw across to right hand side. Clean ragged edges with edge of trowel.
9. When mortar is nearly hard, brush over with a stiff brush to remove bits.
10. Stand back and feel justifiably proud.

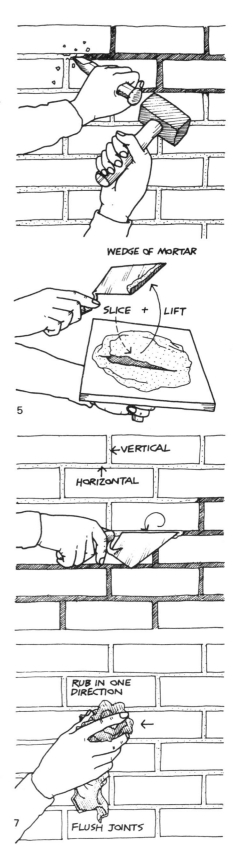

WEDGE OF MORTAR

SLICE + LIFT

5

←VERTICAL

HORIZONTAL

RUB IN ONE DIRECTION

7   FLUSH JOINTS

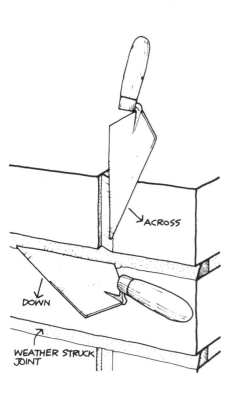

ACROSS

DOWN

WEATHER STRUCK JOINT

# To replace broken sash cords

Sliding sashes are counterbalanced by iron weights, which run up and down inside the 'box' frame. A sash cord runs over a pulley fixed into the frame and connects weight with sash. Always use proper sash cord, specially made for the job. Polypropylene sash cord is available now and is preferable for a longer life.

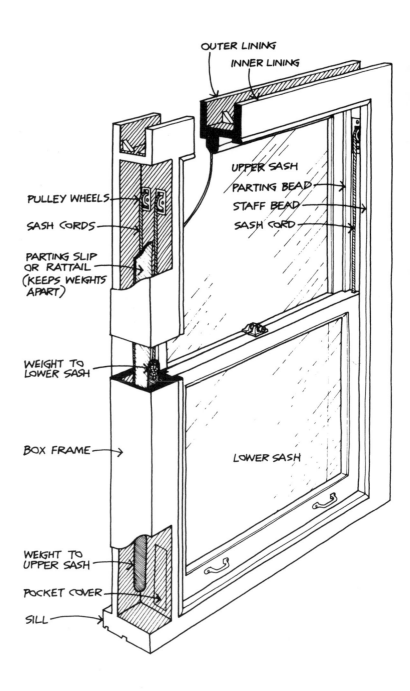

### To remove old cords

1. Carefully lift staff beads on both sides of frame, using an old chisel or screwdriver.
2. Lift out lower sash, cut sash cords and lower weights to bottom of frame.
3. Prise out parting beads and remove upper sash in same way.
4. Remove old cords and nails from groove in edge of sashes; clean and paint sashes if necessary.
5. Locate pocket covers on inner linings (tap old paintwork until joint appears) and prise out. These are often fitted loose but may be fixed with small nails around edge.
6. Reach in, take out weights and untie old sash cords.
7. Inspect pulley wheels — oil wheels or replace if damaged.

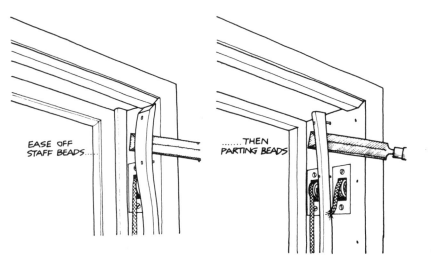

EASE OFF STAFF BEADS....

.......THEN PARTING BEADS

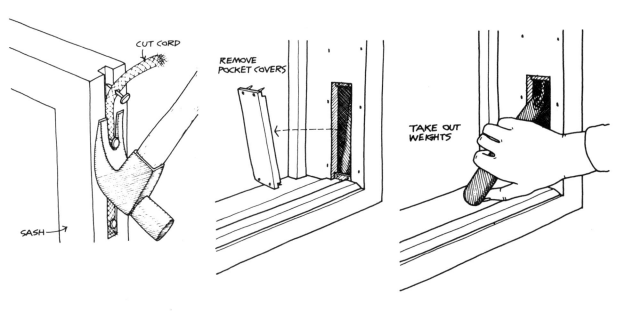

CUT CORD

SASH

REMOVE POCKET COVERS

TAKE OUT WEIGHTS

**To fit new cords**

1. Tie nail to long piece of string. Feed over pulley and pull out through pocket, leaving other end over pulley. Use this to pull new sash cords through. Knot the cord ends to stop them slipping through the pulleys.

2. Thread the cord through the hole in the weight and tie a figure-of-eight knot tightly.

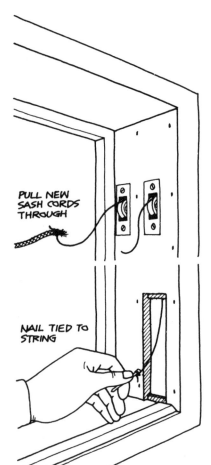

PULL NEW SASH CORDS THROUGH

NAIL TIED TO STRING

KNOT THE CORD-ENDS

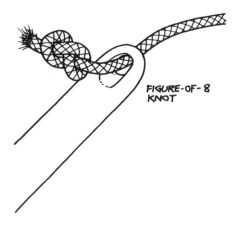

FIGURE-OF-8 KNOT

3. Support sashes against top of frame and mark the level of the pulley wheel centre-line. This will be the position of the highest nail fixing the cords.

4. Fix top (outer) sash first; rest sash in frame on window sill. Pull one sash cord down as far as possible to bring weight up to pulley.

5. Fix cord into groove with 1'' galvanized clout nails (4 minimum), working down from pulley mark. Cut cord end to suit groove length. Repeat with other cord.

6. Test sash: ensure it closes properly without weights hitting bottom of box frame.

7 Replace parting beads now, using 1½'' panel pins.

8. Fit cords to lower (inner) sash and test.

9. Replace pocket covers and ensure tight fit.

10. Replace inner staff beads using panel pins or oval wire nails.

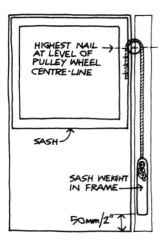

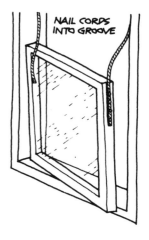

**Note**

New pulley wheels and sash cords are available from builders' merchants or ironmongers. If buying a pulley wheel, take the old one with you to match up.

If parting/staff beads are lost or damaged, new sections are available at most timber merchants. These are standard sections, but take along a measurement or sample just in case.

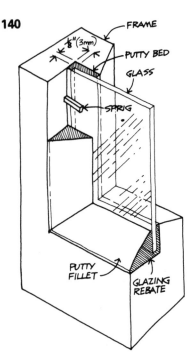

FRAME
⅛"(3mm)
PUTTY BED
GLASS
SPRIG
PUTTY FILLET
GLAZING REBATE

# To glaze windows/doors

### Glass

Before going to buy the glass, find out what size and thickness is needed.

1. Measure height and width of rebate, then subtract ¼" (6 mm.) for glass size.
2. Check frame is square with tri-square — if not, make paper template of rebate.
3. Glass thickness: add width and height of glass; if total is less than 80" (200 mm.), use 3 mm. thickness. If more use 4 mm.

### Re-glazing

1. Tape over old glass and break out from top of window downwards. Wear gloves and protect eyes.
2. Break out old putty with old knife or chisel and hammer.
3. Remove sprigs (flat nails) with pincers from timber frames. Or remove glazing clips from metal frames and keep for re-use.
4. Remove remaining bits of glass.
5. Scrape clean rebate and prepare frame:
   Timber: paint with wood primer
   Metal: rust proofer and zinc-based metal primer

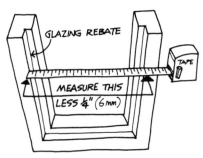

GLAZING REBATE
TAPE
MEASURE THIS LESS ¼" (6mm)

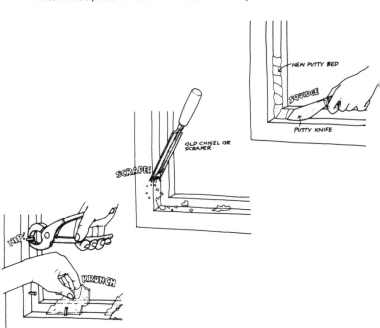

NEW PUTTY BED
SQUIDGE
PUTTY KNIFE
OLD CHISEL OR SCRAPER
SCRAPE!
NIP!
KRUNCH
THWACK!

6. Put new glass into rebate to test for size. Trim with glass cutter if necessary.

7. Apply putty to rebate in equal size blobs to give $\frac{1}{8}$'' maximum thickness of 'bed' for glass.

8. Push glass into frame against putty bed, pressing evenly around edges with fingers.

9. Tap in sprigs tight against glass with side of chisel and hammer. Space 3'' from each corner and 12'' apart in between. For metal frames, tap glazing clips back into slots.

10. Apply putty in blobs to face of frame (having pummelled putty first to a workable consistency) and smooth with putty knife into triangular wedge or fillet. Cut away excess and trim edges with knife.

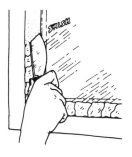

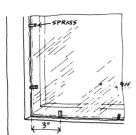

**Note**

There is a special putty to be used for metal frames.

Make sure the sprigs do not project above the surface of the putty fillet.

Allow putty to harden for 2 weeks before painting.

# TOOLS

This is not a comprehensive catalogue, but the basic toolkit for the reluctant handyman. Without it, you will find it difficult to carry out the simplest repair jobs around the house and impossible to do most of the things described in previous chapters. More sophisticated and extravagant tools can be added later; more expensive but little-used tools can be hired.

When setting up the basic toolkit, buy the best you can possibly afford — they will last longer and give better performance than cheaper tools. There's nothing worse than a hammer whose head keeps flying off or a bendy screwdriver. Get to know how they work and try them first, especially tools for cutting, shaping and smoothing. Store them neatly in one place — in a large box, a toolbag or hanging on a wall. Keep them clean, sharp and free of rust for a long, healthy life.

When you buy cutting tools, such as saws or chisels, ask if the shop provides a sharpening service — if it is a proper specialist tool shop it should do. Otherwise find one that does and get saws and chisels regularly serviced.

# The basic toolkit

### Holding operations

#### Bench

The operating table of house surgery. Most jobs require something to support and grip the work in hand: for versatility and value-for-money get a well-known brand of folding work bench with adjustable top, which combines bench, vice and carpenter's trestle.

They are very hi-tech and look good as a TV table or can be used for more strenuous keep-fit exercises.

#### Storage

You're all set to go, but where on earth are those nails, drill-bits, sticky-tape, etc.? Apart from your basic toolkit, you will accumulate a collection of essential bits and pieces which need to be readily identifiable and accessible.

There is great scope for imagination here in assembling a stock of suitable containers organized, categorized, systemized and labelled to suit your own preference and style. To start with you will need containers for:

a    Nails — store different kinds and sizes separately, as it's no joke sorting nails.

b    Screws — same again, but if you want to mix them at least keep screws of same gauge (diameter) together.

c    Drill-bits — best kept in a little flat box or tin. A kid's crayon case can be very handy.

d    Wall-plugs — if you like these can be stored with the screws which fit them.

e    Miscellaneous fixings — clips, staples, bolts, etc.

f    Electrical — fuse-wires, cartridges, cable-clips, etc. . . . and so on.

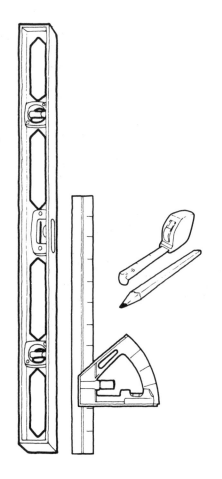

#### Measuring and marking

12ft (3.6 m.) flexible steel tape:
For large or small measuring jobs, marked in feet/inches and metres/millimetres.
Check: locking device for tape and recoil spring.

12″ (300 mm.) steel combination square:
For marking and checking right-angles, also 45° angles.
Check: ease of adjustment, and built-in spirit level for small levelling jobs.

24″ (600 mm.) metal alloy spirit level:
For checking and marking levels and verticals, also as occasional straight-edge for cutting.
Check: bubbles for horizontal and vertical levelling.

Carpenter's pencil:
For marking lines against straight edges. Oval shape with flat, wide lead.

**144**

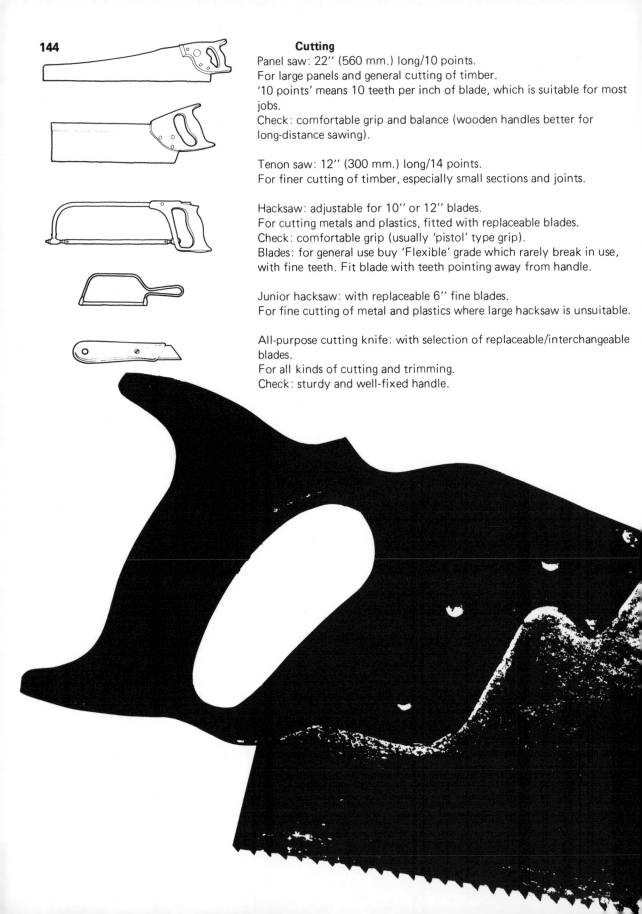

## Cutting

Panel saw: 22″ (560 mm.) long/10 points.
For large panels and general cutting of timber.
'10 points' means 10 teeth per inch of blade, which is suitable for most jobs.
Check: comfortable grip and balance (wooden handles better for long-distance sawing).

Tenon saw: 12″ (300 mm.) long/14 points.
For finer cutting of timber, especially small sections and joints.

Hacksaw: adjustable for 10″ or 12″ blades.
For cutting metals and plastics, fitted with replaceable blades.
Check: comfortable grip (usually 'pistol' type grip).
Blades: for general use buy 'Flexible' grade which rarely break in use, with fine teeth. Fit blade with teeth pointing away from handle.

Junior hacksaw: with replaceable 6″ fine blades.
For fine cutting of metal and plastics where large hacksaw is unsuitable.

All-purpose cutting knife: with selection of replaceable/interchangeable blades.
For all kinds of cutting and trimming.
Check: sturdy and well-fixed handle.

### Shaping and smoothing

Bevel edge chisel: 10 mm./18 mm./25 mm. blade widths.
For cutting recesses and mortises in wood (hinges, locks, joints).
Other blade widths are available between 6 mm. and 25 mm. but the three sizes above should be adequate.
Buy ones with plastic handles, which can be used with a steel hammer.
Check: plastic cap supplied to protect blade.

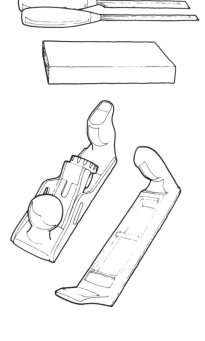

Oilstone: combination medium/fine surfaces 6″ x 2″ x 1″.
For sharpening chisels — essential!
Best fitted (or bought) in an oilstone box.
Use lightly covered with oil and keep free of dust.

Smoothing plane: 10″ (250 mm.) long/replaceable blade type.
For planing-down and smoothing wood (special blades available for plastic laminates).
Depth and angle of blade are adjustable.
Check: for comfortable grip and solid feel.

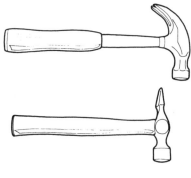

Multi-purpose trimming tool: various sizes/replaceable blades.
For trimming and shaping wood, laminates, metal objects, brick, fibreglass, etc. Used like a plane, but not intended for producing smooth surfaces — can be used instead of a rasp or steel file.

### Hammers

Claw hammer: steel shaft/16-20 oz. weight.
For general hammering work, and removing nails with 'claw'. A good quality wooden handle (hickory) is fine but the head won't come off a steel shaft.
Check: for balance — stand on claw — and weight.
        finely cut 'V' in claw for removing small nails.

Cross pein or Warrington hammer: 10-12 oz. weight.
For nailing, and starting small nails/pins with wedged end (pein).
Check: for balance and quality of head and pein.

## Drills 'n bits

Hand drill (wheelbrace): ¼'' (6.5 mm.) chuck size.
For hand drilling holes $\frac{1}{16}$''-¼'' (1.5-6.5 mm.), usually into wood.
Check: gearing smooth running and not loose.

Hand brace: ½'' (13 mm.) chuck size/10'' sweep.
For hand drilling larger, 'special' holes with square-ended bits (auger and centre-bits).
Can be operated by continuous turning of the handle or by using the ratchet with short push-pulls.
Check: fitted with ratchet device/mushroom-head with ball-race bearings for easy action.

Electric drill: up to $\frac{3}{8}$'' (10 mm.) chuck size/2-speed/hammer action.
For general drilling into wood, metal, masonry.
Many attachments available for other jobs — sanding, sawing, polishing, etc.
Not absolutely essential for the truly reluctant but worth buying in the long term.
Check: range of attachments available.
　　　　cable length — may need extension lead.
　　　　plug fuse 3A.

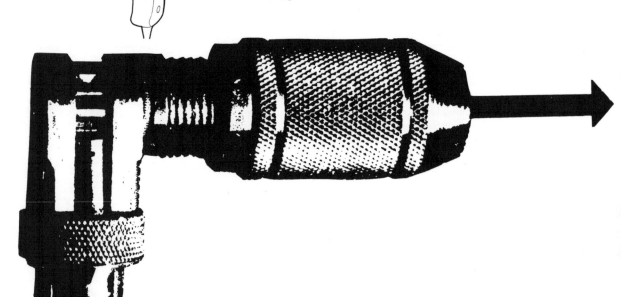

Drill bits:
a　　Twist drill: carbon steel or chrome vanadium for wood.
　　　high speed steel (HSS) for metal — yes, metal!
　　　Use with hand drills or electric drills. For drilling holes up to
　　　¼'' in diameter, usually for screw fixings into wood. Bought
　　　singly or in packs, and available from $\frac{1}{16}$'' (1.5 mm.) to
　　　$\frac{3}{8}$'' (9.5 mm.) diameter. A useful range for most jobs is:

| $\frac{1}{16}$ | $\frac{3}{32}$ | $\frac{1}{8}$ | $\frac{5}{32}$ | $\frac{3}{16}$ | $\frac{7}{32}$ | $\frac{1}{4}$ | ins. |
|---|---|---|---|---|---|---|---|
| 1.5 | 2.5 | 3 | 4 | 4.5 | 6 | 6.5 | mm. |

When screwing pieces of softwood together, first drill a 'clearance hole' in one piece for the screw to pass through tightly, then drill a 'pilot hole' in the other to take the screw thread. Select a drill bit according to the screw gauge (diameter):

| Screw gauge | 2 | 4 | 6 | 8 | 10 | 12 | |
|---|---|---|---|---|---|---|---|
| **Clearance hole:** | | | | | | | |
| bit | $\frac{3}{32}$ | $\frac{1}{8}$ | $\frac{5}{32}$ | $\frac{3}{16}$ | $\frac{3}{16}$ | $\frac{7}{32}$ | ins. |
| diameter | 2.5 | 3 | 4 | 4.5 | 4.5 | 6 | mm. |
| **Pilot hole:** | | | | | | | |
| bit | use | | $\frac{1}{16}$ | $\frac{3}{32}$ | $\frac{3}{32}$ | $\frac{1}{8}$ | ins. |
| diameter | bradawl | | 1.5 | 2.5 | 2.5 | 3 | mm. |

b   Auger bit: usually square-ended and used with a hand-brace. For accurate drilling of deeper and larger holes in wood. Has a screw-point which pulls a cutting-edge into the wood. The spiral body of the bit keeps it straight and removes waste wood whilst cutting.
Buy one as you need it, because they cost about £3-£10 each depending on size.
Available in sizes from ¼'' up to 1½'' diameter.

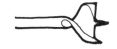

c   Centre bit: usually square-ended and used with a hand-brace. For drilling shallower holes than an auger bit, but often wider. Ideal for cutting holes into the face of panels or doors, especially if fitting cylinder locks.
Available in sizes from ¼'' up to 2¼'' diameter holes. The 1¼'' size is usually used for fitting cylinder locks into doors.

d   Flat bit: for use with electric drills.
An alternative to the centre bit if using an electric drill, although not so accurate and best used for shallow holes.
Available in sizes from $\frac{3}{8}$ '' up to 1¼'' diameter holes.

e   Masonry drill bit: tungsten carbide tipped.
For drilling into brick, concrete blocks, ceramic tiles. Small holes can be drilled with a hand drill, but for best results use an electric drill.
For hard masonry (concrete, stone) use a special percussion drill bit, with the drill set to 'hammer' action.
Available in sizes from $\frac{3}{16}$ '' up to ½'' diameter, sometimes referred to as a masonry bit size number:

| Size no. | 8 | 10 | 12 | 14 | 16 | 20 | 22 | 24 | |
|---|---|---|---|---|---|---|---|---|---|
| Diameter | $\frac{3}{16}$ | $\frac{7}{32}$ | $\frac{1}{4}$ | $\frac{9}{32}$ | $\frac{5}{16}$ | $\frac{3}{8}$ | $\frac{7}{16}$ | $\frac{1}{2}$ | in |
| | 5 | 5.5 | 6.5 | 7 | 8 | 9.5 | 11 | 13 | mm. |

Buy them to suit the diameter of wall plugs or expanding bolts to be fixed — a no. 12 size (¼'') is useful as it suits wall plugs for the most often used screw sizes — 6, 8 and 10 gauge.

## Bradawl and countersinker:

Bradawl: like very small screwdriver, but makes very small holes in wood — for marking the centre of a hole before drilling, forming a pilot hole for small screws.

Counter-sinker: having drilled the hole for your counter-sunk screw you counter-sink the hole for the screw head. This is accomplished by using a counter-sinking bit, either as a bit fitted into a drill or fixed to a handle like a screwdriver. Do not contemplate using counter-sunk screws until you have one!

## Screwdrivers

Single-slot flat-blade screwdriver: for single-slot woodscrews.
Handy sizes: 4-6″ blade for no. 6-8 gauge screws.
            8″ blade for no. 10-12 gauge screws.
These should cover most jobs.
Check: wide handle for maximum grip.
       snug fit of blade into screw-slot.

Electrician's screwdriver: insulated handle.
For most electrical work and very small screws.
Handy sizes: 3 mm. blade.
            5 mm. blade.

The mains-tested version has a neon tube in the handle which lights up if a live wire is touched, and is worth the extra expense.

Ratchet screwdriver: with ratchet device operating in both directions — can be locked and used like an ordinary screwdriver.
Not essential for occasional use.

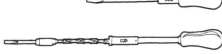

For long-distance screwing, use a long spiral-ratchet screwdriver where the handle is pushed in and out, not turned. Usually sold with a range of different interchangeable blades.

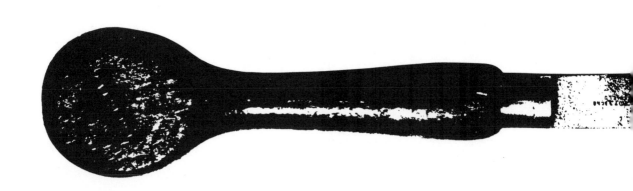

## Pliers/spanner

Pincers: 7" long with small claw on handle end.
For removing nails, nibbling ceramic tiles.

Electrician's pliers: 6" long with insulated handles.
For holding, bending and cutting wire and other small metal bits and
pieces. Have serrated grip and a cutting edge.
Check: comfortable grip, not too stiff.

Wire stripper: adjusts to different cable diameters.
For stripping insulation from wires. Not essential but a great time-
saver if doing a lot of wiring work.
Avoids problem of cutting through the wire.

Adjustable spanner (or wrench): 8" (200 mm.) length. Screw
adjustment to fit most types of plumbing fittings. Buy two for
compression pipe joints — one turning against the other.
Check: for easy screw adjustment (not too stiff or slack).

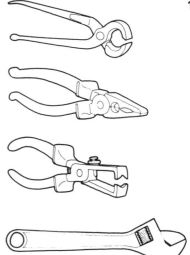

## Ladders

Stepladder: 6 ft (2 m.) minimum height.
For decorating, fixing shelves, getting into the loft and a host of things
that would otherwise be impossible or very dangerous. Don't skimp on
stepladders — buy ones that allow you to reach your highest ceiling
comfortably, or get through the loft hatch without jumping.
If you can afford it, get the aluminium ones, which are light to carry,
long-lasting and can be stored outdoors.
For decorating select a model which has, or allows for, a shelf on top
for holding paint cans/trays.
Check: non-slip feet and sturdy safety struts.

......ASK FOR A DEMONSTRATION

**Tool hire**

Some jobs require tools of a specialist nature which are too expensive to buy unless you're going into the home-improvement business full time. Fortunately, help is at hand with the growing network of tool and plant (machinery, not marigolds) hire shops across the nation. Equipment can usually be hired for half-days, days, weeks or more. Heavier items can be delivered and collected for an extra charge.

If you are not sure exactly which item you need to hire, go to the hire shop and ask. Before you hire:

1   Get all the preparatory work done first — for example, don't hire the concrete mixer until you're ready to lay the concrete.
2   Know how to operate the equipment and check that it works — ask for it to be started in your presence and ask for a demonstration if you need it. Are there any parts or attachments missing?
3   Heavy tools of an industrial nature — drills, saws, cutters — can be very dangerous. Apart from using them properly, wear protective clothing such as goggles, masks (often available from the hire shop) and reinforced shoes.

The range of equipment available can be mind-boggling, and depends on the hire shop you go to. Some of the useful things you should be able to hire are:

*Heavy work:*   concrete mixers (electric if possible)
heavy-duty drills — for masonry and concrete
disc grinders — for cutting masonry
scaffolding — for access to walls and roofs

*Renovation:*   floor sanders (punch the nails down first!)
carpet cleaners — deep cleaning
steam wallpaper strippers
floor rollers — for newly laid vinyl tiles
ceramic tile cutters — the easy way

*Decorating:*   dust sheets — for covering furniture, etc.
ladders and platforms
wallpaper tables

*Plumbing:*   copper tube benders — making bends in pipework
blowlamps — for soldered joints
drain clearing rods — plus attachments

*Emergencies:*   propane gas heater blowers — drying out damp
generators — in case of power failure/shut-off
floodlights

For address of hire shops in your area, see Where to Find It.

When you go off to the builders' merchants to buy one of those things that fits into — well you know, with a round bit on the end — it helps if you can ask for what you want. It's like going on a holiday to a foreign country — a few words from a phrasebook make all the difference. And, like a phrasebook, we don't aim to cover the full range of building materials here, but just some of the things you will most often need — timber, various kinds of building boards, fixings and plumbing fittings.

The sizes and types described here are not comprehensive, but should get you off to a good start. Bon Voyage!

## Timber

**Commonly available timber sizes**

| ¾ in / 19 mm | 1 in / 25 mm | 1½ in / 38 mm | 2 in / 50 mm | 3 in / 75 mm | 4 in / 100 mm | 5 in / 125 mm | 6 in / 150 mm | |
|---|---|---|---|---|---|---|---|---|
| ■ | ■ | ■ | ■ | | ▭ | | | ½ in/13 mm |
| ■ | ■ | ■ | ■ | ▭ | ▭ | ▭ | | $\frac{5}{8}$ in/16 mm |
| ■ | ■ | ■ | ■ | ▭ | | | ■ | ¾ in/19 mm |
| | | | | ▭ | | ■ | ■ | $\frac{7}{8}$ in/22mm |
| | ■ | ■ | ■ | ■ | ■ | ■ | ■ | 1 in/25 mm |
| | | ■ | ■ | | | ▭ | ▭ | 1½ in/38 mm |
| | | | ■ | | | ▭ | ▭ | 2 in/50 mm |
| | | | | | ▭ | ▭ | ▭ | 2½ in/63 mm |
| | | | | | ▭ | ▭ | ▭ | 3 in/75 mm |
| | | | | | ▭ | | ▭ | 4 in/100 mm |

▭ sawn

■ sawn & planed

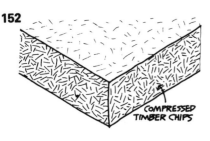

**CHIPBOARD**

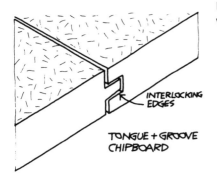

**TONGUE + GROOVE CHIPBOARD**

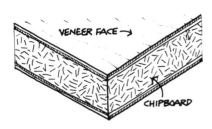

**KERROTEX**

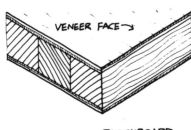

**BLOCKBOARD**

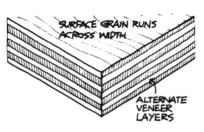

**PLYWOOD**

**Softwood** (most common)
Sawn (rough)
Prepared (planed): sizes are quoted as sawn, so in fact are about ¼'' less

**Three grades of timber:**
Carcassing: for timber stud walls, floors and roofs; if it's to be covered up, it must be 'tanalized' (i.e. impregnated with preservative)
Joinery: for cabinet-making
Standard: for floorboards, door frames, skirtings

NB: knots surrounded with black rings mean that the knot is dead, and will eventually fall out. Beware.

# Boards

**Chipboard** for internal work, non-structural uses

**WPB chipboard:** for structural use (e.g. flooring, roofing)
thicknesses: ½'' (12mm.), $\frac{5}{8}$'' (16mm.), ¾'' (19 mm.), 1'' (25 mm.)
sizes: 8' x 4'0'' (2440 x 1220 mm.)

**T & G chipboard:** for flooring
thicknesses: $\frac{5}{8}$'' (16 mm.), ¾'' (19 mm.)
sizes: 8'0'' x 2'0'' (2440 x 610 mm.)

**Kerrotex**
Laminated board with chipboard core, hardwood veneers: for internal work, cheaper than blockboard
thicknesses: ¾'' (19 mm.), 1'' (25 mm.)
sizes: 8'0'' x 4'0'' (2440 x 1220 mm.), 6'0'' x 3'0'' (1800 x 900 mm.)

**Blockboard**
Strips of softwood between hardwood veneers: for internal work. Stronger than chipboard
thicknesses and sizes as for chipboard

**Plywood**
Hardwood veneers with grain of alternate veneers. Very strong (for external or internal work) many uses, but more expensive than other boards
thicknesses: $\frac{3}{8}$'' (4 mm.), ¼'' (6 mm.)
sizes: as chipboard
sold in 'ply' (number of layers): from 3-ply to 11-ply

### Hardboard

One smooth face and one rough; variety of decorative finishes, from embossed patterns to punched holes; enamelled surfaces available in a variety of hard wearing colours, PVC sheets available suitable for bath panels. Oil-tempered are water resistant: for flooring and lining walls

thickness: ¼'' (6 mm.)

sizes: 8'0'' x 4'0'' (2440 x 1220 mm.), 6'0'' x 3'0'' (1800 x 900 mm.)

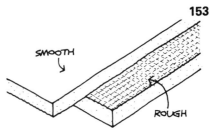

HARDBOARD

### Fibreboard

Lightweight and non-structural: for insulation, especially for sound and thermal insulation.

finishes: white decor paper, fibrous felts

thickness: ⅝'' (16 mm.)

sizes: 8'0'' x 4'0'' (2440 x 1220 mm.), 6'0'' x 3'0'' (1800 x 900 mm.)

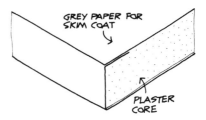

BASEBOARD

### Plasterboards

Lightweight: variety of sizes and types: two main types — those intended to be plastered over ('baseboard'), and those which are ready for decoration ('decorative boards').

### Baseboard

Finished with grey paper on both sides. Require skim coat of plaster, approx $\frac{3}{16}$'' thick.

thicknesses: ⅜'' (9.5 mm.), ½'' (12.7 mm.)

sizes: 4'0'' x 1'6'' (1200 x 450 mm.), 6'0'' x 3'0'' (1800 x 900 mm.)

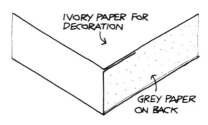

DECORATIVE BOARD

### Decorative board

Finished with one side ivory coloured paper, the other grey. Also available with aluminium over the grey face as insulation: for external walls and beneath roofs.

thicknesses: ⅜'' (9.5 mm.), ½'' (12.7 mm.)

size: 8'0'' x 4'0'' (2440 x 1220 mm.)

⅜'' must be supported by studwork at 18'' centres; ½'' at 24'' centres. Joints between board filled with jointing compound, and scrim (cotton gauze) laid over the joint.

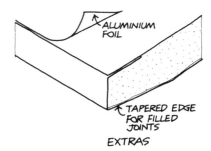

EXTRAS

# Special boards

### Laminated board

Solid plaster partitions made from plasterboard — 4 boards are laminated together: for partitions, requiring only timber plates on floor and ceiling.

### Thermal board

Plasterboard laminated to thick polystyrene sheets: for insulation; can be glued to external walls on pads of plaster containing glue. Called 'dry lining': for old houses.

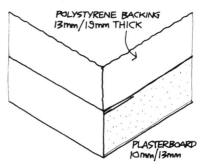

THERMAL BOARD

# Nails

| Type | Use | Sizes | Material |
|------|-----|-------|----------|
| Round wire nail | General purpose carpentry/ structural. Head visible | 20-150 mm. | Bright steel/galvanized |
| Round lost-head nail | General purpose for flush finish | 40-75 mm. | As above |
| Oval wire nail | General purpose for unobtrusive finish. Oval section reduces wood splitting | 25-150 mm. | Bright steel |
| Cut floor brad | Floorboards | 60-65 mm. | Steel |
| Clout or slate nail | Roof felt, slates, sash cords | 13-50 mm. | Galvanized |
| Panel pin | Cabinet work, thin panels, mouldings. Small head punched into surfaces | 13-40 mm. | |
| Hardboard pin | Fixing hardboard. Pointed head is lost in board. Hole can be filled | 10-25 mm. | Copper/zinc to prevent staining |
| Steel tack | Carpets, upholstery. Invisible, easy to remove | 10-20 mm. | Steel |

# Screws selectaguide

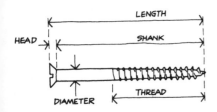

**Gauge**: diameter of shank. 19 British Standard sizes from 0 to 32 (largest), but not all generally available
usual gauges: 4, 5, 6, 7, 8, 9, 10
handy sizes: 6 for cabinet hinges and catches
   8 for light interior room doors
   10 for external doors and heavy work

**Length**: measured from end of thread to surface. 24 British Standard lengths, from $\frac{3}{16}$'' to 6''

**Material**: steel, brass and sheradized steel
steel: most common
brass: for damp areas or brass fittings
sheradized steel: will not rust, also for damp spots (cheaper than brass)

**Head**: counter-sunk, raised counter-sunk and round
counter-sunk: for flush finish (use counter-sinking tool)
raised counter-sunk: for door furniture where counter-sunk recess is in fitting
round: for fixing metal fittings too thin to be counter-sunk

**Drive**: slotted head, cross-head, Pozidrive, one-way anti-thief (clutch-head) mirror screws with dome head: for use with different headed screwdrivers

COUNTERSUNK    RAISED COUNTERSUNK    ROUND        SLOTTED HEAD    CROSS HEAD eg. POZIDRIV    CLUTCH HEAD (ONE-WAY)    MIRROR SCREW + DOME HEAD

# Bolts for wall and partition fixing

**Collapsible anchor bolt**: for partitions

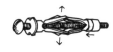

**Rubber sleeve anchor bolt**: for partitions

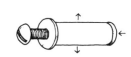

**Toggle bolt**: for partitions

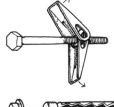

**Expanding bolts**: for masonry

# Copper plumbing

For water supply, central heating
tube sizes: 10 mm., 15 mm., 22 mm., 28 mm. most common
standard lengths: 3 metres, 6 metres

Common compression fittings for all pipe sizes:

straight

elbow

T

T for varying
size pipes

reducer

Common pre-soldered fittings:

straight

elbow

T

T for varying
size pipes

reducer

# Plastic plumbing

ABS plastic: for waste drainage
UPVC: for rainwater goods
pipe sizes: 19 mm., 32 mm., 38 mm., 50 mm., 65 mm., 75 mm.,
100 mm.
length: 4 metres

**Methods of joining**
Solvent weld: where pipes are glued together
Push-fit: where pipes are pushed together, rubber ring holds in position

**Fittings**
Waste plumbing:

straight connector

elbow connector

.135° bend

side inlet

double inlet

access eye

Rainwater:

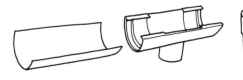

gutter          shoe

straight      elbow
connector    connector

hopper

side inlet

access eye

# TRADESMEN

You might not be happy if, after six months of struggling to install your own central heating system, you find that a heating contractor could have done the job in two weeks and for only 10% more than it cost you in materials alone! Today's increasingly do-it-yourself world assumes that house-owners should practically be able to build their own houses. To read the DIY books or magazines you'd think there's nothing you couldn't do, from laying drains to tiling the roof. Instead of the entrepreneur's aim of maximum return for minimum input, the DIY's aim seems almost the reverse — as much input as possible from the individual. But for us reluctant types the philosophy is definitely minimum effort with maximum return.

Before starting any job, consider whether the cost saving (if any) is worth the extra effort of doing it yourself. It may be easier and less time consuming to do some overtime and pay a builder than to do the job yourself. It's always assumed that doing it yourself is automatically cheaper than having someone do it for you. Well, I had this picture window fitted; the cost of having it fitted was cheaper than installing the window myself because the installer did not have to pay VAT on the window, and his installation charges were the same as the VAT. The anomalies of VAT regulations will be explained later.

You may of course be forced into using builders, as there are some skills you won't be able to master — plastering or bricklaying, for instance. So you're going to need to know how to handle someone else to do it for you.

Obviously the smaller the task the more uneconomical it is to have someone else doing it — for instance unblocking a drain; everybody I know who's used an emergency plumber is furious because the bill seems huge for 5 minutes' work. Most of the cost is simply getting to and from your house. Bear in mind that certain tasks, such as decorating, are labour intensive, whereas plumbing and central heating have proportionately higher material costs. And remember, if you enter into a contract with someone to do work for you, you will have some recompense under common law if the work is done badly, or not done at all. If your own attempts fail you have no one to claim against but yourself.

### Architects and surveyors

The task of establishing exactly what the job entails, obtaining a good price and making sure it's carried out satisfactorily all falls within the sphere of your local building surveyor, or architect should it involve design. Too often the services of both are considered luxuries that can be ill-afforded. However, when you hear stories of people giving money to builders who simply vanish, the 10-15% fee seems insignificant. The prime tasks of both professions are to assist you in establishing what you want, offer you cost-saving alternatives to your original fantasy, obtain approvals from local authorities, make arrangements with statutory bodies if need be, write specifications and prepare drawings where necessary, obtain competitive quotes from suitable contractors, draw up contracts, keep hold of the purse strings and check standards during the course of construction, and even drop in six months later to check that everything is OK.

In my opinion (although I know I'll offend both parties) building surveyors are best suited to repair works, installation of services, etc., and architects to new rear extensions, loft conversions or conversion work. If you want an architect in your area, contact the RIBA Clients' Advisory Service in London and they will provide a list of suitable chaps. Remember we discussed the finding of surveyors in Chapter 1. Bear in mind that both architects and surveyors can be consulted on an hourly basis, so if you only need a small amount of advice, you could pop into their office with your photographs and plans for an hour's worth.

5 MINS. TO GO, MR + MRS. BROWN......

### What do you want?

As mentioned, one of the main tasks of a surveyor or architect is to draw up plans and a 'specification' to describe the work you want done. Well, you'd be amazed how much expensive time you can spend with an architect, just explaining your personal likes and dislikes, whereas with a bit of patience and graph paper you'd be able to work out for yourself far more than you would imagine.

A specification is simply a builder's shopping list or recipe: take 3 lb. of bricks and ½ lb. of concrete, mix together and allow to stand. Once you've done your shopping list there's no end of things you can do with it, such as sending it to builders, showing the building inspector, and even working out roughly how much it should cost. The easiest way to draw up plans is to obtain an A3 or A2 graph paper pad from the stationers, with 1 cm. size squares. A good scale to work to is 1 cm. to 20 cm. To draw a simple roof plan is helpful if getting the roof re-tiled; it will mean that a contractor won't have to call round to take dimensions and he'll know what sort of roof it is — pitched or a valley gutter roof, for example.

To write a specification for re-tiling a roof couldn't be simpler. For instance, for a main pitched roof you'd need to specify:

*What* re-tile roof.
*Where* main roof as shown on sketch.

1      Take off existing tiles and set aside if sound for re-use.
2      Provide new roof covering, with underfelt and new tiles as
       required, on new battens.

You may wish to add further information on the materials: for instance, what colour tiles you want. Or you may require other work done while they're up on the roof, such as pointing of the chimney stack, all of which can form part of your specification.

Another example might be central heating, where your plans can be more explicit, showing where the radiators are to be located, where the boiler is to go, where the existing hot-water storage tank is, etc. This time the specification would need to explain:

*What*  central heating.
*Where*  all rooms except garage and utility room.

1    Provide gas central heating and hot water system with balanced flue boiler.
2    Radiators to be pressed steel panels.
3    All pipework to be hidden below flooring.
4    Existing hot water storage to be used, and cold water tank in main roof space.

Here again, you may specify such things as the particular type of boiler you want because it fits nicely into your kitchen.

To help you clarify your requirements further, endless information is available from your local builders' merchant on materials and equipment, from the local library for information on building technology, or manufacturers' literature for information on products and materials. By simply picking up the phone and asking for details, you may even get a free visit from a representative to discuss your particular requirements. But probably the best starting place for almost any aspect of building work is the Building Centre in London, and in other major cities in England and Wales, who have recently started an advisory service with architects and surveyors installed at desks ready to discuss your personal difficulties for a nominal fee. More information can be obtained from the advisory services of trade associations.

No specification is complete without a few conditions concerning the standard of workmanship, and I recommend the inclusion of the following statement with all specifications: 'All works are to be carried out in a workmanlike manner, in accordance with all relevant codes of practice, to the British Standards, Building Byelaws, and all relevant Government Acts.'

### How much is it all going to cost?

Many people embark on DIY projects without calculating the final cost, only to be amazed at the amount of money they are spending on materials. So it is advisable before going too far to establish crudely the cost involved. An understanding of the total costs involved allows an appreciation of the savings that may be made using alternative methods or materials. Cheap utilitarian white sanitary fittings take on a charm of their own when you discover that the low level coloured syphonic WC suite of your dreams costs three or four times as much.

### How a builder prices a job

Initially builders' prices may look high, but even at these prices builders find it difficult to survive, and an enormous number of small contracting firms go out of business within a couple of years. If a builder's prices are too low he may go bankrupt halfway through the job, so it's better to pay a bit extra and know the job will be finished. A builder's prices are generally made up as follows:

....IT'LL ONLY COST
£20 A DAY FOR ME —
AND £200 FOR
THE OFFICE AND ITS
STAFF.....

— EXCUSE ME, DO YOU
HAVE SPONS?

CERTAINLY NOT,
MADAM!

The cost of materials:
with 10% wastage allowance (or more if the job requires specialized materials that can't be used elsewhere) plus 20% for the handling of materials (arranging for deliveries, unloading them, paying the invoices)

The cost of labour:
(bearing in mind that nobody works 7½ hours every day, even though they get paid for it) plus pension plan, national insurance, disability insurances. The current national trade union rate for labourers is £60 per week, and skilled labour £80. All the bits usually double this figure.

The cost of plant:
as you'll appreciate, cement mixers and the like don't go on indefinitely, and they need to be renewed and maintained from time to time.

Overheads:
each job has to share a portion of the cost of the office and its staff, together with running costs.

Statutory fees and insurances:
like the building inspector's fee. Having worked out that lot a contractor would add a profit of round about 20% and hope to make it.

### Pricing information

Life is made a bit easier when you get to know about 'rates', which are prices for a square metre of this and that. For instance, lightweight plastering costs between £3 and £6 per square metre up and down the country. If you wanted to get an idea of how much it would cost to re-plaster your house you could simply phone your local plastering firm and ask what his current rates are.

Prices for building materials can obviously be obtained from the local builders' merchants. You'll find that if you give a merchant a list you may get better rates than asking for individual prices.

There are pricing books, which you may find interesting but not very useful, and which quantity surveyors use. Ask in your local library for **Spon's** pricing book which is a yearly publication.

### VAT

As you are aware, everything you buy at the DIY shop or builders' merchants carries VAT, and as an individual you are unable to recover this from the Inland Revenue, even though it may be intended for works that do not in the opinion of the Inland Revenue carry VAT.

However, if a contractor or sub-contractor carries out work for you on, say, installing a new central heating system, although he may pay VAT to the builders' merchant, he doesn't pass the tax on to you but recovers it from the Inland Revenue in his quarterly or monthly return. This is because the government has decided that in principle 'repairs' to houses carry VAT whereas 'new works' (additions to the house) are zero-rated. In HM Customs and Excise Notice 715 (Revised August 1975) you will find a detailed list of the items that are zero-rated. The pamphlet, which is entitled **Construction Industry Alterations and Repairs Maintenance**, can easily be obtained by phoning the local Inland Revenue office.

There has been a move by the construction industry to have all works zero-rated. If and when this succeeds, it is hoped that it will increase the incentive to have a builder do your repairs instead of sweating over them yourself.

### How much can a skilled person do?

In *Spon's*, mentioned earlier, you will find an analysis of a number of building tasks which shows you, for instance, the time it takes for a carpenter to hang a door. Be careful when using these figures as they relate to large contracts: always use a safety margin of three, and remember the figures relate specifically to that task, not obtaining materials and discussing with you the type of ironmongery you want.

### Tradesmen

Beware of cowboys! The derivation of the term cowboy in the contracting business comes from the time when real cowboys used to drift into mid-west ranch towns and did any sort of casual work they could get their hands on — not particularly well.

Finding the right people for the job can in itself be the greatest cost saving. Obviously you wouldn't approach a car mechanic to lay a roof. The construction industry has three main divisions: main contractors; sub-contractors; and skilled men. The object of a main contractor is primarily the management of a variety of skills (sub-contractors and tradesmen) which would be needed in the construction of a new rear extension, for example. Sub-contractors are specialists dealing in thousands of different tasks; there are sub-contractors who simply lay insulation (laggers) and there are sub-contractors who simply apply mastics or sealing compounds to buildings. The most common sub-contractors are roofers, plasterers, bricklayers, plumbers, electricians and carpenters. Finally there are individual skilled people, 'jacks of all trades', who can deal with most small jobs. A competent chap is a boon to any home owner. In selecting any person or company to do work, by far and away the best way of deciding is on the last customer's recommendation.

### Main contractors

Because of the problems involved with the handling of contractors for domestic work in recent years, consumer protectionists have been looking for ways to protect home owners from crooked contractors. Recently a group called the 'Home Enlargement Bureau' has been set up by the Institute of British Architects and Institute of Chartered Surveyors, and based in High Wycombe. They keep a list of suitable contractors and it is obviously worth contacting them. There are two builders' associations who also keep a record of contractors throughout the country although regrettably they don't tell you who's good and who's not so good. Finally Yellow Pages generally has an extensive list.

Bear in mind that if you use a main contractor he will add a percentage on to the bill he gets from the sub-contractor. He will save you the hassle of dealing with the various sub-contractors, but it will cost you more.

### Sub-contractors

As with main contractors, each individual sub-contractor has a trade association which keeps lists of its members. We have listed the most common at the back of the book. Again, yellow pages is a good source.

### Establishing the suitability of main contractors or sub-contractors

Having located a number of contractors, try to establish before asking for a price if the contractor is capable of doing the work satisfactorily.

YEAH, WE BELONG
TO MOST OF 'EM....

Start first with looking for his yard or offices and enquire how many years the company has been established. From his notice boards, see whether or not he is a member of any trade association, and contact the association to see if he is a paid-up member. Also establish in your own mind if the company is large enough to handle your work.

### Tendering

It is totally amazing the differences in price contractors give for the same work. And anybody who doesn't have considerable experience in construction would be a fool not to obtain at least three different prices. The main reason for the variance is whether the contractor is interested in doing your job and whether or not he could fit it into his programme if successful. Many contractors return ridiculously high prices to ensure that they don't get the work. Having looked at your specification, strangely enough, many consider that not to give any price will mean that they won't be asked again.

Having obtained your three tenderers, phone them and ask if they would be interested in giving a quote for the job. Describe as much as you can and, if they are interested, ask if they would be able to give you references from a couple of their past customers and if they would be able to give a bank reference. Then post your specification and drawing (if necessary) as described earlier in the chapter and state the date that you would like his price returned. With most small domestic jobs, a contractor should be able to return his price within two weeks.

In your letter be sure to state that the price is to be fixed and to include all plant, labour and materials necessary for completing the task. If you are doing a proper job, also tell him which standard form of contract you wish to use.

### Contracts

Even the simple two page 'National Joint Councils' NJC Contract for Minor Works will give you considerable protection from 'fly-by-night' contractors (see Where to Find It). By the way, if a contractor says he doesn't want to work under a contract simply conclude that he is not a professional. Regrettably, you still may be forced to use him, as there are remarkably few competent contractors in the industry. My advice is that you ask your local surveyor if he would be prepared to act as an arbitrator between you and the contractor should you come to blows.

### Paying

Don't be surprised if the contractor asks you for a bank reference. It's a sign of a good businesslike firm, and certainly preferable to those who ask for a deposit of a third of the contract price and then, for some unknown reason, vanish.

Under the terms of a minor works contract you can pay either at regular intervals or stage payments on completion of certain tasks, such as when the plastering is done. Once you've agreed to pay a stage payment you should ensure that the money is in the contractor's hand within at least two weeks. However, the sooner you pay the better service you'll get, as there is nothing like cash flow for enhancing trust.

A great advantage of standard building contracts is the retention of 5% or an agreed % of the contract sum for defects that may show up in the first six months, or, in the case of central heating, twelve months, which ensures that the contractor returns to repair defective work.

### Labour only

If money is the real problem, the best way to make life easier is to use the labour of skilled persons (e.g. plasterers or plumbers), organize materials for them, and act as their labourer. A very high proportion of the cost of building works is simply in obtaining and preparing materials for use. However, the biggest problem in this approach is finding a skilled person to help you. The only real method is by keeping your ear to the ground or looking at newsagents' notice boards. Again, personal recommendation is the best way.

There are two ways of paying: either on an agreed price assuming you'll get the materials and act as a labourer, a method which will change your mind about the average British workman; or at a daily rate. Avoid paying cash for labour (in order to obtain tax relief), if you can, as you won't be able to keep a clear record of how much you've paid either for proof to the tradesperson or the Inland Revenue.

*YOU OK?*

*NO, I NEED A SKILLED PERSON*

### Quality control supervision

When the contractor is ready to start, arrange to meet him at the house to discuss the following:

1    Where the operatives should defecate/wee.
2    Who is to be the foreman on site.
3    Whether or not you want him using your telephone.
4    What his programme for the work is, written if possible.
5    What precautions will be taken against weather penetration.
6    What the security arrangements are to be.
7    A regular meeting time to discuss problems.

The normal working hours in the construction industry are from 8 a.m. to 5 p.m. with a half an hour breakfast break at 10 a.m., half an hour lunch break at 12.30 p.m. and tea at 3.30 p.m.

To be able to criticize or, better, enquire about the quality of a contractor's work without upsetting him to the point where he downs tools and leaves the site, is to understand the building process. For instance, if you are unhappy about the concrete in the foundations, the best time to discuss it is as soon as possible, not when the contractor is just completing the decorations. Conversely, premature criticism can make anybody edgy. Building work goes through a number of very definite stages which we list below; if you are employing sub-contractors yourself this list will help you to organize their schedules so that, for example, the plasterer comes after the electrician.

### Stage 1   Opening Up                    Demolitions and initial works

This is primarily to do with works to existing buildings where both the contractor and the building owner seek out problems such as dry rot. Also includes the removal of redundant structures such as the outside WC and the protection of valuable parts like the hardwood handrail to the stairs.

**Stage 2  Structure**

Excavations
Underground drains
Hardfill/reinforcement/formwork
Concrete
Brickwork
DPCs and DPMs

Now for the really messy part of putting up the building from the ground.

**Stage 3  Carcassing**

Joinery
Carpentry: first fix

We now reach the ceremony of 'topping out'; the roof structure is complete and subsequently the skeleton of each room is formed with staircases, timber stud walls, door frames and windows being placed; floorboarding is laid but not fixed.

**Stage 4  Closing Up**

Asphalt roofing
Built-up roofing
Zinc/leadwork
Slate roofing
Glazing
External decorations
Surface water and waste plumbing
Timber treatment
External works

At this stage the contractor is getting ready to dismantle the scaffolding that he used when putting up the building, but before 'striking' it (taking it down) he wants to ensure there is no reason for going back up again. So all the unreachable outside works are completed and the building made watertight to protect the future internal works.

**Stage 5  Services First Fix**

Electrics
Plumbing and central heating
Gas, water, electricity boards

OK so everybody is now dry and the services can be installed, or rather those parts to be hidden, such as electric cables, pipework and gas pipes.

**Stage 6  Plastering**

Plastering/plasterboards
Screeds

On to covering up the skeleton with plaster and plasterboard, starting from the top of the house to make sure that finished work is not messed up with plaster droppings. Finally finishing with floor screeds (concrete).

**Stage 7  Second Fix**

Sanitary fittings
Kitchen fittings
Radiators
Carpentry: second fix
Electrics: second fix

In with the posh bits such as the electrical fittings, the sanitary ware, the kitchen fittings, skirtings and doors.

**Stage 8  Finishes**

Internal decorations
Floor and wall tiling
Snagging

The grand finale — the fifteen coats of gloss paint, the silk wall-paper and the marble flooring tiles.

Finally, you can tell a good contractor by how clean he keeps his site. Peter, whose particular skill is plastering, when helping me to build my house, was always insistent that all plaster droppings should be cleaned up before stopping each evening, as it's twice as difficult and time consuming to do it the following day. I can tell you that it takes real courage to do this sort of cleaning up, especially after mixing plaster all day, but it's worth it. If your contractor's work is messy, you can be sure the end product will also be.

# ECONOMY
# PROJECTS

**9**

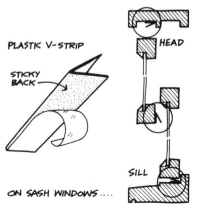

PLASTIC V-STRIP

STICKY
BACK

HEAD

SILL

ON SASH WINDOWS....

External doors and windows

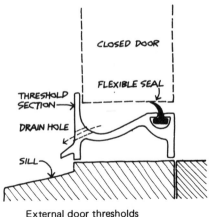

CLOSED DOOR

FLEXIBLE SEAL

THRESHOLD
SECTION

DRAIN HOLE

SILL

External door thresholds

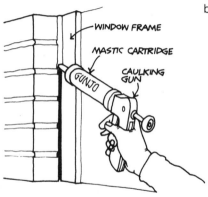

WINDOW FRAME

MASTIC CARTRIDGE

CAULKING
GUN

GUNJO

Window frames

**166**

### Project 1: Draughtproofing the house

In just a couple of weekends you can draughtproof the house for only a few pounds, save up to 10% of your annual fuel bill and above all make yourself and the cat more comfy. Remember that, apart from heating up the fresh air blasting through the windows, you may be using extra heat to overcome the discomfort of draughts passing over your person, or as they say in America, the 'wind chill factor'.

**External doors and windows**: stick self-adhesive foam strip to window or door frames; 'V' type plastic strip if you have sash windows, as foam strip pulls away with the sliding of the sashes. Be sure to clean the surface of the frame thoroughly first with something like coarse wire wool. By the way, don't forget the loft access hatch or cellar door.

**External door thresholds** (bottom of the door): if you are lucky enough to have a water bar (which is fixed to the sill), fit the self-adhesive strip to the door. If no water bar, then install purpose-made threshold bar, available from DIY shops. The one shown allows the rainwater that dribbles down the door to drain away and the door mat to snuggle up behind, and is fitted to the frame on either side. If you need to reduce the door, see Techniques (Ch. 5).

**Gaps between door/window frames and the wall**: use a caulking gun to seal up the gaps between frames and wall; even a hairline crack can cause a considerable draught. Also seal the joint between the purpose-made threshold bars and the doorstep.

**Timber ground floors**: if you are not lucky enough to have tongue-and-groove floorboarding, fill the gaps between the boards and the gap between the skirting and the floorboards with papier mâché.

**Block up flues to disused fireplaces**: block flues with newspaper or, better still, remove unwanted fireplaces, except in the living room where one may come in handy later or just because you like toasting your feet; brick or board up, leaving a grille for ventilation of the flue.

GRILLE

BLOCKED
FIREPLACE

**Keyholes and letterboxes**: provide keyhole covers over external door keyholes and a fibre flap over the letterbox or block it all together to prevent the postman putting the gas and electric bills through.

### Warning!

Don't block up fresh-air vents in rooms with gas-burning appliances, because you may be breaking the Gas Act and may just kill yourself with carbon monoxide poisoning. If in doubt consult the Gas Board.

**Insulation contractors**: if you are unable to manage this project yourself, why not call in the specialist sub-contractors for a free estimate? Look under insulation contractors in the Yellow Pages, and don't forget to obtain three estimates. They will, of course, be able to quote for all types of other insulation, such as cavity fill and loft insulation.

### Project 2: Cure condensation

It is obvious that the object of draught-proofing is to prevent the external cold air coming in. However, assuming success, you will reduce the ability for moisture-laden air to escape from the house, leading to a higher risk of condensation. This is especially true if you are putting quantities of moisture into the air, for instance, by using paraffin heating which emits one pint of water from every five pints of paraffin burnt, or by boiling water in the kitchen for cooking and washing. Moreover, smells from the loo, kitchen and dad's pipe will stay with you unless you open a window. Well! A very modern concept indeed, to the British anyway, is that of central ventilation. This is a system of ducting, with two small electric fans that extract stale, moisture-laden air from the house and draw fresh air in via the loft space, where the fans are located. To save the heat from the outgoing stale air a 'heat recovery' box allows the two streams of air to pass over each other, without mixing, whereby the warm air heats the incoming air. Manufacturers claim that between 60-75% of the heat is recovered. It is possible to buy kits for around £500 and do it yourself. However if you want a specialist to install it, contact the manufacturers (see Where to Find It) and ask for a list of suitable sub-contractors. By the way, the system includes a cooker-extract hood which is noiseless because its fan is in the roof.

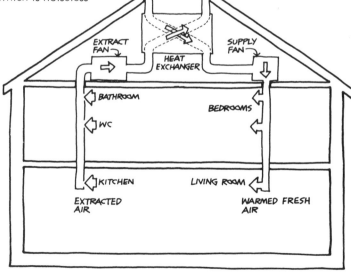

Whole house ventilation and heat recovery

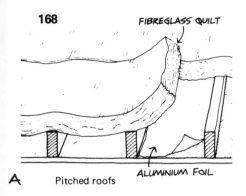

FIBREGLASS QUILT

ALUMINIUM FOIL

**A** Pitched roofs

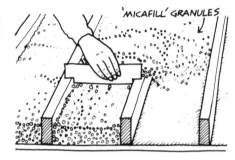

'MICAFILL' GRANULES

**B** Pitched roofs

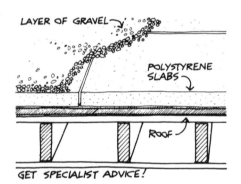

LAYER OF GRAVEL

POLYSTYRENE SLABS

ROOF

GET SPECIALIST ADVICE!

Flat roofs

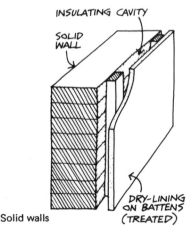

INSULATING CAVITY

SOLID WALL

DRY-LINING ON BATTENS (TREATED)

Solid walls

## Project 3: Increase your resistance (thermal)

If you are not resistible enough already, go up into the loft and lay some roof insulation and attempt to reduce the 25% of your fuel bill floating upwards to the great outer atmosphere.

**Pitched roofs**: lay at least 4″ (100 mm.) of fibreglass quilt over the joists or fill between them with 'Micafill', if you dislike touching fibreglass. If you are having your cavity walls injected with mineral wool you can have the roof space done at the same time. Enthusiasts will wish to lay aluminium foil between the joists to prevent heat being radiated upwards. If you are having the house re-roofed you could request the roofing sub-contractor to fix a fibreglass quilt over the rafters under the roofing felt so that you will be able to use the roof space at a later date.

**Flat roofs**: very popular nowadays is the 'upside-down roof', which simply means the laying of 2″ (50 mm.) thick polystyrene slabs over the roof covering. You'll require specialist advice on doing this to avoid the problems of condensation forming inside the roof structure, as well as the approval of the Building Inspector (see Where to Find It).

**Cavity walls**: fill them with either injected expanding foam (Urea Formaldehyde Foam), Thermobeads, which are tiny polystyrene beads blown into the cavity, or mineral wool, which is 100% rock melted down and spun into a soft cotton-wool like texture, and blown into the cavity. For advice on filling your cavities contact the National Cavity Insulation Association, who also provide a list of suitable installers.

**Solid walls**: either dry-line them internally or externally. If your plaster is in poor condition, instead of re-plastering use 'thermal board', which is 1″ (25 mm.) thick polystyrene foam stuck to sheets of plasterboard and manufactured by British Gypsum, who will give a list of suitable 'dry-lining' sub-contractors. Whilst on the 'phone ask for a copy of their booklet on dry-lining (see Where to Find It). Subject to obtaining planning permission, you could insulate solid walls by providing a layer of 4″ (100 mm.) fibreglass on the outside of the house, supported by a grid of timber battens. The insulation could be protected in various ways to suit the original design of the house, for instance, tiles or boarding. Of course there would be problems where the dry lining met windows, roofs and waste pipes.

**Porous brickwork**: the purpose of most insulation materials is to trap air, which surprising enough is an excellent insulator. But porous brickwork will lose its insulating qualities if it becomes saturated with water. To prevent porous bricks soaking up the rain, paint brickwork with a colourless silicone paint. Ensure before applying that it is of the permeable type, allowing the wall to breathe, so that residual moisture contained within the wall can escape.

**Windows**: at night time you might as well have a hole in the wall when it comes to glazed areas, and double glazing doesn't improve the situation that much. Essential equipment therefore is snug, heavy curtains, lined with aluminium foil to prevent heat loss and down draughts, but don't allow them to cover the radiators. If you are fortunate enough to have window shutters, put them into use and provide them with draught seals. The modern equivalents of window shutters are thermal shutters constructed from polystyrene panels, which fold aside like curtains and are tailormade for your own window.

Lined curtains

**Floors**: there isn't much that can be done to existing floors apart from nice thick, woolly carpets with felt or foam underlays (make sure that concrete floors aren't damp with your damp meter before laying a carpet). Of course, if you are building a wing to the mansion, provide polystyrene slabs in the concrete floor, as shown in manufacturer's leaflets, which will greatly reduce the downward heat loss of up to 10% of the annual fuel bill.

**Radiators on external walls**: prevent the rear of the radiators radiating heat to the outside by the use of aluminium foil panels obtainable from DIY shops.

**Pipework and storage tanks**: drop by the builders' merchant and buy ½" (12mm.) and ¾" (20mm.) foam pipe insulation and slip it on the pipes in the loft space, below the timber suspended ground floor and, most important, on the incoming water mains. Obtain also a 3" (76mm.) thick hot-water cylinder jacket. Before going to buy, check the rough dimensions of the hot-water cylinder and whether or not it's factory insulated, which many modern cylinders are. If it is, you will be unable to see the copper of the cylinder. Lastly make sure the cold-water storage tank and boiler feed tanks have lids and are insulated.

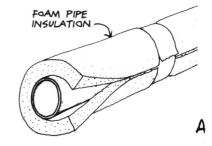

### Project 4: Control your energy

The average fuel bill in the country is £400 per annum per household; for the average family house this works out at £100 per person; 10p per year per cubic foot of house. At the Homeworld 1981 Exhibition held at Milton Keynes an energy-saving house used only a quarter of this energy. So why not establish if you are a 'fuel guzzler' by working out the cost of your yearly fuel bills per person and per cubic foot of your house? Which in turn will assist you to establish the cost effectiveness of curbing your energy excesses.

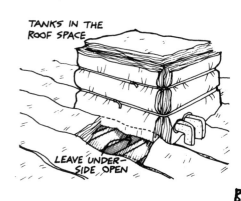

Pipework and storage tanks

**Time clocks**: most central heating systems use simple, inexpensive twin period time clocks to turn on the heating for set periods in the morning and evening. A variety of similar time clocks can be obtained from electrical shops, which plug into 13-amp wall sockets, and which can time control oil-filled electrical radiators or electric immersion heaters for hot water. Then you could time the dishwasher, washing machine or tumble dryer to come on in the middle of the night, thereby using cheap electricity. (Insert ear plugs before retiring to bed.)

**Economy Seven**: if you have a white meter or can guarantee to use 40% of your electricity between the hours of 11 p.m. and 7 a.m., rush down to the electric showrooms and order an Economy Seven Meter. This will reduce your fuel bill by a third for the power used in Economy Seven Time.

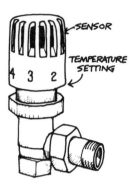

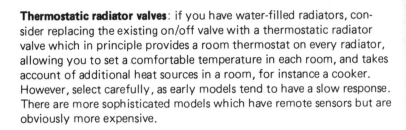

Thermostatic valves

**Thermostatic radiator valves**: if you have water-filled radiators, consider replacing the existing on/off valve with a thermostatic radiator valve which in principle provides a room thermostat on every radiator, allowing you to set a comfortable temperature in each room, and takes account of additional heat sources in a room, for instance a cooker. However, select carefully, as early models tend to have a slow response. There are more sophisticated models which have remote sensors but are obviously more expensive.

**Control yourself**: keep windows and doors closed during the winter months, also keep internal doors closed to prevent heat drifting up the stairs. Use a shower instead of filling the bath and completely fill washing machines, tumble dryers and dishwashers when using them. Keep the room thermostat down to a temperature not greater than 21°C if it's located in the living room or 18°C elsewhere. Put on additional clothing if you feel cold. Should the living room not reach 21°C when the hall reaches 18°C, which you can obviously check with the aid of two thermostats, either have the heating system balanced by a heating engineer who will adjust the 'lockshield valves' on the radiators, or replace the living room radiator with a larger one.

### Project 5: Home heating

As a result of the energy crisis, a previously simple choice of central heating systems has been revolutionized. Systems considered experimental only a couple of years ago, such as solar heating, are now marketable products. Anybody installing a new system is therefore in need of unbiased advice from, for instance, one of the country's building centres, which are currently offering free advice on heating and energy. You could also appoint your own consultant heating engineer by contacting the Institute of Domestic Heating and Environmental Engineers. Your engineer will, for a fee, advise you on the most suitable system for your house, as well as the appropriate thermal insulation and ventilation. Furthermore, he will be able to draw up specifications for tendering and supervise under contract the successful sub-contractor. Who knows, you may find that with increased insulation your present forms of heating are adequate?

**Economy Seven**: only ten years ago electric heating with the aid of off-peak energy and night storage heaters was seen as the heating of the future. Clean, economical, dry, and cheap to install. Then Mr Therm rose from the North Sea and destroyed the whole idea of clean living. Electricity Boards are staging a come-back of the old formula with the Economy Seven meter, which I mentioned in Project 4. And new houses that are well insulated and heated by electricity are given the 'Medallion Award' by the Electricity Board.

From the reluctant person's point of view electric heating is ideal in that it has low maintenance, is clean and avoids water sloshing about the house. However, night storage heaters are not as flexible to the user as other installations, as they work on a twenty-four hour cycle and cannot be simply turned on and off like a gas boiler. For cost comparison ask your local electricity showroom for a quote.

**Gas central heating**: high installation costs but cheap to run, unless someone has a mind to push the price of gas up to be comparable with ordinary electricity rates. Be sure that you've insulated the house thoroughly before embarking on such a high-cost investment, because, if you haven't, the money would more profitably be spent on higher standards of insulation. If you've lived with an Ascot for some years and grown used to instantaneous hot water, investigate the gas boilers from Germany and France which not only provide instantaneous hot water but also central heating. With one of these boilers you can simply remove the old Ascot, substitute the new boiler and connect it to the existing hot water pipe, draw off down services and run pipes directly to the radiators anywhere. The central heating system is sealed and does not require a feed and expansion tank in the roof. Furthermore, as the hot water comes directly off the mains you can have a high-pressure cheap shower whenever you want.

If you are not too keen on water sloshing around the house you could go for gas warm-air heating if the layout of your house is suitably planned.

When obtaining quotations for gas central heating with either radiators or warm air, be sure that the sub-contractors are 'Corgi' registered. Also obtain a quote from your local Gas Board. Check with the sub-contractors that their work will be acceptable to the board so that you can, if you wish, have the board's 5-star maintenance programme when it's finished — they are a bit choosy.

**Solar energy**: systems work on a similar basis to any wet system of central heating, the only difference being the method by which the water is heated. The substitute boiler, located on the roof to catch the sun's rays, is formed with a glass-fronted box with matt black base. Within the box run loops of pipework filled with water to carry the heat away. The heat from the sun makes the inside of the box very hot, rather like a greenhouse or being in the loft below a slate roof on a hot day. In principle a solar convector is a combination of both. Off-the-peg systems at the moment are for pre-heating the hot-water storage tank. The systems are expensive but developments abound and costs are coming down; and of course you have no running costs.

**Heat pumps**: on the same principle — in reverse — as a refrigerator, heat pumps extract low-grade heat from, say, the ground to provide heat for central heating and hot water. The other evening on *Tomorrow's World* a heat pump driven by an old Ford engine was extracting low-grade heat from the ground to provide boiling water. Admittedly heat pumps do cost money to run but the cost is substantially below other forms of energy. Heat pumps are already extensively used for heating swimming pools and obviously the boys in the back room will soon have domestic heat pumps suitable for doing the house. Your consultant engineer will, of course, be conversant with up-to-date developments.

**Totem**: if you are really friendly with the neighbours and they are also in need of a new heating system, why not co-operatively invest in your very own small-scale power station called 'Totem'? The principle here is to produce energy in exactly the same manner as a power station, with the use of a car engine, but save the wasted energy that's lost in sending electricity to your home. A staggering 75% of the energy produced by power stations is lost up the cooling towers and in the national grid cables. 'Totem' is stuck in a box at the bottom of the garden and from oil generates electricity and hot water by water cooling the engine.

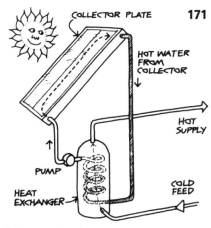

Solar water heating

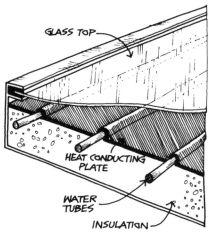

Solar collector

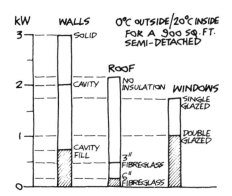

Comparative heat losses in KW

The brief to an engineer

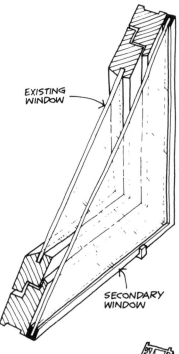

EXISTING WINDOW

SECONDARY WINDOW

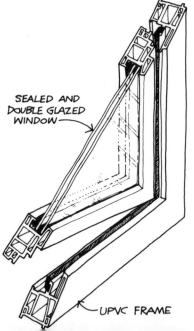

SEALED AND DOUBLE GLAZED WINDOW

UPVC FRAME

**Conclusion**: obviously only a few of the multitude of methods of heating your home have been mentioned above. The reluctant person's brief to a consulting engineer should be to provide a system with low capital cost, low running costs, minimum maintenance and the ability to have heat within seconds.

### Project 6: Window replacement

Almost as confusing as central heating is the topic of window improvement and double glazing. A vast market has grown up for secondary window systems leading the home-owner to believe that the system will double-glaze his window. Well it will, but not as originally intended. The original idea was to double the ridiculously low thermal resistance of a single sheet of glass by trapping air within two hermetically sealed sheets of glass not more than ¾" apart. Moisture-free dry air is an excellent insulating medium, as long as it's kept still. When the panels of glass are spaced further apart, convection currents develop between the sheets of glass.

The importance of double glazing is that heat loss depends heavily on the extent of glazing; the statutory minimum of glazing in homes is 10% of the floor area.

If you live in a greenhouse, obviously double glazing would have a significant effect on your comfort and energy costs. If you consider your windows are in such a poor state that draught-proofing wouldn't improve the situation, you should look into window replacement. Although more expensive than simple secondary windows the benefits to the reluctant home-owner can be enormous.

If you upgrade your single glazing to double, the work may be free of VAT if considered an improvement. The same applies to sliding patio doors, so check with installer.

**UPVC windows** are the most attractive proposal. They can be made to measure to fit into the existing opening, and, more importantly, can be reproduced in the original style of your period house. They have the advantages of proper double-glazing, built-in draught-proofing and above all do not require decorating every five years. No need with this one to do it yourself as the cost saving would be minimal, the manufacturers supply and fix. The manufacturers have set up an association called British Plastics Window Group; why not ring and ask for a list of their members and obtain three free quotes? Manufacturers of other replacement windows are working in keen competition and also have associations such as the British Woodworking Association, the Steel Window Association and the Aluminium Window Association. Be sure too that the manufacturers have checked with the local planning office and Building Inspector for clearance.

Take care to check that existing windows are not a part of the structure of the house. Some windows cannot be replaced with plastic as they are supporting the structure above, notably sash windows in Victorian bays.

Once upon a time a shower was considered to be a luxury, but with ever-increasing fuel prices, baths, which use four to five times as much energy as a shower, have taken over the luxury market, as can be seen by the rocketing sales of fun whirlpool baths. For those who are only too well aware that heating water consumes 25% of their fuel bills, showers are an essential cost saver. To be sure that the family will use the shower in preference to the bath, a proper installation is required, not simply a rubber hose shower extension to the bath taps. The most economic location is of course over the bath, so as to use the existing drainage and eliminate the need for a shower tray.

**Conventional showers:** are served from the existing hot- and cold-water storage tanks. To achieve adequate shower pressure, the base of the cold-water storage tank must be at least 3'0'' above the shower head. Below this height electric shower pumps need to be installed, which may make a conventional shower more expensive than an instantaneous shower. To overcome fluctuations in the shower pressure due to the loo being flushed, a separate ½'' downpipe from the cold-water tank is required for the shower. Finally there is the choice between mixer showers and thermostatic showers at twice the price. Provided a separate cold-water downpipe is installed a mixer shower should be adequate. The object of thermostatic showers is to maintain a constant temperature by automatically increasing or decreasing the hot or cold water pressure.

**Instantaneous showers:** are served directly off the cold water rising main, with the water being electrically heated when needed. Although they have over the past ten years suffered a poor reputation, recent models are much improved. The cost of a shower is surprisingly cheap at 2p per shower; at that rate a family of four could shower twice a week for £8 a year. The installation requires a ½'' 'T' pipe off the rising main before other supplies to the kitchen sink or cold-water storage tanks, and a separate electrical supply from the fuseboard. Local Electricity Boards install instantaneous showers with shower curtains for between £100 and £200, so ask for a free quote today. An added bonus being that the installation of a shower is VAT free.

**Shower screens:** I find that with a shower curtain the curtain is attracted to my body, distracting me from my purpose. A variety of shower screen kits can be obtained and fixed to the side of the bath and when installed more effectively prevent water splashing about on the timber bathroom floor (possibly causing timber decay).

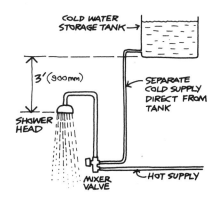

Shower from cold water tank

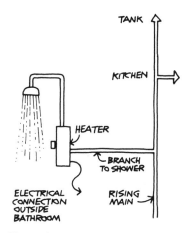

Shower from mains

## 1 Fund raising

So how are you going to pay for all these house improvements?
Borrowing money is the usual answer, unless you happen to have plenty
of cash hidden under the floorboards. There may be the possibility of
a Local Authority Improvement Grant, which will contribute a percentage of the total cost of the work.

Before you dive into the money market, do your homework and
sort out a few facts:

### Is it worth it?

Whatever it is you have in mind, make sure you really want to go
through with it. Will the improvement be worth all the trouble and will
it add to the resale value of the house? You can't take home improvements when you move. Some 'improvements' cost thousands but add
only hundreds to the value of the house.

### How much will it cost?

Make sure you have a clear idea of the total cost — including all the
work associated with your improvement. New kitchen units, for
example, may mean bits of re-plastering, new plumbing, altering electrical points and complete re-decoration.

Set out a detailed list of all the bits of work involved and then
price them (see Chapter 8). Best of all, get a firm-price quotation from
a builder who is willing to do the work — you will need this in any
case when applying for a mortgage loan or grant. Find out when the
work can start, how long it will take and make sure the quotation is
firm, or fixed for the length of time required. Don't forget to add VAT
if necessary, as this can make quite a difference.

### Can you afford it?

When you know how much you want to borrow, you can start shopping around for the best deal. You will be most interested in:

1    *Interest rates*: these days the 'true annual percentage rate of
     interest' (APR) has to be quoted by anyone lending money.
     Any reputable lender will tell you how much interest you will
     pay.

2    *Monthly repayments*: these depend on the length of the repay-
     ment period and the current bank interest rate. Generally the
     longer the repayment period, the lower the monthly repayments.

Don't forget that there is tax relief on interest paid for home improvement loans, whatever the source. By home improvement the tax man
has in mind alterations and additions such as rebuilding and enlarging
your kitchen but not repairs and replacements, such as new kitchen
units. Only loans up to a total of £25,000 (including mortgage) qualify
for tax relief on interest — if you already have a mortgage of £25,000
a further loan will not attract tax relief on the interest.

HOUSE + IMPROVEMENTS TO SUPPORT THANKS

If you've already bought a house and want to find the cash for essential repairs or improvements first try the original mortgagee or lender. The additional improvement loan can be added to the first and repaid over the remaining repayment period. This will certainly mean lower monthly repayments than any other shorter-term loan.

Normally loans are available for all kinds of improvements — central heating, double glazing, new kitchens — but when funds are scarce, loans may be restricted to essential repairs such as new roofs.

Even if you get an Improvement Grant, you may still have to find about 50% of the total cost yourself.

### Building societies

If you have a mortgage with one of the building societies, try them first. This is usually the cheapest way of borrowing for improvements although priority may be given to house purchase loans. They should be able to lend you money for house improvements as a 're-advance' on your mortgage — you repay over the remaining loan period with adjusted monthly payments.

You will need to give them full details of the proposed improvements, with a builder's estimate, and you may have to pay for a survey and valuation to be carried out by the lender's surveyor, as well as the legal costs of drawing up any necessary documents. This can make it an expensive way of borrowing small amounts.

Loans will generally be given for anything which will enhance the value of your home. The security for these loans is, after all, the increased value of your house over its original mortgage value.

Remember that with this kind of loan you receive the cash on completion of the work (or stages of it) and a temporary 'bridging' loan may be needed to get the job started — for buying materials, paying builders or tradesmen in progress payments. If you have the building society's promise of a loan in writing you should be able to organize this with your bank manager.

### Banks

Short-term bridging loans are usually given at the same interest rate as an overdraft, which is really what they are. Remember you can get tax relief on interest paid in some cases.

There are two levels of loan available for home improvements — unsecured and secured. Both offer a flexible and quick way of borrowing money and you will not need to give the same detailed information about your proposals as you would to a building society, which obviously saves time if you're in a hurry. Loans over £3,000 will need to be secured — probably by a second mortgage, an endowment insurance policy or a guarantee from a rich aunt. Loans under £3,000 are not usually secured and you only have to show you can afford the monthly repayments. You do not need to have an account with the bank from whom you are borrowing, but it does help if you're an owner-occupier.

Repayment periods tend to be between 6 months and 5 years and the interest rates are higher than a building society loan. The interest can be either fixed or variable: if you think interest rates may fall, then variable is a better bet, since your payments vary with current interest rates.

## Insurance companies

Insurance companies do not usually give full mortgage loans, but they are a source of smaller loans (below about £5,000) in addition to your existing building society mortgage. Loans are secured against a life insurance policy: the amount you borrow is repaid when the policy matures (or on your death if before), but instead of receiving the cash benefit at the end, you get it at the beginning. If you already have an endowment or life insurance policy, you may find it can be used as security against a loan.

The minimum period of such a policy is 10 years and the interest rates can be competitive with those offered by building societies. There are many life insurance schemes on the market and you will have to shop around for the cheapest. This is best done through a trusty broker or by contacting the Insurance Brokers' Association (see Where to Find It) and asking their advice.

## Finance houses

Loans from this source are arranged in much the same way as a home improvement loan from the bank. You can apply through a branch office, through suppliers of goods or services, or by sending off one of their coupons which you find in magazines or newspapers.

As with a bank, loans up to £4,000 are usually unsecured and repayable within 5 years — loans over £3,000 require security and are repayable within 10 years. Interest rates are usually higher than those quoted by the banks, but not always.

The advantage of this type of loan is that it is easier to arrange and there are no extra charges for surveys or processing applications. All you have to do is show that you can make the monthly repayments and off you go!

## House renovation grants

The Housing Act 1974 graciously made available grants for the improvement and repair of older houses, normally meaning those built before 1961. They are available to freeholders or leaseholders with a lease of 5 years minimum to run.

For anyone disabled, grants are available to make a dwelling of any age more suited to the disabled person's needs — this could mean installing a ground-floor bathroom or widening a doorway for a wheelchair.

There are four kinds of renovation grant, covering different levels of repair work to improve the standard of old houses and keep them in good repair for 15-30 years longer. All but one are given at your local council's discretion: if you qualify for an Intermediate Grant (which covers the provision of basic washing and toilet facilities) the council is obliged to pay (good news for all of you with an outside loo!). The other three are: repair grants, which, obviously enough, are for repairs, but only to houses in General Improvement Areas (GIAs) or Housing Action Areas (HAAs); Improvement Grants, which are for improvements and conversions; and Special Grants, which are for houses with multiple occupation.

Improvement Grants can be used for converting a large house into flats, but not for making your existing house larger. Note that grants apply to all dwellings, so that you may qualify if you live in a flat rather than a house.

The chart gives an insight into the deeper mysteries of Renovation Grants.

If you accept a grant, you will be expected to meet a certain standard of repairs and amenities. This is nothing to be frightened of, because if you've read this book you will want a proper job. You will be expected to complete the work in 12 months from the grant approval date unless you have a good reason for not doing so. (Six months' holiday in the Caribbean is not a good reason.)

The grant amount is determined as a proportion of the total cost of the work up to a limit for the particular grant. This limit is called the 'eligible expense', which is the total cost, of which they pay you a percentage; for a normal Improvement Grant this is £11,500 and the grant-aided percentage is 50%. That means you get £5,750 if the cost of the work eligible for a grant is £11,500 or more. If it is less, say £5,000, you would get £2,500 (50%).

The grant-aided percentage varies according to location and need, being higher in cases of personal financial hardship.

Normal areas — 50% (65% financial hardship)
General Improvement Areas — 65%
Housing Action Areas — 75% (90% financial hardship)

Applications for grants are made to your local council, but discuss your proposals with them first — they can tell you whether your area is normal, General Improvement or a Housing Action Area. The application itself will need to include details of the proposed works (a specification) and a builder's estimate of the costs, although it is possible for you to do the work yourself. Make sure the estimate is not too low (you may not get the full grant available) or so high that you can't afford it even with a grant. In any case do **not** start work before the grant is approved or you may be disqualified.

### Insulation grant

In 1978 the Government introduced Home Insulation Grants as a contribution to the cost of insulating your roof and hot-water cylinder. If you already have your roof space insulated you won't get a grant for re-doing it — if you don't have insulation this grant is well worth applying for. Pensioners are given a higher percentage of the total cost — see the chart.

Anyone, owners or tenants, can apply for a grant. Application forms are obtained from your local council, who may make an inspection first. As with renovation grants, do not start the work until your application is approved, and remember you get the money after the work is completed.

### 2 Insurance

If you have any sort of financial interest in a house, you should make sure you are insured against all those disasters that can and do happen. There are over 100 burglaries every hour all over Britain, not to mention numerous fires, floods and the occasional earth tremor.

If you have a mortgage, the building society will have arranged insurance for the house itself (but not the contents); it's worth checking the policy, and ensuring that it is in your opinion correct. If no building society is involved, you are responsible for insuring the building yourself. You will also need to insure the contents. The two kinds of insurance can be arranged separately if you wish, from different companies. A third kind of insurance is a mortgage-linked life

WELL THAT'S A RELIEF, DEAR — THEY SAY OUR AREA IS NORMAL

insurance, by which, should you have an unfortunate accident while fixing loose tiles on the roof, your outstanding debt to the mortgage company is paid in your absence. If you have an endowment mortgage, this is not necessary.

### Buildings insurance

This covers the structure of your dwelling, together with outbuildings, garden fences, landlord's fixtures (if a tenancy) and, for some, drives and swimming pools. Check to see whether it includes decorations.

The various disasters, or 'contingencies', covered by this policy include fire, explosion, subsidence, floods, falling trees and even impact by animals. They will be listed on the Certificate of Insurance — if you don't have one, ask your insurance company for a copy.

The sum insured is the maximum amount the company will pay if your house is completely destroyed; if it is partly destroyed, the company will pay the proportion of the total they believe has been destroyed. The sum insured should represent the rebuilding cost. It is not the same as the resale value of the property, which can easily be much less than the rebuilding cost. If the property is under-insured the insurance company is not obliged to meet the full amount of any claims made, so it is important that the rebuilding cost is as accurate as possible.

Insurance companies publish a chart of house re-building costs for different types and sizes of house in variious locations. The costs are given in £ per square foot of floor area and are prepared by the Royal Institution of Chartered Surveyors; contact your insurers and ask for a copy of this chart.

If you think the resulting cost seems high, it probably isn't; a typical 2-storey Victorian terrace house can cost £40 per square foot

## SELECTA GRANT CHART

| Repair grant | Special grant | Insulation grant |
|---|---|---|
| At council's discretion | At council's discretion | Subject to government funds |
| Houses built pre-1919 in HAAs or GIAs Rateable value as for Improvement Grants | Houses in multiple occupation by two or more households | Dwellings without existing insulation |
| Structural repairs but not improvements, e.g. roofs, foundations | Providing basic amenities* which will be shared | Insulating roof space, cold-water tank in roof, hot-water cylinder |
| Be in good repair structurally | Have basic amenities | Provide required insulation standard (e.g. 80 mm. fibre-glass quilt in roof space) |
| £5,500 £4,000 (can be increased for works unforeseen when applying for grant) | Set by council but not exceeding limits for Intermediate Grants | Maximum grant is: £65 or 2/3 cost of work<br><br>For pensioners receiving rent rebate/allowance: £90 or 90% cost of work |

to rebuild in the London area down to £35 anywhere else. If it still seems high, don't forget that rebuilding includes the cost of demolition and clearance, architects' or surveyors' fees, legal fees and probably an improved standard of building.

### Index-linking
Having got the right sum insured, you want to keep it that way. Building costs keep on rising, and every year you should review the sum insured and amend it as necessary. Also allow for any improvements or additions to the house such as extensions, garages, double-glazing, which will add to the rebuilding cost.

Index-linked policies are available, which adjust the sum insured

| | Improvement grant | Intermediate grant |
|---|---|---|
| Availability: | At council's discretion | council obliged to pay |
| Given for: | Dwellings with rateable value under<br>£400 — GLC area<br>£225 — elsewhere<br>No limit Housing Action Areas | Dwellings of any rateable value |
| Towards the cost of: | Improving older houses<br>Converting single older houses into flats | Providing basic amenities*<br>in older houses<br>Repairs in connection with the above |
| On completion the dwelling must: | Have basic amenities*<br>Be in good repair<br>Have a useful life of 30 years<br>Conform to the 10 point standard:<br>1 Free from damp<br>2 Natural light and ventilation<br>3 Adequate electrical points<br>4 Adequate drainage<br>5 Structurally stable<br>6 Acceptable room layout<br>7 Kitchen facilities<br>8 Heating facilities<br>9 Fuel Storage (if needed)<br>10 Roof insulation | Have basic amenities<br>Be in good repair<br>Have a useful life of 15 years<br>Be fit for habitation<br>Have roof insulation<br><br><br><br><br>*Basic amenities are:<br>— bath or shower<br>— wash basin<br>— sink<br>— H & C water supply to above<br>— WC |

| Eligible expense limits: | Priority cases | Others | Basic amenities | Associated repairs |
|---|---|---|---|---|
| GLC | £11,500 | £7,500 | £2,500 | £3,500 |
| Elsewhere | £ 8,500 | £5,500 | £1,900 | £2,500 |

Grant Aided Percentage:
| | |
|---|---|
| Normal | 50% (65% financial hardships cases) |
| GIA | 65% |
| HAA | 75% (90%     "           "         "  ) |

every year in accordance with a Building Costs Index prepared by the Building Cost Information Service of the Royal Institution of Chartered Surveyors. This index reflects changing costs of materials and labour in the construction industry. When your policy falls due for renewal each year the premium is revised to suit the new insured sum.

### Contents insurance

This covers the contents of your house against loss or damage by theft, fire, accidental breakage, burst pipes and other similarly unhappy happenings. If interior decorations are not covered in your building insurance, it should include them. It will also cover legal liability for any accidents which injure the policy holder and family in the home or even outside it ('all risks' cover); and 'third-party' risk, when someone gets hit by a flying slate from your roof and wants to sue you.

There are two kinds of policy: 'replacement' cover or the more usual 'new-for-old' cover. The first kind is basic insurance — you receive the replacement cost less an amount for wear and tear — and not much good for replacing things as new. The second kind is the better choice. 'New-for-old' policies provide the full cost of replacing new whatever the age of the article, except for clothes, sheets, towels and household linen.

With any insurance policy the company will not pay more than the sum insured if you make a claim, and you may not receive the full amount of a claim if you are under-insured. Again it is important that you have accurately assessed the value of your home's contents.

The best way is simply to go from top to bottom and make a list of everything in the house: furniture, electrical goods, kitchen equipment, clothes, jewellery, pictures, and so on. Then you go through the list adding the price of buying each item new. You will be amazed how valuable all that rubbish is! Keep a copy of your list so that you can update it regularly.

### Index-linking

There are also index-linked contents policies, where your sum insured is updated in line with inflation. This time the index used is the Retail Price Index, which is published monthly, although your premium is adjusted annually. And even if your policy is index-linked, don't forget to update the sum insured to take into account your ever-increasing, or decreasing, collection of household accoutrements.

### Mortgage protection policy

Is there life after death? Certainly, but only if you've paid the premiums. If you wondered who pays off the mortgage when you've gone, the answer could be an insurance company — through a form of life insurance called a mortgage protection policy. At its simplest it covers the outstanding loan. If you have an endowment mortgage (where the loan is linked to an insurance policy) you will not need this kind of insurance.

### 3 Legislation

This is an introduction to the areas of legislation which reluctant handypersons may encounter in their domestic adventures. The main areas of interest are land law, legislation covering planning and building construction, public health, and the regulations applying to gas, water and electricity installations. If you are building a rear extension or trying to annex your neighbour's vegetable patch (or is it yours?), you may run into some of them.

## Land Law

The definition of 'land' in the Law of Property Act 1925 includes the buildings on it, so any reference to 'land' means buildings as well. Do not think of this as an easy guide to DIY litigation — if it's got that far, find yourself a lawyer.

## Boundaries

These separate me from you, but you might not be able to see them. If a house is not registered at the Land Registry, the boundaries will be shown in the deeds on a plan of dubious accuracy. If registered, the plan accompanying the Land Certificate will be an Ordnance Survey map at a scale of 1:1250 (very small) with a note telling you that the exact line of the boundary will be left undetermined; not much use in either case. Boundaries when they are determined are most usually decided by:

a   'Provable Acts' The definition of Title Deeds by words or by reference to plans or existing buildings — also by ownership obtained by 12 years' unhindered possession of land.

b   'Presumption' Deeds do not usually show who owns a fence and owners are not obliged to fence their property, so often you just have to guess. When not clearly defined in Title Deeds or Land Certificate, a boundary may be presumed, although your presumption can be rebutted by someone who doesn't agree with you.

**Fences**: in towns or cities where fences are used as boundaries, it is presumed that they belong to the person on whose side the fence-posts stand. With a dividing hedge each neighbour is presumed to own half.

**Walls**: a wall dividing two gardens (for example) is presumed to be the boundary and assumed to be similar to a party wall and is shared unless there is evidence to the contrary, such as a sign, fixed on the wall.

## Party walls

These also separate me from you but are different to boundaries in that they form part of a building.

Outside London and Bristol, party walls are subject to Common Law — there is no exact definition of what makes a wall a party wall. In principle the wall on either side of a line down the middle belongs to the owner of the land it stands on. Each half is subject to an 'easement', or right, of support in favour of the other — in other words, each half is expected to hold up the other. You can take down your half as long as you prevent the other half falling down (not very easy). If building a rear extension against a party wall, you may only build on top of your own half unless you reach an agreement with your neighbour to build on the whole wall.

London and Bristol have their own ideas on party walls which are defined in the London Building Acts and the Bristol Improvement Act. Section 44 of the London Act, for example, defines a party wall as one 'which forms part of a building and stands on lands of different owners' . . . In other words the wall is the *common* property of both adjoining owners and any works or alterations involving a party wall must be commonly consented to. There is a definite procedure set out

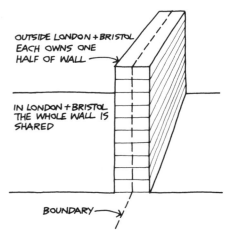

Party walls

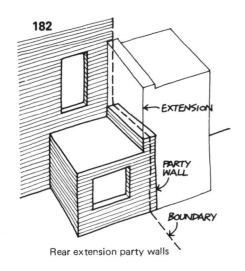

Rear extension party walls

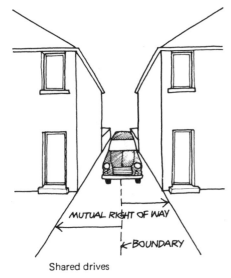

Shared drives

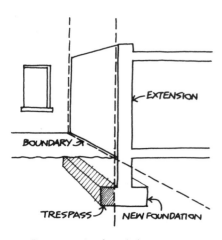

Rear extension foundations

for reaching a party wall agreement, which provides a life's work for some surveyors and architects. However, you can start the ball rolling yourself by serving the formal written notice on the adjoining owner of your intention to carry out work on the wall in question. If you both come to a mutual agreement, in writing, you can relax. If you don't, the life's work begins and you all start appointing surveyors. It's great fun and a wonderful topic of conversation at parties. (Party wall parties.)

### Easements

These are rights acquired over the land of another person, not necessarily an adjoining owner. Generally they give rights of way, light or support but are always concisely defined (unlike boundaries).

Easements (in Scotland 'Servitudes') are most commonly acquired 'expressly' — in other words by deed which gives to one person a right over another, and also to that person's successors in ownership, or 'title'. Otherwise they are acquired by 'prescription', uninterrupted use for a long time, as with well-established Rights of Way.

Many houses have a shared drive between them, and the ownership is usually shown in the Title Deeds or Land Certificate of the properties. It is common for the boundary to run down the middle, with each neighbour owning one half of the drive with a Right of Way over the other. It may be that one owns the whole drive and the other has a Right of Way over it. In either case no one can obstruct the other's Right of Way.

### Trespass

This covers any unauthorized intrusion by one person onto another's land. Apart from simply walking onto or into their property, it can mean hammering a nail into their wall, growing Virginia creeper up it or even propping a ladder against it.

Also generally included is the intrusion into air space or ground space (over-flying and under-mining excepted). A roof eaves overhanging adjoining land is therefore a trespass, so before extending your eaves make sure your trespass is authorized by negotiating a 'licence' (consent given for a certain time) or, better still, by acquiring an 'easement' over the neighbour's land. If you are building a rear extension, the wall may be built up to a boundary line but the foundation will need to project beyond the width of the wall and into your neighbour's land. To do this you will need your neighbour's consent — if you don't get it, you must re-design the foundations or move the wall.

### Trees

Yes, the ones with leaves and branches. But this is not an excursion into landscape gardening, just a little word about some of the problems trees can cause.

First of all, the neighbour's tree with those overhanging branches dropping leaves all over your marigolds. Can you cut them off? Overhanging branches and roots projecting onto a neighbour's land are trespassing and what the legal eagles call an 'actionable nuisance', meaning you can do something about it. First ask the neighbour to cut back the branches; if this meets with no response you are entitled to cut them back yourself, gloriously applying the remedy of 'abatement'. You can similarly cut back roots to the boundary, and if the tree subsequently dies, your neighbour has no redress in law. Neither does it matter for how long the branches have been overhanging.

However, do remember to return all these bits of root and branch, because they remain the neighbour's property.

What about old trees on adjoining land causing damage to your property? The adjoining owner has a duty to look after the tree carefully but has to be proved negligent before you can claim damages. If the neighbour had no knowledge or no reasonable grounds for knowing the tree was unsafe or causing damage there is no negligence, and no liability. If you have any good reason to consider a tree is causing damage or is unsafe you should notify the owner in writing and say so. If the owner does nothing about it and it falls on your house, you would be able to prove negligence and claim damages.

Finally, if you own a tree and you want to axe it to make way for the second garage, check with your local council to find out if there is a tree preservation order on it. If there is, you need the council's permission to remove it, or face a large fine. Anyway it's much nicer having the tree than a second car.

BOUNDARY

### Restrictive covenants

If you have plans for alterations or extensions, watch out for restrictive covenants, conditions written into the Deeds by a vendor to control the future use of land. They may simply forbid certain things happening or require someone's consent. In olden days members of the landed gentry, short of cash, would sell a few spare acres but throw in a covenant forbidding any buildings, thereby protecting the lovely view from the west wing.

In theory such aged covenants apply to all successors (in ownership) of the original vendor and purchaser, but in practice it is often impossible to find anyone who can rightfully enforce them. If uncertain, ask a solicitor for advice — if your uncertainty is confirmed you can insure for a small premium against someone turning up and enforcing the covenant.

Purchasers of houses on newly built estates are more likely to come across covenants imposed by the builder or owner of the site. These control such things as the use of your house (no pet tigers) or its maintenance, or where you can put garden sheds. They may even forbid you extending or altering your house — after all, it was architect-designed and we don't want to spoil it, do we?

### Planning permission

A more common obstacle in the home improvements game will be planning permission. First of all you have to decide if you need it.

All development of land in England and Wales is controlled by the Town & Country Planning Act (similarly in Scotland). Planning controls can be very complicated, but as far as the reluctant handyman is concerned: 'Development' means (a) the carrying out of operations such as building (or mining), and (b) Making a material change in the use of the land (which includes buildings on it).

Converting a house into 2 flats or materially changing the external appearance by, for example, putting dormer windows into the roof, will need to have planning permission.

If your house is in a conservation area, or listed as being of historic interest, there may be other things for which permission for change will be needed, such as the type of windows or colour of external paintwork. It is always safest to contact your local authority planning department, who will determine what constitutes 'develop-

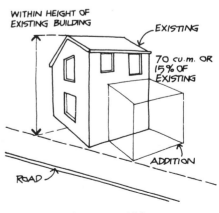

WITHIN HEIGHT OF EXISTING BUILDING

EXISTING

70 cu.m. OR 15% OF EXISTING

ADDITION

ROAD

Permitted development - additions

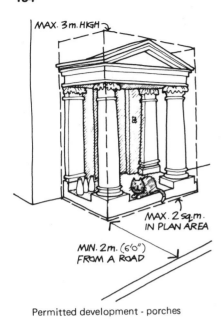

MAX. 3m. HIGH

MAX. 2 sq.m.
IN PLAN AREA

MIN. 2m. (6'0")
FROM A ROAD

Permitted development - porches

ment' and advise generally on any special conditions applying.

There are some things, however, which do not require planning permission, even though they may alter the external appearance of your house. These are called 'Permitted Developments' and there are 23 separate clauses of developments for which planning permission is automatically given; there is no need to make an application although it is advisable to check first.

The clause of most interest to home improvers relates to house extensions; it allows every single-family dwelling (without special conditions applying) to be enlarged without planning permission by 70 cubic metres or 15% of the cubic volume to a maximum of 115 cubic metres. The addition must not exceed the height of the existing building nor extend further than the nearest point of the building fronting onto a road. Small porches are also allowed without permission if no more than 3 metres high, 2 square metres in area and no nearer than 2 metres to a road. If you do need planning permission, you apply to your local authority using forms which they will supply. The application will probably need to include drawings of your proposal if it involves the external appearance or internal layout of your house. Always arrange to discuss any proposals with the Planning Officer before making an application as this can save a lot of time in getting approval; you will also find out if you are likely to get approval before going too far.

### Building Regulations

Once you've got your planning permission sorted out, you can get down to the bricks and mortar stage, which is where the Building Regulations come in. These are standards laid down by Acts of Parliament to protect the health, safety and welfare of a building's inhabitants, covering structure, drainage, natural lighting and ventilation, room heights, insulation and fire precautions.

In England and Wales the 'Building Regulations' apply, made under the Public Health Acts and enforced by the Local Authorities' Building Inspectors.

In Scotland building control is based on the 'Building Standards (Scotland) Regulations' made under the Building (Scotland) Act, and similarly enforced.

Building in the 12 inner London Boroughs is controlled by the 'London Building Acts and By-Laws' which apply to all work on existing buildings as well as new ones. They are administered by the GLC through local District Surveyors, the policemen of the built environment.

If you are planning to do any structural alterations or new building you will need to have your proposals approved before starting any work. In all cases applications for approval must be made to the local authority (Building Inspectors or Surveyors) or the District Surveyor in Inner London. District Surveyors also require 48 hours' notice in writing of starting any building works, from digging the foundation trench onwards.

Applications for Building Regulations or By-laws approval must be accompanied by details of the proposed new construction in the form of plans and specification of materials. You may need the services of an architect or surveyor here.

A building owner who fails to make an application and submit plans for approval under the Building Regulations is guilty of an offence under the Public Health Act; work carried out without approval may have to be removed or altered. District Surveyors have similar powers in London — 'excuse me, sir, 'ave you got a licence for that wall'?

### 4 Public utilities

**Water authorities:** each of the nine water authorities has its own local bye-laws governing the installation of plumbing within your house. Why not ring and ask for a free copy before carrying out your re-plumbing? The authorities are empowered to insist on you complying with their bye-laws (the 1948 Water Act); they are most concerned with waste misuse and contamination.

**Electricity boards:** there are no bye-laws for home electrics. Installations are expected to comply with the Institute of Electrical Engineers' wiring regulations, the 16th edition of which has just reached your local library. The electricity boards' main concern is with their supply; should your installation damage their supply, they are allowed (the 1899 Electric Lighting Clauses Act) to turn you off. A word of warning: should your electrics not comply with the IEE regulations, then your insurance company may refuse to pay up in case of a fire.

JUST A FEW ROUTINE QUESTIONS, SIR....

**Gas Boards:** None of the twelve gas boards are keen on anyone not considered technically competent handling gas service pipes or appliances. As a result they have a nationwide register of approved installers, named the 'CORGI' Register. Gas boards also expect installations to comply with the relevant British Standards and Codes of Practice, such as BS 540 'Flues and Ventilation For Boilers' and BS 5376 'Boiler Installations'. There are, of course, many more which you can either inspect at the local library or obtain from HMSO.

The gas boards are empowered under the 1972 Gas Safety Act and the 1939 London Gas Undertakings Regulations to turn off the gas supply if they consider installations to be 'potentially lethal' and impose if they so wish fines up to £400 for each contravention of a British Standard or Code of Practice. If you are doubtful whether your installation complies, you can ask the local gas showroom for an inspection for a small fee. The greatest misdemeanour, however, is tampering with the gas pipework before the meter.

# WHERE TO FIND IT

| | | |
|---|---|---|
| Chapter 1 | **Damp aids** | Hometer House, Marlow, Bucks SL7 1LX (06284) 72722 |
| Chapter 3 | **Leaf guards** | Gutterfast Ltd, 67 Victoria Rd, Horley, Surrey RH6 7QH (02934) 73409 |
| | **Building centres** | Birmingham: Engineering and Building Centre (021) 454 2629<br>Bristol: The Building Centre Information (0272) 27002<br>Cambridge: The Building Centre (0223) 59625<br>Coventry: Building Information Centre (0203) 25555 (ext. 2512)<br>Durham: Northern Counties Building Information Centre (0385) 62611<br>Glasgow: The Building Centre Scotland (041) 332 7399<br>Liverpool: Building and Design Centre Information (051) 709 8484<br>London: The Building Centre, 26 Store Street, London WC1E 7BT: information (01) 637 8361; international section (01) 636 1197; brick advisory centre (01) 637 0047; build electric information bureau (01) 580 4986; solid fuel advisory service (01) 637 1022<br>Manchester: The Building Centre Information (061) 236 6933<br>Southampton: The Building Centre (0703) 27350<br>Stoke-on-Trent: The Building Information Centre (0782) 29561 |
| | **Glue blocks for slipped slates** | Roof-Bond (London) Ltd, 2 Engelwood Rd, London SW12 9NZ (01) 673 6574 |
| | **Central heating water inhibitors** | Fernox, Industrial (Anti-Corrosion) Services, 214-44 High St, Waltham Cross, Herts (0992) 22368 |
| | **Water softeners** | Permutit, Houseman (Burnham) Ltd, Permutit Domestic Division, The Priory, Burnham, Slough SL1 7LS (06286) 4488 |
| | **Hard water scale inhibitors** | Salamander (Engineering) Ltd, Reddicap Trading Estate, Sutton Coldfield, West Midlands B75 7BU (021) 378 0952 |
| Chapter 6 | **Hire shops** | Hire Association (Europe), Idenden House, Medway St, Maidstone, Kent ME14 1NX (0622) 679645 |
| Chapter 8 | **Architects** (also NJC 'minor works' contract) | Clients Advisory Service, Royal Institute of British Architects, 66 Portland Place, London W1N 4AD (01) 580 5533/(01) 323 0687 |
| | **Main contractors** (builders) | National Home Enlargement Bureau, PO Box 67, High Wycombe (0494) 711649; Federation of Master Builders, 33 John St, London WC1N 2BB (01) 242 7583 |
| | **Sub-contractors** | Federation of Building Sub-Contractors, 82 New Cavendish St, London W1M 8AD (01) 580 5588 |
| | **Plasterers** | National Federation of Plastering Contractors, 82 Cavendish St, London W1M 8AD (01) 580 4041 |
| | **Ready-mixed concrete suppliers** | British Ready Mixed Concrete Association, Shepperton House, Green Lane, Shepperton, Middx TW17 8DN (093 22) 43232 |

| | |
|---|---|
| **Roofers** | National Federation of Roofing Contractors, 15 Soho Square, London **187** W1V 5FB (01) 439 1753; Felt Roofing Contractor Advisory Board, Maxwelton House, 41 Boltro Rd, Haywards Heath, W. Sussex RH16 1BJ (0444) 51835; Mastic Asphalt Council and Employers' Federation, Construction House, Paddockhail Rd, Haywards Heath, W. Sussex RH 16 1HE (0444) 57786; Lead Development Association, 34 Berkeley Square, London W1X 6AJ (01) 499 8422 |
| **Timber treatment specialists** | British Wood Preserving Association, Premier House, 150 Southampton Row, London WC1B 5AL (01) 837 8217 |
| **Chemical damp-proof course contractors** | British Chemical Damp Course Association, 51 High Street, Broom, Bidford-on-Avon, Warwicks B50 4HL (078988) 2716 |
| **Glaziers** | Glass & Tiling Federation, 6 Mount Row, London W1Y 6DY (01) 629 8334 |
| **Decorators** | British Decorator Association, 6 Haywra St, Harrogate, Yorks HG5 BL (0423) 67292 ; National Federation of Painting and Decorating Contractors, 82 New Cavendish St, London W1M 8AD (01) 580 4041 |
| **Carpenters & joiners** | Institute of Carpenters, 24 Ormond Rd, Richmond, Surrey (01) 948 4151; British Woodworking Federation, 82 New Cavendish St, London W1 (01) 580 5588 |
| **Plumbers** | Institute of Plumbing, Scottish Mutual House, North St, Hornchurch, Essex RM11 1RU (040 24) 51236 |
| **Heating engineers** | Gas Board showrooms; Heating and Ventilation Contractors Association, Esca House, 34 Palace Court, London W2 4JG (01) 229 2488; home heating enquiries (01) 229 5543 |
| **Electricians** | Electricity Board showrooms; Institution of Electrical Engineers, Savoy Pl., London WC2R OBL (01) 240 1871; National Inspection Council for Electrical Installation Contracting, 237 Kennington Lane, London SE11 5QJ (01) 582 7746; Electrical Contractors Association, Esca House, 34 Palace Court, London W2 4HY (01) 229 1266 |
| Chapter 9    Project 1: **Insulation contractors** | Thermal Insulation Contractors Association, 24 Ormond Rd, Richmond, Surrey TW10 6TH (01) 948 4151 |
| Project 2: **Central ventilation equipment** | Colchester Fan Marketing Co. Ltd, Hillbottom Rd, Sands Industrial Estate, High Wycombe, Bucks (0494) 28905 |
| Project 3: **Insulation for laying on top of flat roofs** | Dow Chemical Co. Ltd, Heathrow House, Bath Rd, Hounslow, TW5 9QY (01) 759 2600 |
| **Filling cavity walls** | National Cavity Insulation Association, 178-202 Gt Portland St, London W1N 6AQ (01) 637 7481; Association of British Manufacturers of Mineral Insulating Fibres, 64 Wilton Rd, London SW1V 1DE (01) 828 0151 |
| **Internal dry lining** | British Gypsum, Ferguson House, 15-17 Marylebone Rd, London NW1 5JE (01) 486 1282; Dry Lining and Partition Association, 82 New Cavendish St, London W1M 8AD (01) 580 5588 |

| | |
|---|---|
| **188** Project 5: **Consultant heating engineers** | Institute of Domestic Heating and Environmental Engineers, 93 High Rd, Benfleet, Essex (037 45) 54266 |
| **Combined instantaneous gas water heaters and central heating boilers** | Vaillant Boilers, Vaillant House, Unit 5, Heston industrial Estate, Aerodrome Way, Hounslow, Middx TW5 9PU (01) 897 6037 |
| **Solar energy** | Solar Trade Association, 26 Store St, London WC1E 7BT (01) 637 8361 |
| **Advice on heat pumps** | Electricity Council, 30 Millbank, London SW1P 4RD (01) 834 2333 |
| Project 6: **Plastic replacement windows** | British Plastics Window Group, British Plastics Federation, 5 Belgrave Sq., London SW1 (01) 235 9896 |
| **Aluminium replacement windows** | Aluminium Window Association, 26 Store St, London WC1E 7EL (01) 637 3578 |
| **Steel replacement windows** | Steel Window Association, 26 Store St, London WC1E 7JR (01) 637 3571 |
| **Timber replacement windows** | Steel Window Association, 26 Store St, London WC1 7JR (01) 637 3571 |
| **Timber replacement windows** | British Woodworking Federation, 82 New Cavendish St, London W1M 8AD |
| Chapter 10 **Insurance** | Insurance Brokers Association, Fountain House, 130 Fenchurch St, London EC3 |

# INDEX